Helping Young Children Learn

Third Edition

Helping
Young
Children
Learn

Third Edition

Evelyn Goodenough Pitcher

Eliot-Pearson Department of Child Study
Tufts University

Miriam G. Lasher

Cambridge-Somerville Mental Health Center
Cambridge, Massachusetts

Sylvia G. Feinburg

Eliot-Pearson Department of Child Study
Tufts University

Linda Abrams Braun

Belmont Public Schools
Belmont, Massachusetts

CHARLES E. MERRILL PUBLISHING COMPANY
A Bell & Howell Company
Columbus, Ohio 43216

The illustrations that appear on pages 20, 27, 46, 50, 58, 65, 66, 108, 112, 113, 114, 126, 127, 129, 140, 158, 177, and 192 are the work of and were provided by Sylvia G. Feinburg. All photographs were taken and provided by Miriam G. Lasher.

Published by
CHARLES E. MERRILL PUBLISHING COMPANY
A Bell & Howell Company
Columbus, Ohio 43216

This book was set in Paladium.
The production editor was Dawna Ramage Ayers.
The cover was prepared by Will Chenoweth.

Library of Congress Catalog Card Number: 79-83639
International Standard Book Number: 0-675-08256-0

1 2 3 4 5 6 7 8 9 10/85 84 83 82 81 80 79

Printed in the United States of America

Preface to the Third Edition

This revised third edition is again a book for teachers and future teachers about things to do with children and ways to understand them in the classroom. It attempts to retain major elements of the first two editions: the emphasis on children's own experimentation, self-direction, and self-expression and encouragement for teachers to be innovative and creative. But it also attempts to reflect newer understandings of how children learn and what kinds of help they need; indeed, it tries to reflect the broader range of backgrounds now represented among children in preschool programs.

To emphasize our belief that play will enhance, not displace, learning, we begin this edition with a new section on its crucial role. We have also interwoven throughout the text our bias toward a Piagetian, cognitive-developmental point of view, prompting teachers to provide appropriate challenges to stimulate the child's successive mastery of certain concepts. Teachers are encouraged throughout the book to consider how the total environment of the child is in reality a curriculum that promotes learning.

New bibliographies and approaches to curriculum materials document the best of what is currently available. The chapter "Adapting to Learning Problems in the Classroom," which deals with informal teacher assessment and programming for children with behavior and learning problems, has been updated to reflect newer ideas about the use of behavioral objectives.

Throughout the book there has been an attempt to remain true to the philosophy imparted in the original edition: Children are unique human beings with their own unique individual ways of learning. A good preschool program provides the raw materials, the responsive well-prepared evironment, and, most of all, a teacher who is ready both to lead and follow the child as he learns and grows.

NOTE: In this edition we have made some effort to recast sentences so that not all teachers will be *she* nor all children *he*. But that is frequently awkward, and so we ask our readers' understanding while we continue to perpetuate a stereotype. In real life we know some superb male teachers of young children, but the majority of our colleagues continue to be women.

Evelyn Goodenough Pitcher
Miriam G. Lasher
Sylvia G. Feinburg
Linda Abrams Braun

Acknowledgments

We are grateful to Miss Beatrice Spaulding who wrote chapter three, "Music for Young Children"; to Samuel J. Braun, M.D., who helped with the chapter, "Learning Problems in the Classroom"; and to Miss Martha Chandler, who gave overall helpful suggestions.

We also would like to acknowledge the contribution that was made by the late Dr. Esther P. Edwards, formerly a member of the Eliot-Pearson Department of Child Study at Tufts University, who assisted in writing parts of the first edition. Her devotion to young children and the entire process of education was a source of enormous inspiration to all who knew her.

We would like to dedicate this edition of *Helping Young Children Learn* to the staff, parents, and children of Eliot-Pearson Children's School. Much of what we write about originated in our shared association with the developing school and the community of adults and children working together there. The photographs for this edition of the book were taken in the school in November 1978. Barely two days after the work was completed, the building and all its contents burned to the ground. The courage of the staff to face the task of rebuilding and to begin school in temporary quarters, after only a two-day break, is an inspiration to us all.

Evelyn Goodenough Pitcher
Miriam G. Lasher
Sylvia G. Feinburg
Linda Abrams Braun

Contents

ONE

Guiding the Young Child   1

The Crucial Role of Play   1
The Child and the Teacher   3
Parents and the School   9
Selected Reference Materials in Early Childhood Education   12
Bibliography   15

TWO

Art for Young Children   17

Why Is Art Important?   18
What Should You Know about Scribbling?   20
What Should you Know about the Early
     Representational Stage?   21
The Importance of Materials   22
What Are Appropriate Materials?   23
Vegetable Printing   29
Thing Printing   30
Sculpture   31
Beautiful Junk   33
What Can You Do with Straws?   33
Children Love to Make Collages   34
Organizing the Environment   35
What Is Motivation?   36
In Regard to Praise   38
Individual Differences   39
A Few Important Things to Keep in Mind about
     Art Education   42

Selected Reference Materials in Art Education
   for Young Children   43

THREE

Music for Young Children   45

Learning to Listen   45
Time for Singing   46
Musical Instruments   48
Rhythmic Movement and Dancing   50
Dramatic Play and Music   51
Direction and Control   52
The Selection of Music   52
The Search   53
Selected Reference Materials in Music and Dance   54
Bibliography   55

FOUR

Literature for Children:
General Considerations   57

Why Do We Read Books to Young Children?   57
How Do We Recognize a Good Book?   57
It Is Not Enough Just to Find a Good Book!   58
Age Differences   61
Special Concerns   68
Conclusion   74
Bibliography   74

FIVE

Literature for Children:
A Bibliography   75

Animals and Creatures   76
Bibliographies of Multiethnic Books   78
Books about Children's Literature   78
Children in School   80
Children's Concerns, Fears, and Special Needs   81
Close Relationships: Family and Friends   83
Concepts and Academic Preliminaries   85
Good Stories with Real Plots   88
Humor and Nonsense   89
International Friends   90
Minority Groups   93
Nature and Science   96

Poetry, Songs, and Verse   98
Religion and Holidays   99
Sex Role Diversity   100
The Urban Community   101
Sources for Locating Media Books   103
Sources for Reviews, Lists, and Evaluations of Good
      Children's Books   103
Key to Publishers   104

SIX

Important Activities in the Classroom   105

Variety in the Curriculum   105
Water Play   108
Cooking with Young Children   111
Block Play   116
Carpentry for Young Children   120
Animals in the Classroom   126
A Word about Scrounged Materials   130
Helping Children Learn from Everyday Activities   131
Selected Reference Materials on Variety in the
      Curriculum for Teachers of Young Children   132

SEVEN

Academic Preliminaries   135

Academic Skills Belong in the Preschool   135
Motivation Is Critical   137
Teachers Must Be Alert to the Everyday
      Opportunities to Foster Skill Development   137
Sometimes You Do Isolate a Skill   139
Skills on Which Reading, Writing, and
      Arithmetic Are Based   139
Selected Reference Materials on Integrating Academic
      Preliminaries into the Curriculum of Teachers of
      Young Children   155

EIGHT

Understanding the Physical and Social World   157

Children Know a Great Deal   157
What Is the Responsibility of the Teacher?   157
Children Need to Know about Their Own Environments   158
How Does the Teacher Plan?   159

Some Specific Examples of How to Proceed   165
Plants   166
Soil   170
Hair   174
Epilogue   175
Selected Reference Materials on Integrating
    Academic Environment for Teachers of
    Young Children   175

NINE

Adapting to Learning Problems in the Classroom   179

Teacher Assessment of Children in the Classroom   179
Motor Development   181
Speech and Language Development   184
Cognitive Development   187
Social and Emotional Development   189
Interrelatedness of Problems   195
Providing for Special Needs   195
Summary   201
Selected Reference Materials on Learning
    Problems for Teachers of Young Children   202

Index   205

Helping
Young
Children
Learn

Third Edition

One

Guiding the Young Child

THE CRUCIAL ROLE OF PLAY

In an effort to provide specific help for those adults helping young children learn, the chapter headings of this book have been designed to quickly reveal that we are considering major traditional subject areas of learning, together with the materials or equipment commonly associated with them. But we must underscore at the outset our conviction that *optimal learning in young children occurs when they play*. Educators of young children must therefore acquaint themselves with the crucial role of play in the development of the individual human child. In recent years, a great number of important books studying the nature and importance of play have appeared. While good teachers of young children have always acknowledged the inevitability of play in the child and protested that play was the young child's work, recent scholars are documenting the reasons for this and are increasing our sensitivity to play learnings and skill learnings and the relationship of one to the other.

It is especially important to the present generation for us to be cognizant of the significance of play since there is now a prevailing and insidious swing of the educational pendulum in favor of more structure and skill learnings and less play in educational settings. The proponents of this change demand more vigorous attention to basic skill development; there is a plea that education provide children with specific instruments that may be useful to them as adult members of their culture.

It is important that we do not allow this popular bombardment of protest to prompt us to try to undermine the role of play in the learning process of young children. A most provocative and cogent article on this subject is Jerome Bruner's "Nature and Uses of Immaturity." Bruner calls our attention to the psychological importance of immaturity. Human beings, unlike animals, experience a delayed maturation of the brain for a considerable time and, particularly during this period of immaturity, spontaneously engage in play. Bruner sees play as serving important functions. "It minimizes the consequences of actions and learning; one can test limits without risk. Also play provides excellent opportunities to try combinations of behavior that would, under functional pressure, never be tried" (1).*

Play occurs optimally in a pressure-free, safe environment. Children do not play in an environment laden with fear or stress. As their development progresses, they slowly learn

---

*Numbers in parentheses refer to entries in the bibliography at the end of this chapter.

about the physical and social properties of the world; each year brings with it a greater neurological maturity and a greater ability to plan as well as to play.

Play is motion, adventure, friendship: learning.

As children play, they learn to make their world predictable, at first constructing it for themselves in a fashion that makes it more simple than it really is. It takes a number of years, for instance, for children to understand how water, sand, and air behave, how their own bodies operate, and how to use language. Through play the child copes with object permanence; in spite of the fact that things look different, they may be the same—a veritable beginning of philosophy! As he walks and jumps, pokes and prods, he uses the physically maturing skills of his body to probe the properties of physical objects. He discovers how to use things as means to solve problems; through his play, he becomes a user of tools. In order to use tools, he must develop skills. The development of these skills requires repetitive acts, which children apparently enjoy. Through repetition they develop enough small modular acts, or subroutines, requiring minimal attention, that they are able to attend to longer and more complicated tasks.

Sylva reports an interesting study exploring the relationship between play and the solving of mechanical problems. In this investigation, children with prior play experience solved a problem as well as those who had been previously instructed in the principle of making a tool appropriate to the task. Furthermore, the children with play experience seemed to be less frustrated and more goal-directed than the other children. The children with play experience were also more attentive to means, rather than ends, to process rather than product (4).

Do not assume that we are suggesting that there is no place for instruction or teachers in the supervision of play or in skill development. We will discuss the role of the teacher more fully later, but we do need to emphasize here that the teacher's role in instruction is often highly important—in how to use scissors, for example. But the teaching of specific skills to young children should not preempt the child's own skill development and problem solving in play. In general, the teacher's role in such learnings is to provide appropriate challenges and to introduce novelties when needed. The teacher needs to know the developmental and cognitive capacities of each child and to match the curriculum to these capacities (2).

As we allow freedom for play within educational programs for young children, we foster important principles of basic research in the minds of these learners. We can think of play as basic research. Play provides the means for a fundamental quest for knowledge in human beings; it is a vehicle for probing insatiable curiosities and minimizing uncertainties in the universe. Basic research fosters information-getters as contrasted with applied research, in which information from basic research is used to develop skills and make products. Of course, children need to engage in applied research as well as basic research in order to enjoy the products or crafts they can make. A program of only basic research could be boring; a program with an orientation only to the applied could be stultifying.

As we observe young children in their play, we are reminded of our true basic scientists who play with plastics, play with sound, and play with light. These basic scientists are different from the applied scientists who make the toasters, the cars, the rockets, and all products that are useful but dependent on the vision of the scholars.

In play young children are scholar-scientists.* During their period of immaturity, they explore and promote a high degree of intellectual flexibility that is important for later adjustments and explorations in the changing culture of the adult world.

The learnings we discuss, then, have at their base the environment of play. Such an environment is characterized by self-initiation, by opportunities to explore a wide variety of alternate combinations or solutions to problems, and by a freedom from stress to achieve the "right" answer. In such an environment, the child learns the disciplines of art, music, mathematics, and literature appropriate to his understandings. He also learns to play with the ideas in such disciplines. His capacity and freedom to play allow him to become a potential creator as well as practitioner of learnings.

THE CHILD AND THE TEACHER

This book offers teachers of young children an orientation to curriculum, which we would like to interpret as being those experiences which help children learn. We want to encourage an attitude toward the children—what they do and what they do *with*—so that they will dare and *care* to learn. We present materials and approaches which we believe will promote constructive learnings in children aged three through five.

Our focus attempts to be suggestive rather than exhaustive. We want to comment briefly and specifically on important concerns in the hope of communicating a theory of early childhood education through practical and varied suggestions. Our focus is also selective; there are many areas that we do not approach here except by inference: the child's physical and mental health, various problems in individual children, matters of grouping and scheduling, outdoor play, dramatic play, trips, games, efforts at keeping records, or evaluation. However, bibliographies at the end of the chapters will direct readers to books that present a more comprehensive picture.

An important beginning for every teacher is to find out about the children she will teach. She must start where the child is, aware that every child will bring different and irregular patterns of growth and abilities, different experiences and backgrounds, and different perceptions to her classroom. She will recognize, too, that children are unique individuals, social animals, and *children*, not small adults.

*The metaphor of the young child as a scholar-scientist was suggested by Prof. David Rose, who utilizes this concept in his course, "Intellectual Development of Young Children," taught in Child Study at Tufts University.

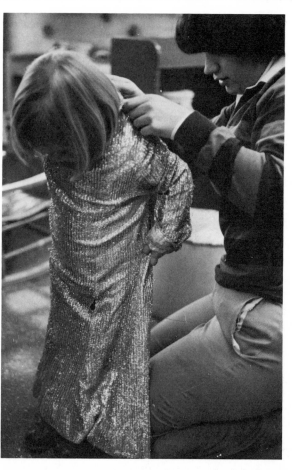

In much of their dramatic play, children act out the life they see around them.

Yet many educational programs for children founder because there is not sufficient awareness that *very young children* are different from *children.* First, there is a difference in the rapidity of a young child's development. Perhaps the most rapid and significant growth and learning already has taken place by the time a child is three years old. Also, many failures to develop can take place in the period between birth and the age of three. We must consider what experiences and what lack of usual experiences, what personality, and what constellation of learnings the child already has had. During the time he is with us in nursery school and kindergarten, he will grow very rapidly, too. The observable differences between a two-, a three-, and a four-year-old child are much more striking than those between a seven, an eight, and a nine year old. But although these areas and others—sight, hearing, ability to pay attention, speech—develop rapidly, they cannot be developed overnight. We must resist pressures that overrate the swift, the verbal, and the measurable, remembering that learning is not the shortest distance between two points. The way is complicated, and many hidden learnings accompany the main lesson. There are often periods, too, when nothing seems to be happening and the child seems just to be "fooling around." He may need such periods of quiet and absorption to gather strength for the next push, to assimilate what he has learned, and to rest.

Our bias is toward a Piagetian, cognitive-developmental point of view in which the teacher strives to provide appropriate conflict to stimulate the child's successive mastery of certain concepts. From this viewpoint, the adult's primary concern is with challenging the child to consider ways of raising questions, testing hypotheses, and analyzing events. A teacher committed to this approach, for example, would not be content to leave the water table in the exact same stage week after week, month after month, without considering ways in which the media could be altered to provide greater provocation for the child. If the child accidentally discovers a syphon, the teacher might capitalize on this event spontaneously, posing questions, adding additional materials, and heightening the child's awareness of the particular set of ideas involved. Although teacher dissemination of some information is of obvious importance in the teaching process, the teacher's major emphasis should be on influencing the basic process of conceptualization in ways that are compatible with the child's developmental level.

Learning and growth are irregular. Because a child is four does not mean he will display a full set of four-year-old abilities. He may have the language mastery of a five year old, the motor abilities of a three year old, and a relationship to people and himself of a baby of two. The teacher should familiarize herself with the general expectancies in various areas of development so that she is ready to back up or move forward to meet the child. She will help him meet success and challenge him with what can come next. Because of the irregularity of growth, critical periods for the development of any behavior or the incorporation of any learnings can be considered to some extent unique for each person. There is likely to be some overlapping of the periods no matter what conceptual scheme is considered.

Young children generally are more active than older children. They can sometimes be quiet for long periods of time, but they also move around a lot, want to touch or manipulate objects, make spontaneous noises, and demand adult attention. Children are not born with a zeal to be clean, quiet, punctual, orderly, and well-mannered.

The younger the child, the more likely he is to be self-centered in every respect. He first wants the complete attention of an adult. Enlightened adults tend to take it for granted that when the toddler is present, an adult must be aware of him almost constantly—watch what he touches, where he goes, what he sees. Adults usually accompany their watchfulness with verbalizations so that the child is protected and stimulated almost constantly. He wants to control materials as well as adults. When he is first in the company of other children, his play tends to be solitary or parallel. His socialization is basic, but it takes a long time to evolve.

His motivation to learn is bound up with his activity, his interest, and his feelings. Since he understands so little of verbal directions or expectations, so little of time sequences, he cannot be motivated through future rewards of some worthwhile outcome. He must experience an immediate stimulating pleasure through his immediate personal involvement in activity. He must have a good, pleasurable feeling that his teacher will be readily responsive to his need for attention, will accept as natural his regressions to more babyish ways of behaving when he needs to regress, will pick up clues that indicate his interest in something so that she can help him succeed, will comment favorably on his good intentions, and will prompt him to be curious and engage in appropriate explorations about himself, his friends, and the objects in his environment.

Because young children are just beginning to develop an awareness of time and other intangible concepts, the younger the child the less is his tolerance for frustrations. Also, the more pervasive is his need for recognizable, loving support. The development of trust begins in infancy with the attentive, loving care of a parenting adult. The very young child cannot yet tolerate the possible threat of withdrawal of support and love easily. He enjoys and needs repetition of activities so that he can build a sense of mastery that allows him to go on to something new. He is also strikingly immature in his ability to conceptualize. Although he may use many words—and even be able to read—he does not have the wide experience that assures a mature use and understanding of language. He may understandably be perplexed, for example, by the distinction between shots for your arms and shots that make you dead. And he may wonder what "hold your horses" means.

He also can be confused easily and quickly by apparent changes in sizes of objects, as Piaget has strikingly demonstrated. Although he may see the same amount of water poured into a tall, thin glass and a short, wide one, he believes that the tall one contains more liquid.

He cannot understand the concept of four initially, although he may be able to count by rote to ten. When he plays store, he cannot be depended upon to distinguish between the role of the seller and buyer and understand the interchange of money. The very young child cannot play hide-and-seek because he cannot grasp the idea of what it means to be hidden and yet present. Similarly, a young child cannot play many simple games which involve taking turns and making choices because he cannot understand these concepts. Related also is his poor ability to distinguish between reality and fantasy; he is easily frightened or confused by what appears to be so since his limited experience has not yet allowed him the time to determine what is true and what is fanciful. The young child has strong feelings about his parents, and he may have anxieties about being separated from them. He is concerned about being little and ineffectual and realizes a real thrill when he controls a situation or material, when he is master. He is puzzled about the beginning and end of things, about birth and death. Anything unseen or covered is of great interest—God, roots, worms. And he is worried about remaining intact—sometimes there is terror at cutting fingernails or hair, perhaps because he is afraid of losing some other parts of his body. His emerging sense of self is very gradual—he needs to look at himself in a mirror and in photographs. It is helpful to observe with him such things as his freckles, the color of his hair and eyes, the color of his skin, his sex, his size, his name and to comment on similar aspects of other children.

All the foregoing information, which comes from our general observations of young children, seems to apply to young children in general. Various unfortunate labels have been attached to certain children from economically poor areas, including "deprived," "disadvantaged," "segregated," "different," and "poor." We increasingly realize that any of these terms can be applied to any group of children, depending upon whose value judgment is represented. From the point of view of many children in low socioeconomic environments, the middle-class child may be "culturally different." The most important label, however, is that of "young child"; and children of many backgrounds have their basic childhood as a common background. An understanding of childhood can help us to provide appropriate learning experiences.

We must meet all groups of children with open minds, with a desire to learn as much about them as we can, and with the conviction that the only way to find out when and how various things can be taught them is to try—not *just* try, but try intelligently and thoughtfully. Among some groups of children, there will be more than the average number from one-parent homes, large families, or environments sparse in a variety of stimuli. Such backgrounds may result in more children than the average having immature behaviors, since such children may not have had many or stimulating experiences between birth and the age of three. Teachers need to pick up these lost experiences in order to satisfy children's needs. These children may demand more individual attention and show less autonomy or initiative because there has been too little affection or a poverty of relationships in their lives. Teachers may need to give more than the usual amount of personal warmth, physical contact, and listening. They may have to accept a child's need to control them as a toddler controls his mother. But touching and handling must be approached carefully since children may withdraw from people who rush in too quickly with personal contact. We must plan judiciously so that these children can be gradually led to involve themselves with objects as well as with teachers, in social interaction with one another and then in the independent, creative, self-motivated learning that is so excitingly characteristic of young children who have not been frustrated or blocked.

Our levels of expectation about how any child can grow must not be low. And we must not approach any child *a priori* as a problem child. Many come from multiproblem homes and show extreme feelings of hostility, aggression, or withdrawal. Many have acquired only limited vocabularies and have had little experience in expressing themselves. But such deficiencies do not necessarily provoke extraordinary physical or emotional problems, for children impoverished in some areas may be strong in others. They may have rich—although different—vocabularies; or they may have extraordinary gross-motor skills, unusual sensitivities to music and rhythm, or remarkable courage, daring, ingenuity, or resourcefulness. We must recognize, cultivate, and stimulate strengths as we seek to understand each child.

Finally, we must not lose our perspective and expect too much to happen in whatever brief period is allotted to us. Learning is sometimes rapid, more often gradual; it is not often visible, and what sometimes may seem to be visible one day vanishes the next. At the beginning, a lot of learning and energy goes into introducing the child to a group experience that is initially foreign to him so that he accepts it, even likes it. A teacher must work especially hard to discover something about a child's unique style so that she can deal in a better way with his learning processes. It is good, if possible, to involve him even in a few exploratory beginnings of learning.

Thus, we believe that it is neither necessary nor advisable to alter the aims of early childhood education or to create a different curriculum for any one group of children. A good program will bring together children of differing backgrounds and talents. Although it is not necessary to alter the curriculum, we may, as has been indicated, need to alter our notions of when and how different aspects of the curriculum are introduced for different children. All children will be involved in reading, mathematics, science, literature, music, art, and social studies as well as in unique personal learnings. What we need to do is to mesh the child's living and play and feeling into frameworks of conceptualization and problem solving characteristic of young children's ways of learning. And we mustn't think of the importance of these years only in future-oriented ways—children need what they need now. We must remember that some of these children have not had experiences with a consistent and predictable environment. In school we must be especially careful to present things in a sensible progression of manageable steps in order to begin to build up in the child the feeling that he can dare to try something new.

This book is directed primarily to teachers, and teachers are the key persons in the whole endeavor. If they do not understand developmental sequences and expectancies, they cannot very well adapt the curriculum to them. And if they themselves do not have well-developed concepts in the fields of mathematics, science, language, and art as well as a certain zeal about these studies, they cannot very well use their knowledge to mesh appropriate learnings into the emotional and social life of children or inspire the children with a love of learning. They must have standards of excellence in arts and sciences so that they can demonstrate and inspire academic excellence in children. They do not impart their knowledge through lectures or precepts, however; they translate what they know into classroom action through listening, observing, and participating.

These are times in which there is often tremendous pressure for teachers to deny children the kind of educational experiences that are in their best interest. Pressures for accountability, a return to basics, and the elimination of "frills" often result in teachers' imposing excessive use of workbooks, teaching reading skills prematurely, and using paper/pencil lessons in ways that are not always appropriate for individual children. The sustaining of standards is frequently equated with the superiority of one teaching method over another and with the assumption that allowing children to explore, to play, and to engage in concrete, direct activity is wasting time instead of leading to meaningful learning.

Teachers need to have the strength of their convictions, helping parents and colleagues who work with older children understand that the ways in which young children learn are qualitatively different from those of the elementary-school-aged child. The teacher who attempts to honor the pressures and expectations of others without honoring her own commitment to what she knows is appropriate and best for the young child will ultimately accomplish little. Too, parents must feel that the teacher is a professional who holds a set of understandings and beliefs about the nature of the educational experience and is willing to stand by those beliefs. This is not to suggest that the teacher should remain insensitive to the opinions and expectations of parents and the community but rather that she has the responsibility for defining the program and for promoting greater understanding of her knowledge and educational objectives.

The teacher must not have her ideas regarding the educational program bound up in a "system," for then there will be a real danger of taking one path to the exclusion of others. Children must have ideas presented in many different ways at appropriate times, thereby learning how tasks are similar before they can understand abstract principles or basic structures.

The wise teacher will recognize that subject matter which is compelling to children offers the most meaningful way to stimulate their learning. She will listen to children's conversations and play with a sensitive ear, extracting the issues and events that hold special importance, and build upon these areas in designing curriculum. "I have a new baby at home." "Phillip is adopted." "The cookie monster isn't really alive." Statements such as these are dynamic sources for building curriculum, and the creative adult will find within them the potential for a unit on babies, on increased understanding of adoption, and on the clarification of reality and fantasy. The teacher who holds a clear grasp of the concepts and skills that are basic to a given stage of development will be able to address these objectives through subject matter emanating from the child.

Children's conversations can be an important source of subject matter for designing curriculum.

The teacher will also want to consider that individual children may be predisposed towards a particular way of learning and that for some children the visual modality will dominate; with others, auditory or tactile experiences will be of great importance. Children's preferences for a given media or kind of activity should also influence the teacher in planning curriculum. For one child, the use of three-dimensional construction may serve to reinforce a particular set of ideas, while, for another, drawing, speaking into a tape recorder, or listening to a story would be a more strategic approach.

The delicate balance of freedom and structure is of central importance to the educational environment. The teacher who speaks of self-expression, creativity, and individuality must understand that these cannot take place in an environment in which there is not order, predictability, and the setting of limits. The adult must have a keen understanding of how to order the physical environment, define time and sequence, effect transitions, and communicate to children expectations about behavior in order for them to live harmoniously together.

Order and predictability are of special importance for young children since their sense of time, space, and reality is only tentatively formed. School rooms that are disorganized, confusing, and lack consistency and stability tax the child's capacity to feel safe, confident, and able to function independently and creatively. The child must feel secure in knowing that what is inappropriate behavior or use of materials today will be so tomorrow and that each day will unfold in a relatively consistent manner. This is not to suggest that the teacher should be rigid or inflexible but rather that children will feel freer to take risks, to be adventuresome, and tackle new areas of investigation when they are living within an environment that they thoroughly understand. Sometimes one sees classrooms in which it is next to impossible to find a pair of scissors or to know where to return tools. The environment of a classroom in which housekeeping has been dealt with in such a lax manner discourages productivity. Likewise, a child whose emotional energies are consumed with survival from the aggression of others or who feels compelled to challenge limits in order to define the authority of significant adults is not able to maximize the school environment. The teacher must be secure in the knowledge that she holds the ultimate authority for the classroom and everything that occurs within it. Clearly, authoritarian abuse of this responsibility would be inappropriate, but the teacher's denial of or equivocation about this important role can be equally injurious.

The general public, never fully understanding or appreciating education except when it deals with subject matter, is very much intent that academic subjects be taught in the crib, playpen, and nursery school. However, instead of estimating only the academic preparation and competence of teachers, we must consider the kind of person a teacher is, the values she incorporates and represents. It is useless to try to teach values or ideals as formulae or catechetical magic. Teachers (and parents) must have ideals and values as controlling principles in their own conduct.

An adult who is not genuinely and constructively loving, tolerant, or gracious has nothing to teach a child about such qualities. The child learns from concrete representation and feelings; the teacher must be the model of the values she wishes to impart, and she will begin forming a child by first forming herself.

PARENTS AND THE SCHOOL

Since the young child is extremely dependent on his home and family, it is unrealistic to think of his education apart from his parents. Parents provide or deny stimulating environments; they are models to imitate in sex roles, values, language, personal idiosyncrasies, beliefs. Parents themselves are often "in love" with their children in ways that arouse strong emotions of love or hate or something in between. It is highly unusual to find a "disinterested" parent. Parents testify their love by their eagerness to talk about their children and their obvious pleasure at what they consider to be their children's accomplishments. Although many parents seem to be duplicating a way of life for their children that reflects the way they themselves were brought up, most parents hope for something "better" for their children and respond positively when opportunities to further their children's education or well-being are presented.

In recent years, changes have taken place in our understanding of families of young children and the interrelationships established with care-giving persons such as teachers and day-care providers. A decade ago there were primarily two general types of settings in which young children were cared for in groups. Private preschools served largely a privileged group of families who could afford to pay tuition for their children's early educational experiences. Many of these families fitted into a stereotype of the two-parent family in which the father went out to work each day and the mother cared for the home and the children. Her life was punctuated by a series of station-wagon trips to take children to school, recreational activities, music lessons, and doctors' appointments. There were also urban day-care centers sponsored by private philanthropic groups with funding supplemented by groups such as United Fund or the Salvation Army. "Poor" children attended these centers while parents worked or because parents were unable to give adequate daytime care. Family problems were concentrated in these centers, which were usually staffed by social workers as well as educators. There was little overlap in the types of clientele served by these two general types of centers. With the exception of a small handful of cooperative nursery schools, parents were not generally involved in the administration of the preschools that their children attended. They dropped children off, and in the better schools they attended one or two individual parent-teacher conferences and an occasional evening meeting. These conferences were often a source of anxiety for both teachers and parents, each presuming they would be evaluated and judged by the other. As a result, little real sharing took place during these formal contacts.

Many of the trends of the last fifteen years have brought about changes in this system. More mothers work outside their homes, necessitating complicated child-care arrangements. According to data presented to the House Select Committee on Population in May 1978, (3) there were (in 1975) "an estimated 27,400 day care centers . . . (and) 950,000 licensed and unlicensed day care homes." In 1977, 44 percent of under-age-three children had mothers who worked outside their homes sometime during the year. This represents a marked increase over earlier years. In addition, alternative family living styles are more prevalent, and we have had to broaden our understanding of what constitutes a family. Fewer children have experienced a traditional two-parent family. Unmarried couples, single, separated, or divorced parents, parents in communal living arrangements, separated parents equally sharing their children and child-care responsibilities, couples who reverse or redistribute their wage-earning and child-rearing roles all may be found among the families represented in the average preschool center. A mixture of socioeconomic levels is also common as privately incorporated schools and day-care centers make formal contracts with welfare departments for a certain number of "slots" in their enrollment. Too, schools are making a concerted effort to increase their cultural diversity and, more recently, to serve children with various special needs or handicaps.

In some areas, day-care centers predominate in response to the increasing number of single-parent families and families in which both parents work regularly outside the home. All kinds of children, not just those who are "poor," attend these centers. Family day care has also become institutionalized as an alternative or complement to center-based day care.

The age of consumerism has also caught up with us. Parent and community boards have heavy input into decisions about how centers will be administered, how funds will be spent, what kinds of people will be chosen to teach, and what kind of educational program will be presented for children. Teachers feel accountable to parents, and they may actively struggle together over what sets of values will be represented in child-care centers. Since, now, children from a variety of backgrounds may be attending any one center, there may be periodic turmoil as center staffs attempt to define their own identity while, at the same time, satisfying the wishes of families who choose to enroll their children. How much freedom or structure there will be, what methods of discipline will be used, how younger children will be toilet trained, whether academics will be taught, what kind of food will be served for snacks and even whether hands will be washed before eating—all these and more are topics for open-forum discussions among teachers and families. The traditional twice-yearly parent conference/teacher report has become an ongoing dialogue among parties with presumably equal input.

But another trend runs concurrently. There is increasing realization that parenting is a specialized and difficult task; one is not automatically an expert at parenting. Experiences are therefore being provided for junior and senior high school students in preparation for parenthood. These may include practice experiences in public school primary classrooms, day-care centers, and nursery schools as well as classroom discussions focused on child development, child-rearing practices, and family communication systems. Support groups and courses to help adults become effective parents now abound in certain areas, as do support groups to help adults cope with a variety of life situations, such as separation and divorce, death, child abuse, sexual abuse, and many others. This trend toward reaching out to share common life experiences occurs in response to a shift toward smaller families lacking the traditional built-in supports of older extended families in a less complex society. Parents have fewer models around them and a greater need to share the burden of the decision making regarding their children as well as their actual care.

The adults who provide a young child with his first school experience are in a uniquely influential position. Parents turn to them as models but also may be especially critical of things they do differently than the parents themselves do at home, especially if the differences result from basic variations in value systems. Establishing a meaningful dialogue with parents can therefore be a time-consuming responsibility for teachers. It can seldom be done at the doorway of the school when the teacher may be at her busiest, handling arrivals and departures. It can seldom be done by a teacher's putting in long hours in a day-care classroom or by teaching double session in a kindergarten with as many as fifty or sixty different children each day. Rarely is it accomplished within a teacher's traditional working hours.

Parents, children, and teachers need time to share the details of a first school experience.

Working with parents may demand a redefinition of a teacher's job description so that both time and energy are available for late afternoon and evening conferences and home visits and so that there are time periods during the day and evening for relaxed telephone conversations with families. Trusting relationships and true dialogues do not happen in semiannual conferences routinely scheduled in November and May. They develop because a teacher takes time to call a parent to say how things went on a child's first full day alone in school, or because a teacher realizes that a child seems sad and different on a Monday morning. Such gestures on a teacher's part suggest a way of doing business together; caregivers responsible for different parts of a child's day have many questions to ask each other and many observations and aspirations to share. No one party is the expert. The teacher, rather than being an agent for the child, is an advocate for the family as a whole. For teachers to recommend or admonish parents that they spend more time alone with the child each day, that they read stories to the child or allow the child to help in the kitchen without first getting fully acquainted with the physical setting of the home and the unique problems the parents have to cope with, is naive and may only serve to shut off communication.

SELECTED REFERENCE MATERIALS IN EARLY CHILDHOOD EDUCATION

Books

Ashton-Warner, Sylvia. *Teacher.* New York: Simon & Schuster, 1963.

Association for Childhood Education International. *Parenting.* Washington, D.C.: Association for Childhood Education International, 1973.

Bell, Donald R., and Low, Roberta M. *Observing and Recording Children's Behavior.* Richland, Va.: Performance Associates, 1977.

Boehm, Ann E., and Weinberg, Richard A. *The Classroom Observer: A Guide to Developing Observation Skills.* New York: Teachers College Press, 1977.

Braun, Samuel, and Edwards, Esther. *History and Theory of Early Childhood Education.* Worthington, Ohio: Charles A. Jones Publishing Co., 1972.

Braun, Samuel, and Lasher, Miriam. *Are You Ready to Mainstream?* Columbus, Ohio: Charles E. Merrill Publishing Co., 1978.

Brazelton, T. Berry. *Infants and Mothers, Differences in Development.* New York: Delacorte Press, 1970.

Bruner, Jerome. *Beyond the Information Given,* edited by Jeremy Anglin. New York: W.W. W.W. Norton & Co., 1973.

Bruner, Jerome; Jolly, Alison; and Sylva, Kathy, eds. *Play: Its Role in Development and Evolution.* New York: Basic Books, 1976.

Chomsky, Carol. "Write First, Read Later." *Childhood Education* 47 (March 1971): 296–99.

Chukovsky, K. *Two to Five.* Berkeley: University of California Press, 1963.

Cohen, D.H. "Continuity from Pre-Kindergarten to Kindergarten." *Young Children* 26 (1971): 282–86.

_____. *The Learning Child.* New York: Pantheon, 1972.

Cohen, Dorothy, and Rudolph, Marguerita. *Kindergarten and Early Schooling.* Englewood Cliffs, N.J.: Prentice-Hall, Inc., 1977.

Cohen, Dorothy, and Stern, Virginia. "Observing and Recording the Behavior of Young Children." *Teachers College Practical Suggestions in Teaching,* No. 18. New York: Columbia University Teachers College, 1958.

Coles, Robert. *Privileged Ones: Volume V of Children in Crisis.* Boston: Little, Brown & Co., 1977.

Crocker, Eleanor C. "Consultation with Parents." *Young Children* 20 (November 1964): 91–99.

Dennison, George. *The Lives of Children.* New York: Random House, 1969.

Dittman, L.L., ed. *Early Child Care: The New Perspectives.* New York: Atherton Press, 1968.

Elkind, David. *Child Development and Education: A Piagetian Perspective.* New York: Oxfort University Press, 1976.

Erikson, Erik. *Childhood and Society*, rev. ed. New York: W. W. Norton & Co., 1963.

Featherstone, Joseph. *Schools Where Children Learn.* New York: Liveright, 1971.

Fraiberg, S. *Every Child's Birthright: In Defense of Mothering.* New York: Basic Books, 1977.

———. *The Magic Years.* New York: Charles Scribner's Sons, 1959.

Frost, Joe L. *The Young Child and the Educative Process.* New York: Holt, Rinehart & Winston, 1976.

Ginsburg, H., and Opper, S. *Piaget's Theory of Intellectual Development.* Englewood Cliffs, N.J.: Prentice-Hall, Inc., 1969.

Golubcheck, Leonard H., and Persky, Barry, eds. *Early Childhood Education.* Wayne, N.J.: Avery Publishing Group, Inc., 1977.

Greenberg, Polly. "Seminars in Parenting Preschoolers." In *Early Childhood Education: It's an Art? It's a Science,* edited by J. D. Andrews, pp. 27–39. Washington, D.C.: National Association for the Education of Young Children, 1976.

Hess, Robert D., and Croft, Doreen J. *Teachers of Young Children,* 2d ed. Boston: Houghton Mifflin, 1975.

Honig, Alice S. *Parent Involvement in Early Childhood Education.* Washington, D.C.: National Association for the Education of Young Children, 1975.

Katz, Lillian G. *Current Topics in Early Childhood Education.* Norwood, N.J.: Ablex Publishing Co., 1977.

Kohlberg, L. "Early Education: A Cognitive-Developmental View." *Child Development* 39 (1968): 1013–62.

Lane, Mary B. *Education for Parenting.* Washington, D.C.: National Association for the Education of Young Children, 1975.

Lay, Margaret Z., and Dopyera, John E. *Becoming a Teacher of Young Children.* Lexington, Mass.: D. C. Heath & Co., 1977.

Leeper, Sarah Hammond; Dales, Ruth J.; Skipper, Dora Sikes; Witherspoon, Ralph L. *Good School for Young Children,* 2d ed. New York: Macmillan Publishing Co., Inc.; London: Collier Macmillan Publishers, 1974.

Maccoby, Eleanor E., and Jacklin, Carol. *The Psychology of Sex Differences.* Stanford, Calif.: Stanford University Press, 1974.

MacEwan, P. T. *Liberating Young Children from Sex Roles: Experiences in Day Care Centers, Play Groups and Free Schools.* Boston: The New England Free Press, 1972.

Mattick, I., and Perkins, F. *Guidelines for Observation and Assessment: An Approach to Evaluating the Learning Environment of a Day Care Center.* New York: Day Care and Child Development Council of America, 1974.

Morrison, George S. *Early Childhood Education Today.* Columbus, Ohio: Charles E. Merrill Publishing Co., 1976.

Neill, A. A. *Summerhill.* New York: Hart Publishing Co., 1960.

Parker, Ronald, ed. *The Preschool in Action, Exploring Early Childhood Programs.* Boston: Allyn & Bacon, 1972.

Pitcher, Evelyn G., and Ames, Louise B. *The Guidance Nursery School,* 2d ed. New York: Harper & Row, Publishers, 1974.

Provence, Sally, with Naylor, A., and Patterson, J. *The Challenge of Day Care.* New Haven and London: Yale University Press, 1977.

Read, Katherine. *The Nursery School,* 6th ed. Philadelphia: W. B. Saunders, 1976.

Silberman, Charles. *Crises in the Classroom.* New York: Random House, 1970.

———. *The Open Classroom Reader.* New York: Vantage Books, 1973.

Smilansky, Sara. *The Effects of Socio-Dramatic Play on Disadvantaged Pre-School Children.* New York: John Wiley & Sons, 1968.

Spodek, Bernard. *Teaching in the Early Years.* Englewood Cliffs, N.J.: Prentice-Hall, Inc. 1972.

Stone, Joseph, and Church, Joseph. *Childhood and Adolescence.* New York: Random House, 1968.

Todd, V. C., and Heffernan, H. *The Years before School: Guiding Preschool Children.* New York: The Macmillan Co., 1970.

Weber, Lillian. *The English Infant School and Informal Education.* Englewood Cliffs, N.J.: Prentice-Hall, Inc., 1971.

Weikart, David P.; Rogers, Linda; Adcock, Carolyn; and McClelland, Donna. "Home Visits." In *The Cognitively Oriented Curriculum,* pp. 79–88. Washington, D.C.: ERIC/National Association for the Education of Young Children, 1971.

White, Robert. "Competence and the Psychological Stages of Development." In *Nebraska Symposium on Motivation,* edited by M. R. Jones, pp. 97–141. Lincoln: University of Nebraska Press, 1960.

Wright, Herbert F. "Observational Child Study." In *Handbook of Research Methods in Child Development,* edited by Paul H. Mussen. New York: Harper & Row, Publishers, 1967.

Journals

Child Care Quarterly. Behavioral Publications, 2852 Broadway, New York, New York 10025.

Child Development. University of Chicago Press for the Society for Research in Child Development, University of Chicago Press, Chicago, Illinois 60637.

Children Today. Children's Bureau, Superintendent of Documents, United States Government Printing Office, Washington, D.C. 20402.

Day Care and Early Education. Behavioral Publications, 2852 Broadway, New York, New York 10025.

Merrill-Palmer Quarterly. 71 East Ferry Avenue, Detroit, Michigan.

Teaching Exceptional Children. Quarterly Journal of the Council for Exceptional Children Information Center, CEC ERIC Clearinghouse and the Special Education IMC/RMC Network, Council for Exceptional Children, 1411 South Jefferson Davis Highway, Arlington, Virginia 22202.

Young Children. Bimonthly journal of the National Association for the Education of Young Children, 1834 Connecticut Avenue, Washington, D.C. 20009.

Organizations

The organizations listed below may be contacted for their publication lists. Pamphlets available from these groups at nominal cost cover a wide range of information, including items on general child care, creative experiences, equipment, child rearing, and various problems connected with nursery and public schools.

Association for Childhood Education International (ACEI). 3615 Wisconsin Avenue, N.W., Washington, D.C. 20016.

Bank Street College of Education. 610 West 112th Street, New York, New York 10025.

Child Study Association of America. 9 East 89th Street, New York, New York 10028.

Day Care and Child Development Council of America. 1426 H Street, N.W., Washington, D.C. 20005.

ERIC Clearinghouse in Early Childhood Education. University of Illinois, 805 West Pennsylvania Avenue, Urbana, Illinois 61801.

National Education Association (NEA). Department of Elementary-Kindergarten-Nursery Education, 1201 Sixteenth Street, N.W., Washington, D.C. 20036.

National Association for the Education of Young Children (NAEYC). 1629 21st Street, N.W., Washington, D.C. 20009.

BIBLIOGRAPHY

1.   Bruner, J. "Nature and Uses of Immaturity." In *Play, Its Role in Developmental Evolution*, edited by J. Bruner, A. Jolly, and K. Sylva. New York: Basic Books, 1976.

2.   Hunt, J. McVicker. *Intelligence and Experience.* New York: Ronald Press, 1961.

3.   *Report on Preschool Education,* 20 June 1978.

4.   Sylva, K., and Geneva, Paul. "The Role of Play in the Problem-Solving of Children 3—5 Years Old." In *Play, Its Role in Developmental Evolution,* edited by J. Bruner, A. Jolly, and K. Sylva. New York: Basic Books, 1976.

Two

Art for Young Children

The inclusion of a good creative art program within the early education curriculum offers the teacher a powerful tool for furthering the total development of the young child. Most children thoroughly enjoy art and gravitate toward it with little prodding since it is a primary source of symbolic production which flows naturally and organically. It is directly reflective of the child's perceptions and emerging sense of reality. Through art, a child clarifies his understandings of the physical and social world, is able to give tangible form to his feelings and responses, and gains an appreciation of himself and the ways in which he is unique and significant as an individual.

Children are highly motivated by the fact that the thing that they sense, feel, or want to express can be made visually tangible by the act of bringing a crayon and a piece of paper into contact with one another. Even in their earliest experiences with art media—when involvement is primarily in the kinesthetic, sensory, and physical act—they delight in the knowledge that this paper with its varied marks exists because of them. What fascination; what power! "I have brought something into being that did not exist before!" This is the essence of the activity.

Independent of culture, all children move sequentially through a series of stages, beginning in a crude, somewhat random manner and continuing systematically through a process of establishing increasingly complex forms and ideas. Since this growth is interwoven with the child's total intellectual and emotional existence, it should not be viewed in isolation as being simply a series of activities intended to enable the child to pass time happily independent of the larger developmental ramifications.

It is also important to remember that the emotional and intellectual contributions of art expression far exceed the dividends of the final product (i.e., the pictures or the objects produced) and are important for all children, not simply "the talented ones," to experience. It is the process, with its concomitant learnings, wherein the most significant learnings rest.

Total aims of art education are many and complex. Only the most significant ones are being given consideration here, and it should be recognized that this represents an abbreviated and minimal discussion.

WHY IS ART IMPORTANT?

Art is important because it gives children the opportunity to learn that people think and feel differently about the same things, that there is not always one single "right" way of doing things, and that the individual has the right to his own point of view. Sharing the other fellow's responses and developing tolerance for different ideas are another critical part of learning.

Art is important because it heightens the child's awareness and responsiveness to the rich physical environment which surrounds him. Activities which involve him in handling different materials, in exploring their textures, colors, patterns, and natural properties, extend and develop his visual and sensory capacities. It is imperative that the young child have the opportunity to feel and examine sand, wood, pebbles, springy wire, smooth velvet, and so on. Not only does this examination contribute to his perceptual development, but it assists him in understanding himself in relationship to that which surrounds him.

Art is important because it allows the child to express feelings and responses which he may have but be unable to verbalize. Emotions (particularly those of a frightening or upsetting nature) are easier for the individual to cope with when they are expressed. It is important that the teacher allow and encourage youngsters to draw and talk about things that seem important to them emotionally (even if such subjects do not always make "comfortable" conversation). Often, what appears to be a most routine drawing has afforded the youngster much expressive satisfaction during the process of its creation.

Typical Examples of Self-expression

If the child who is feeling tense or angry paints for a few minutes in a rapid, involved manner, much emotion may be released.

The six year old who paints "the dragon who's after me in my bad dream" may feel eminently better about the threat of nightmares. He also may feel less threatened when he comes to realize that other children have bad dreams, too.

The four-year-old boy who paints himself as the fire chief experiences a marvelous moment of complete self-realization!

Art is important because it furthers the child's capacity to think in an original, fresh manner. When a teacher challenges a child to utilize his own imagination (rather than hers) in art, she aids him in becoming a more inventive, independent thinker in *all* that he undertakes.

The following kinds of ideas are typical of those that might be ultilized by a teacher to encourage creative thinking:

"If you could invent a new way of traveling, what could it be? How would it look?"

"If you had a funny-shaped piece of paper like this ⌣ or like this ⌔ what kind of an animal (or an automobile or a house) could you make it into?"

"How many different shapes of paper can you cut?"

"What could you do with this empty box, this stick, this card-board (beautiful junk)? How could you place it or arrange it to make something that's your very own idea?"

Art, whether it involves the mature adult or the very young, by definition is related to *self*. Consequently, it is fundamental that any individual involved in the furthering of art activity recognize that *conceptual freedom* is the most important concern.

For a child to feel free to work in his own manner, he needs encouragement and support from the teacher. He needs to feel secure in the knowledge that she is genuinely accepting of his ideas and approach and that *she values his concepts*, even if they are very different from those she is familiar with or is expecting to receive. **Important to Remember**

The child who is confident will plunge freely into art materials and not be unduly dependent upon others' approval. The less secure child will need immediate indication of teacher acceptance. Such simple comments as the following can be very effective in encouraging the dubious beginner:

"I like the way you put that shape next to that other thin shape."

"My goodness, you have good ideas."

"It was hard to make those two pieces of cardboard stick together, but you did it. My, you should be proud!"

The adult who is accepting of "your picture," "your idea," is accepting of "you." This is fundamental to a productive teacher-child relationship and to the inculcating of *self-confidence*.

Teacher acceptance is a broad concept which presupposes that evaluation and guidance exist in relationship to the individual's particular needs rather than as preconceived notions of how something "ought to look" or be.

Art is important because it enables the child to resolve, examine, and clarify ideas and concepts about which he is learning. The child who has learned about the parts of a fire truck or the way to store the fire hose, for example, will often think through his new learnings during the process of drawing.

Originality of ideas
Independence
Confidence in one's own resources
Freedom to express personally meaningful ideas and feelings
Acceptance of self as unique and valuable
Clarification of ideas and concepts

Helping the child to gain these things is important.

Not all methods of teaching art to children are to be considered equally desirable. Lessons in which the final product is predetermined by the adult rob the child of the opportunity to accomplish the aforementioned goals. **Are there undesirable methods of teaching art in terms of achieving these aims?**

These methods are often called "dictated art."

Some examples of dictated art are:

> Coloring books
> Mimeographed or hexographed forms of animals, people, historical figures, and so on
> "Follow the directions" lessons in which a step-by-step process provides the child with a product identical to those of his classmates
> Demonstrations by the teacher of how to draw an object or an idea

Educational research indicates that this kind of teaching in art is detrimental to creative thinking and tends to make children dependent upon adults for inspiration and dissatisfied with their own attempts.

If *conceptual freedom* is truly understood and valued, it is obvious that lessons that do the thinking for the child have no part in a program that purports to be a creative one.

If he says, "I can't make a dog; you do it for me."

He needs reassurance that you want *his* concept; he needs encouragement and, perhaps, help on how to think through what it is that's keeping him from feeling able to create the dog. Discussion in such a case is helpful.

You may say, "If I make it, then it's *my* dog, not yours; and I want to see *your* dog, the way you think of it. How many legs does he have? Is the tail long or short? What are the ears like?" If the child is too insecure to start, urge him to make just one part—maybe the head; then praise his result, no matter how meager, and encourage him onward. Solving this problem by making the dog for him leaves you in the same position on subsequent occasions; the youngster is thoroughly convinced that *you* know how and he doesn't.

When he asks for help, guide his conceptual understanding, not his hand. As one five year old once said, "Drawing is easy. You just think your thought and draw your think!"

WHAT SHOULD YOU KNOW ABOUT SCRIBBLING?

There are wide distinctions among individual children in terms of the sophistication of their scribbling. Most children begin to scribble between the ages of two and four and continue to scribble even after they have begun to make representational objects. The capacity to "make real things" does not result in the abandonment of scribbling; the two activities travel hand-in-hand. Both are important. The child is not necessarily in difficulty if he scribbles into the fifth year, especially if he has had fewer opportunities than other children to work with art materials. In this case, his development is apt to be slower.

Scribbling begins with crude, uncontrolled markings which eventually give way to more discrete, specific forms (circles, rectilinear forms, crosses, etc.) In her book *Analyzing Children's Art*, Rhoda Kellogg has documented the sequence of schemata that children produce. The adult who is familiar with this progression will be able to make important assessments as to an individual child's growth and development during the preschool years.

Scribbling is an important activity; children need to do it, for it is one of the first means of nonverbal self-expression. Consequently, the thorough exploration of scribbling is a prerequisite for all subsequent activity in graphic work.

It is important that the adult not degrade scribbling. Children should not be made to feel that scribbling is a "babyish" thing; nor should adults interfere and make such comments as, "Why don't you make a nice doggie instead of just scribbling?" Such comments inhibit growth.

Big crayons and large paper are good materials for the scribbler.

During the latter part of the scribbling stage, children name their markings and manipulations and often fabricate great stories about their pictures. Enjoy the stories . . . even if the correlations are not obvious. These associations evolve during or after the process of working and reflect the youngster's increasing capacity to utilize symbols. Objective, representational work will soon follow in the majority of children between the ages of three and five years, although scribbling may still continue with some youngsters.

The representational stage is of major significance because it indicates that the child understands that there is a relationship between his markings and his thoughts. He is now able to conceptualize and to project his ideas in a more complete, highly integrated manner.

His drawings will lack detail, and what the adult may consider to be fundamental parts at this stage, for the child will include only what is of paramount importance to him at the time that he makes a given drawing,

WHAT SHOULD YOU KNOW ABOUT THE EARLY REPRESENTATIONAL STAGE?

not all that he knows about a particular phenomenon. Consequently, if the drawing concerns a policeman involved in important work, he may be depicted complete with gun belt and hat but without fingers and other clothing. The child does not lack understanding that these other elements exist; rather, he is selective about what is relevant at a given moment. Essentially, early representationalism is an abstract form of art which includes, eliminates, or distorts sizes and shapes according to highly subjective notions of an immediate reality.

**Important
to Remember**

If the child eliminates the ears or nose or makes the proportions incorrectly on the head—this is as it should be! The teacher should not consider these to be errors; she should not attempt to "fix" his drawings and tell him how they ought to be. It is *imperative* at this stage of development that the child feel free to create symbols as they occur to him without any awareness of possible adult standards of "right and wrong." Failure to acknowledge this fact can inhibit and dissuade a youngster from further personal expression.

**If You Take the
Time to look**

You will realize that young children's early representational drawings are often intelligently conceived, humorous, insightful, and very beautiful! Bear in mind that the child's immature motoric skills frequently make it difficult for the adult to recognize the scope of his expression.

**THE IMPORTANCE
OF MATERIALS**

Materials are important not only because they are the vehicles which enable children to project ideas and feelings, but also because they challenge the child's sense of competence and mastery. As he learns to cut with dexterity, to control exactly the right amount of glue as it oozes from the plastic container, he strengthens both his fine motor skills and his confidence in being able to manage the environment. The wise adult will minimize her part in completing technical challenges for the child and, instead, provide only the necessary reinforcement. "Let's see if you can really get the stapler to go through that heavy paper." "I think that you can get that piece of Scotch tape free from the dispenser, if you grip it more firmly."

Crayons

In general, the younger the child the larger the crayon should be. Order boxes of large and small widths of a good enough quality so that they do not leave waxy deposits that can be easily rubbed off the paper. Broken crayons offer much opportunity for exploration. Encourage youngsters to use the sides as well as the ends.

Kindergarten Chalk

This is fat, wonderfully soft chalk which comes in a wide range of basic and vibrant colors. Since it creates a powdery residue, use newspapers underneath for protection. Colors mix together with ease. This is a grand beginning, freeing material; it discourages tight, inhibited work and makes free experimentation easy.

Try wetting the paper (big paper bags work well) and then applying chalk. It's luminous!

Oil-Base Pastels

Oil-base pastels are a cross between an oily crayon and a chalk. These sticks are narrow in shape and luminous in color. The largest box offers a rich selection of unusual colors to which children are most responsive. Oil pastels work well on a variety of surfaces; their oil base makes them suitable for even waxy papers.

Felt-Tip Pens

The felt-tip pen is a luxury item, but one that children love. Use by a few children, with supervision, is feasible. They are splendid on all surfaces, especially exciting when used on finger paint or shelf paper. They are available in both waterproof and washable inks. The waterproof variety can be used on fabric (old sheets are great!) and will withstand many washings. How about using them on doll clothes and equipment, bean bags, party napkins, flags—what can you think of?

Pastes and Glues

When Young Children Use Paste

Sometimes little children are unaware of the whole concept of *why* and *how* to paste. It is important to demonstrate and explain these concepts to beginners.

Increase children's skill and dexterity and provide them with rich manipulative experiences by making pasting activities frequent and diverse. Consider the following as only a beginning:

> Pasting—egg shells, sand, pebbles, other natural materials, unusual papers and cardboards, the macaroni products, dried lima beans, peas

Many youngsters enjoy the sensory activity of pasting. They want to smear and mess in paste rather than use it functionally. Be tolerant of this as a basic need and offer these youngsters other materials (finger paints, mud and water, etc.) which provide good outlets for this drive.

Homemade paste

Combine one-half cup flour and cold water; mix to creamy consistency; boil slowly for five minutes while stirring; cool; add a few drops of oil of wintergreen to retard spoiling and give a pleasing odor; store in covered jar and refrigerate, if possible.

Felt-tip pens appeal to the child's sense of order, control, and aesthetics.

Ordinary commercial paper paste

This paste is adequate for the majority of paper projects; dispense either on individual scraps of paper or in small baby-food jars with covers.

White all-purpose glue

This is a *must.* It seems expensive—and is when purchased in small containers. However, if the glue is purchased in a gallon container, expense is minimized, and the glue can be diluted with water for many activities. This glue will allow anything to adhere to almost any surface. It can make the difference between successful, rewarding art experiences and those leading to frustration and disappointment. You will use it with beautiful junk; in adhering grasses, wood, branches, etc.; in all three-dimensional construction work; and in tissue-paper work, to mention only a few areas.

Dispense white glue either in individual jars or in small paper cups with Q-tips.

Scissors

Please—make sure they *cut!* There's nothing more frustrating than trying to learn to cut with a pair of scissors that are too blunt. Provide "learning to cut" times for beginners in which the only aim is to snip a pile of cut scraps. Feel free to emphasize the skill! Let them paste the results with a big sign saying, "We are learning to cut!"

Paper

Paper is commonly available in sizes nine inches by twelve inches, twelve by eighteen, and eighteen by twenty-four. Offer children an opportunity to work with each size. Paper measuring eighteen by twenty-four is most satisfactory for the majority of painting experiences.

Basic Papers

This paper is available commercially and is the least expensive. It is adequate for painting, coloring, etc. but is far from ideal for older children who are growing in their visual awareness. **Newsprint (unprinted newspaper)**

Heavier than newsprint, this paper is good for crayons, chalk, felt-tip pens, etc.; it is substantial enough for some three-dimensional work. Have a good supply on hand. **Manila paper**

Provide this heavier, better-quality paper on occasion for painting. **Heavy white paper**

This is ordinary colored paper. Make it available to children; it's excellent with cray-pas, chalk, felt-tip pens, paint, etc. **Construction or poster paper**

Since finger-paint paper is expensive, good shelf paper can be substituted. **Finger-paint paper**

Supplementary, Commercially Available Papers

Flint paper (comes in geometric shapes)
Metallic paper
Gummed colored paper
Rice or absorbent paper
Gold and silver squares
Cellophane—rolls of wonderful colors (Use this for teaching mixing colors; use it on windows; overlap it.)
Sandpaper (Color on it and use it in collages.)
Origami (It is available in small and large squares and in vivid colors. It is easily cut.)
Contact paper
Glazed and unglazed shelf paper (glazed for finger painting)
Tracing paper
Tissue paper

Salvage and Remnant Papers

Children, like adults, respond to variety and change. A teacher who recognizes this and who is resourceful and imaginative can offer her group a wealth of stimulation through the utilization of remnant and inexpensively obtained paper products. The following list provides just a beginning.

Printer's remnants. Herein is one of your best sources of interesting and varied paper goods. Printers dispose of vast amounts of scrap paper; much of it is cut in unusual sizes and shapes and is of a higher quality than most schools can hope to obtain. Don't overlook this free, excellent source!

Aluminum foil. Use two- and three-dimensionally.

Stocking-box paper. It is colorful and is often printed with handsome patterns.

Wallpaper books. Available free at certain times from dealers.

Meat-store paper. Whom do you know in the business?

Old newspaper. Paint on it; use it for papier-mache.

Used or unused holiday and wrapping paper.

Paper bags.

Magazines. Save pages with large areas of color and pattern; allow children to make collections of these.

Waxed paper. Scratch on it with tooth picks; add it to a collage.

Department-store box tissue. Good for painting; use with chalk, construction work.

*Important
Reminders
About Paper*

Change frequently the *size* and *shape* that you offer children; this is a strong means of motivation.

Offer a rich variety of textures. Capitalize on these not only in art but also as a means of increasing *vocabulary* and *general understanding.* Discuss such things as "Which one feels bumpy? Smooth? Wiggly? What other things feel this way?"

Tearing paper is an important activity. Not only does it develop motor dexterity and free children, but it produces fascinating irregular shapes which are suggestive of objects and abstract designs. Try having youngsters tear shapes freely and then discuss what *they* think could be done with them.

"Who can tear an *enormous* shape? A *little* shape? A *narrow* shape? Such questions will aid vocabulary building!

**Challenging
conceptualization**

Older children can be challenged to confront notions of conservation and quantity through simple provocations while utilizing papers and other materials. Suppose that a small group of children each had only one piece of nine-by-twelve paper which he or she could tear or cut . . . alter in any chosen way . . . and then reassemble, utilizing all the parts. The resultant varied shapes of a highly diverse nature could be compared and would help to establish greater understanding of a complicated but important concept.

**Additional activities
using paper**

"If we tear this piece of paper up and join the pieces end to end, how long do you think we could make it?" This small group project encourages children's cooperation and exchange of ideas while providing them with a basis for dealing with notions of length and quantity.

"How many different ways are there to join paper?" Try asking this of a group of children. Acknowledge all solutions, no matter how outlandish! Bobby pins, saliva, squeezing and folding, toothpicks, and sewing are just a few of the possible solutions that little ones will offer to this interesting question. An activity such as this strengthens the idea that you value the children's ideas and that there are many ways to solve the same problem.

Poster or
Tempera Paint

Availability

Powdered tempera is inexpensive but needs to be made up. Do not dilute it so much that it becomes too pallid and watery.

Bottled prepared paint is preferable; dilute it *only* to a consistency which spreads readily without undue dripping. You save money when you purchase it by the gallon.

Containers

Fruit-juice cans or *baby-food jars*—as many as possible—can be used. Plastic covers make these ideal for storage. An individual brush for each color is desirable. These containers fit nicely into cardboard soda-pop containers and offer great flexibility of use and minimize spilling.

Muffin tins provide an adequate means of distribution; using these requires a child to wash the brush between each color. Tins can be stored with asphalt tile squares as covers, then stacked.

For the most part, it's best if brushes are large and full and cover a *Brushes*
large area rapidly, although do provide a few narrower ones for those
who feel the need for them. It's advisable to have a separate brush for
each color, along with some extra ones with empty jars to enable
children to mix new colors at will. This is part of the excitement of
painting. Don't discourage it!

Easels can be fun; a clear plastic easel, for instance, enables children to *General Tips*
paint interactively. Easels are not necessary, however. In fact, working
on a flat surface (floor or table) minimizes dripping and is appealing to
many children.

Use newspapers, a large tarpaulin, or an old shower curtain under
easels and for floor painting.

Include children in the clean-up process. This is an important part of
their learning! Collecting and washing brushes is an important part of the
total experience!

Old clothes racks make good drying areas. So do clotheslines (and
clothespins)!

Paint is more difficult to control than linear, less fluid materials. Don't *Things to Be*
be surprised if children do not produce the same kinds of complex forms *Aware of*
that they do when working with markers or crayons.

Young children are more involved in the act of painting than they are
in the picture itself. They may obliterate what seems beautiful to you. Let
them. They may mix and smear colors together on the paper. Let them.
(They're investigating and discovering as well as often expending some
strong feelings!)

Don't impose stereotyped attitudes about what color the sky or the
ground should be; this limits freedom of choice and aesthetic growth.
There need be no literal correlation between a painting and reality. This
defeats personal expression and all that art implies.

The children need to be reminded that derogatory comments about
another's work are unacceptable and that it is the prerogative of the
individual to decide how his painting should look! This is important to
learn!

Children at a clear plastic easel delight in each other's productions.

Tapes

Cellophane

For young children who have difficulty dispensing tape or who utilize too much at one time, cut many small pieces and attach them lightly to the edge of a table or shelf. The children can take them one at a time as needed.

Masking Tape

Good for affixing things in three-dimensional as well as two-dimensional work; can easily be painted over.

Vinyl and Holiday Tapes

Lots of fun. Use them in collage work or by themselves.

Finger Painting

Finger painting is an important activity which frees youngsters and encourages them to partake of sensory experiences. Demonstrate how one can utilize arms, elbows, backs and fronts of hands, twisting arms, etc. Although some will enjoy "drawing" with a finger in the paint, this is not the primary goal of using this medium, and children should be encouraged (not compelled) to utilize it in a freer manner.

Finger Paint

Commercial

Finger paint can be bought in ready-to-use jars of varying colors.

Formulas for homemade paint

1. 1 cup liquid starch
   6 cups water
   1½ cup soap chips
   Dissolve the soap chips in water until not lumpy. Mix well with starch.

2. Mix wheat paste (ordinary wallpaper paste) into slightly warm water. Stir. Pour into individual containers; add pigment to each one.

Commercially available finger-paint paper is excellent but expensive. *Paper*
More economical substitutes are shelf paper; commercial dime-store glazed papers; or an enameled table top—as is!
Wet paper or table before beginning with wet hands or sponge. Have fun!

What are stick and gum materials? Everything you can obtain that can **Stick and Gum**
be licked and adhered—*all gummed commodities*, such as labels, air- **Materials**
mail stickers, reinforcements, colored dots, book-club stamps, stars, letters, paper strips, numbers, seals, etc.
Use them with any kind of paper, although they work well with interestingly shaped printer's remnants and cardboard.

Some children will see the shapes as parts of objects (a circle as an eye, *Remember*
for example, or the wheel of a wagon), while others will prefer to organize them in a nonobjective manner. Both ways are right; do not indicate a preference for only one way!
Organization (designing and composing) is the important aspect of this activity. Motor development is also furthered.

The following list contains readily available materials which are ex- **Linear Three-**
cellent to have on hand for children to use. The first time each is utilized, **Dimensional**
it would seem wise to limit the number of other materials which are **Materials**
present. (New materials are adequate motivation, and too many at once confuse the beginner and reduce his possible involvement.) Once the material has been used enough for the child to be thoroughly familiar with its potentialities, have it available for general use. All of these articles can be pasted down in conjunction with crayon, paint, etc. and are satisfactory for inclusion with a lesson in sculpture.

String, thread *Examples*
Yarn
Rick-rack, sewing tape
Bias tapes
Thin rubber tubing (from a hardware store)
Basket reed
Colored sticks
Toothpicks
Pipe cleaners
Spaghetti (all noodle products)
Thin dowels (medical sticks)
Q-Tips

VEGETABLE PRINTING

You need carrots, green peppers, potatoes, lemons, oranges, lettuce, **What do you need?**
and anything else which provides an interesting cross section when cut.
You need tempera paint in several different colors. Place the paint and a few paper towels in a shallow container; this creates a homemade equivalent of a stamp pad and requires less skill in the printing procedure.

You need a surface on which to print. Ordinary white or colored construction paper is fine; rice paper or other highly absorbent surfaces are exciting! Tissue and newspaper are good, too.

A brush is optional, but helpful in applying paint.

How do you do it?   For little ones, simply slice flat sections of vegetables; one potato cut into many small shapes and forms will provide enough pieces for a dozen children.

Dip—and print!

For Variety   Try printing on cloth; tempera is still all right, but with older children, textile paint makes it permanent! Old sheets are great.

Try printing on continuous rolls of shelf paper or mural paper.

Hardware stores that sell window shades will frequently give away the remnant pieces that they have trimmed when filling custom-sized orders. These are superb for printing and are natural scrolls.

THING PRINTING

Do you know that everything prints?   It's fascinating to discover that all kinds of small objects can be dipped in paint and used to print. Ordinary things that are about the room, including salvage articles, produce a variety of shapes and textures. All you need is:

Brushes
A few pans of paints
A surface on which to print (Everything from small pieces of paper to fabric is appropriate.)

and *things*, such as:

Keys
Sponges
Corrugated cardboard
Hair rollers
Paper clips
Clothespins
Cardboard strips
Empty film spools
Natural materials (leaves, sticks, etc.)

Keep in Mind   Some children will drag and push the printing implement back and forth instead of printing. This is a natural instinct and part of exploration. Don't be too quick to say, "Oh, no."

Extending Printing   After children have had abundant experiences on a primary level of experimentation and are ready for more complex undertakings, the teacher can encourage repetition and elaboration in a variety of ways. Help children to understand the basic concept of the same form repeated over and over again. Look at fabrics, wallpaper, etc. Clarify the idea of "making the same thing again and again." What does it mean to "repeat a design?" You may want to introduce the fascinating thought that a single total design can be made up of many individual parts or aggregates. Once older children understand this concept, there is high motivation to print with greater deliberation and purposefulness. Specific activities, such as making wallpaper for "our house," clothing for the dolls, decorative panels for block structures, etc. can lend a note of significance.

What fun it is to see whether others can guess what the object was that **After You're Done** you used to print with. This not only serves the skill of visual discrimination but also provides an opportunity for a verbal give-and-take.

Working in three dimensions is an exciting experience and offers **SCULPTURE** technical and cognitive challenges that do not exist when utilizing two-dimensional materials. Although all children should be encouraged to explore a variety of approaches in art, the teacher will observe that some youngsters seem more at home with three-dimensional activities than with two-dimensional ones. All too frequently, the curriculum is slanted too heavily in one direction, and many youngsters who appear disinterested in art would readily respond if the diet were balanced.

Working with clay—and modeling media of all descriptions—is a **Modeling Materials of a** meaningful occupation for children from the simple standpoint of **Manipulative Nature** sensory and manipulative satisfaction. They love to *squish, squeeze, roll* and *play with* soft, pliable materials. Let them! Early experiences should be precisely this. As children grow older (five, six), they still retain this need, but they also begin to explore clay in a more representational manner and to show interest in creating objects, such as animals, simple containers, and people.

Explain to them, if it seems necessary, about smoothing out adjoined sections so they don't break when dry but *don't* show them what to make. This should be their decision.

Challenge their thinking by raising appropriate questions related to weight, balance, three dimensionality, etc.

"How can you keep those legs from falling down when you place something heavy on top?"

"What else could you do to help it stay together?"

"How does it look all the way around? You know, that's what's exciting about sculpture, you can see all of its sides."

Muddling Dough   *Simple Formulas*

Mix and knead:

1   cup salt
1   cup flour
½   cup water

(As used, add more flour to avoid stickiness.) Store in covered jar or wax paper in refrigerator.

Modeling Dough

Mix together:

1   cup salt
½   cup cornstarch
⅔   cup water

Cook and stir constantly until mixture thickens. Remove from heat.
Cool; knead in vegetable coloring. Store in refrigerator.

Sugar Dough

Mix:

1   tablespoon water
2   tablespoons sugar
3   tablespoons flour

Add vegetable coloring.

*Commercially
Available
Modeling Material*

Potters and school suppliers package five- and ten-pound plastic bags of excellent ready-to-use clay. It keeps well a long time in an airtight bin or crock. Some kinds are self-hardening; others can be commercially fired at low cost. Inquire.

Clay pieces can be painted with ordinary tempera paint. If desired, they can be shellacked, too.

Other Sculptural Materials

Potato Sculpture

Use potatoes, straws, toothpicks, wire, yarn, pipe cleaners, paper nut cups, and anything else you think of! Encourage youngsters to be re-sourceful figuring out *how* to affix and organize objects! Straws can be cut and slipped over sticks, which are inserted into base.

Other Bases

Appropriate alternate bases include:

Plasticine (a firm, nonhardening clay)
Play-Doh
Soap
Small boxes
Styrofoam

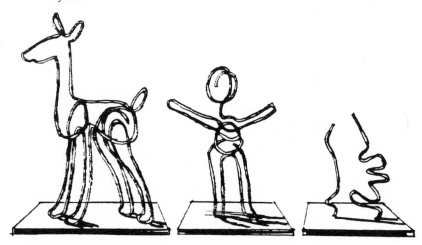

Box Sculpture

Assemble all the empty boxes you can—everything from cigarette to cookie and cereal containers. What can you build? Spraying or brush painting embellishes them.

Wire

Wire is material not commonly offered children, but they love its manipulative, suggestive qualities. Electrician's wire (plastic-coated in bright, beautiful colors) is available in hardware stores. Other spooled wires of narrow gauge are excellent for sculpture. Utilize scraps of wood from the woodworking bin as handsome, simple bases. A good stapler will hold the wire firm. Remember that the children may have other ideas as how to utilize these materials. Help them to express and implement these ideas! Don't insist on *realism*. Nonobjective organizations are equally worthwhile.

BEAUTIFUL JUNK

What is it?

Empty boxes, paper-towel tubes, old ribbons, cookie-box paper, egg boxes, all types of kitchen salvage, plastic spools from cameras, containers that slide and move—*anything* you have left over!

Why do you use it?

Beautiful junk is used because its various sizes, shapes, and forms suggest infinite possibilities and challenge children to *use their imaginations, think independently, and express feelings and ideas that belong to them as individuals.* It also allows them the opportunity to work in a three-dimensional manner.

How do you present it the first time?

You could say (holding up a sliding box, for example), "What could you make this into? What could you add to it that's here on the table? How would you make it stick?" "What could you do with this and this and this?" "It can be anything you like. It needn't look like anything anyone else is making." "Anything you want to make is fine. It should be your own idea."

How do you present it at subsequent times?

The first few experiences with a new material should be motivated in terms of personal exploration—the teacher should emphasize that *whatever the child decides is valid and acceptable!* Later experiences can include such specific motivations as: "Let's make something that an animal or a person could live in" or "Let's make something that moves."

Accompanying Materials

White liquid glue (which can be purchased in a one-gallon container and watered down slightly), scissors, a paper punch.

Keep in Mind

Early attempts will be *crude.* Do not expect representational results from all children. Accept all solutions to the problem; evaluate in terms of *organizing things in an original way*, working hard to join and affix, etc.

If you interfere and edit the results, fix the product, or impose your ideas, you're defeating your initial aims.

WHAT CAN YOU DO WITH STRAWS?

Children are challenged and stimulated by ordinary drinking straws in their art activities. The straws can be included with collage materials and beautiful junk, can be offered as a primary material, or can be offered in conjunction with only one or two other materials. Straws are available in clear or colored cellophane also.

Simple Motivation with Straws, White Glue, Scissors, and Paper

"What can you do with these materials?"

Cut the straws.
Bend them.
Twist them.
Slit them open and past them flat, etc.

"How could you make a picture or design with them?"
"How could you make them stick? Yes, you must wait for the glue to dry!"

"And, *how* could you make something fat?" Paste lots of them together!

"Make whatever you'd like. It may be a house or a friend or an animal, or maybe it will be an interesting arrangement of shapes!"

What are the values?

Using imagination to see the potential in a material and learning that the teacher values *the child's idea, his solution;* developing motor control in handling a material, manual dexterity. The straws, because they are so appealing to the senses, encourage artistic expression—they make the child *want* to create a picture!

How else can straws be used?

Cut and string them; combine them with other small objects that can be utilized in the same manner (gummed paper reinforcements, foil paper with holes cut in it, etc.).

An Idea Most Children Love!

Straws can be used in sculpture—along with potatoes (as a base), thin sticks, wire, and other such materials. Inserting thin sticks or wire within the pieces of straw makes it possible to form a multitude of shapes and constructions. These can be painted.

Use straws as a material in constructing hats, masks, costumes, etc.

Use them as a means of *learning to count* and do simple number games.

With older children, you can use straws and white glue alone as a marvelously challenging construction material.

Managing paste and collage items is a demanding task.

CHILDREN LOVE TO MAKE COLLAGES.

Bits and scraps of papers, flat objects, newspaper, cloth, cookie-box papers, etc., can be pasted down to create fascinating pictures. Try to assemble materials which are *visually appealing* and offer a wide range of possibilities for individual selection. Combine articles of different textures, too (smooth, rough, crinkly, fluffy, scratchy, etc.). Language growth is developed through discussion and expression of "how it feels to me."

Encourage youngsters to talk about which colors and textures they like together, what color background paper seems best, what the articles remind them of, etc.

Strong glue
Scissors
Background paper
An assortment of challenging collage materials

Very young children cannot cut or alter the shapes of collage objects with ease. Use variety in the sizes and shapes of pieces you offer them.

It will be sufficient to have children simply select, arrange, and adhere materials without any particular focus involved. Later, when the medium is familiar and the capacity for representational work is firmly established, you might suggest ideas like the following:

"A make-believe animal; one that never lived."
"A place where you'd like to live."
"A happy or sad feeling." (Emphasize here that some objects make you feel one way; others, another. "Which colors, textures, etc., make you feel happy, sad, cool, hot, etc.?")

Keep in mind that things to stress are one's selections, color and textural relationships, how well the things have been affixed, and the mood of the picture, rather than "how much it looks like a house."

ORGANIZING THE ENVIRONMENT

Storing Basics

Certain materials are fundamental and will be utilized with frequency by children in a classroom. It is best if these are easily accessible on low shelves so that children can go to them at will, utilize them spontaneously, and share the responsibility of getting them and returning them to their storage places. Simple uniform containers, neatly stacked and readily identifiable, are a most important investment, since haphazard disorganization does not promote creative activity. Although there are many alternatives for boxing, Alexander boxes (utilized by many hardware stores) are an excellent option. They are available in many different sizes, have a lowered front for easy accessibility, and line up in an orderly, inviting manner. Labeling each one with its written name or an appropriate symbol helps children develop the capacity for classification and build reading readiness skills.

Certainly a teacher would want to modify her list of basics in terms of the time of year, the age, experience, and general disposition of the group, etc., but the following list might be considered as containing items appropriate for most young children:

Crayons and chalks
Scissors
Various papers
Paper punches
Staplers
Glues and pastes
Felt-tip pens
Scotch and masking tapes
Miscellaneous beautiful junk
Strings and yarns
Painting equipment

Children can help.

If individual boxes are available within the classroom for different kinds of salvage (large, small, linear, bulk, metallic, cardboard, etc.), children can be encouraged to bring appropriate things from home in order to insure a continuous flow of materials. This is important not only in terms of practicality but also because it cultivates an awareness of objects in the environment, their physical properties, and their potential for translation into new forms and symbols. It also serves to enrich home-school interrelationships.

Children need repetition and novelty.

Other materials might be brought out only every now and then or for a stretch of a week or more, depending upon the nature of the experience and the teacher's goals. Electrician's wire, straws, toothpicks, Styrofoam balls might be the kinds of things that are rotated from time to time into the basic storage area and then removed intermittently in order to retain a sense of fresh stimulation. This is important. Although children gain much from predictability and a thorough awareness of what is available, they are also responsive to the novel, the freshly perceived. Retaining the balance between the old and the new, the familiar and the unfamiliar, is a subtle but crucial part of classroom organization and curriculum. It is also important to recognize that many children need repeated contact with the new before they feel free to really explore and extend the potentialities of a medium. The adult should avoid the "flash in the pan" syndrome in which a material or activity is presented once, then removed indefinitely, and the child never has the opportunity to gain a sense of competence and familiarity.

WHAT IS MOTIVATION?

Whenever the teacher talks about the ways in which the children can utilize materials, raises questions, comments, or even sets up the environment in a specific provocative manner, she is, of course, "motivating children."

When should the teacher use it?

When children are very young or have not had many experiences with materials, it is inadvisable for the teacher to feel any need to furnish additional motivation. Self-motivation is always the highest possible form, and when the child seems highly involved in exploring what paint will do or how to handle clay, it would seem obvious that he should be left undisturbed to do just that.

As children grow older and have used materials with frequency, simple discussion of a concept often will encourage them to work with greater enthusiasm and intent. It should be remembered that since art is *self-expression*, the teacher should recognize that all youngsters will not be equally responsive to ideas that are not self-initiated and should treat with deference those children who choose to dismiss her discussion.

Motivation can be enriched by the utilization of objects and devices (animals, slides, pictures, etc.) and by the control over materials exerted at any one given time. Nevertheless, verbalization is frequently an active ingredient of the total process. Essentially, the adult attempts to increase active awareness of both affective and perceptual processes in order to enable the child to produce a richer, more highly integrated form of expression.

Motivation should be kept broad enough to include personal interpretation.

It is critical that the teacher recognize this point. There's a world of difference between having a teacher say, "What is it about the city that you like? Is it the tall, tall buildings? The taxis? The high bridges? How about the busy, busy feeling? What do you like, Jimmy? Oh, the fire escapes, the people rushing about! Or is it riding up high on the elevated?" and "We're going to make a picture of the city. I want everyone to draw the big, high buildings."

The teacher should strive to obtain individual responses to a given concept rather than her own preconceived ones. Some youngsters, if motivated about the visual aspects of the city, may respond by making a picture of their barber. This is as it should be! Remember that motivation is a *means* of activating latent awareness. The response is the important thing, not whether or not it is the specific one the adult envisioned.

The topics selected should be ones that are personally meaningful to **About Topics** the child, either through actual personal involvement or through prior study. Do not ask them to draw or paint Eskimos, fishing ships, or jungle animals if these things are outside their experience. Honest art experience grows out of identification and experience. You cannot express what you do not know! Take your cues from their world. Children of this age are highly egocentric. The teacher would do well to recognize this and select ideas and topics for exploration which are personally pertinent.

Typical subjects might include:

Your house
Your family
Where you like to play
Your favorite thing to play with
An animal you know
How you feel when you're lonely
The city
Stores—where you shop
What you want to be when you grow up
Favorite clothes
How you can help other people
A self-portrait
Things that scare you
Things that make you happy
When it rains
What you like to do when it's hot
Broken things
Dreams
Friends
Old people
Someone you love
How babies are different
Dark places
Shapes and lines you like
When you get angry

This list could go on and on, but it is best to take your cues from the interests of your group.

For the most part, simple discussion works best. Ask questions; seek *How would you* out responses. Emphasize the fact that everyone will feel differently *present topics?* about the same ideas: "It's *your* idea I want."

Voice and dramatics are very important. Ask questions and conduct discussions with enthusiasm! This often makes the difference between the children's listening or not listening. Keep discussions brief; they should not become unwieldy. Don't allow responses to be so thoroughly expressed verbally that there's nothing left to draw about.

Utilize physical objects and demonstrations where they might heighten interest. For example:

An umbrella (when discussing rain)
Hats (different jobs that workers do)
Toy cars (discussing traffic and cars in general)
A key ("if you had a private place with a lock")
Mittens and gloves
Musical instruments
A broom
A shoe, costumes

IN REGARD TO PRAISE

Praise is a vital tool in the socialization of children. Through both verbal and nonverbal reinforcement, children come to understand and internalize the value systems of the adults who are important to them. But there are dangers in too much praise, just as there is in praise that is mechanically and insensitively delivered. It is important that children work primarily for the satisfaction inherent in an activity and because of their own personal preferences rather than to elicit platitudes from teachers. Use praise sparingly and honestly, encouraging children to do their own job of evaluation and responding. "How do you feel about it? Is this one of your favorites . . . or not?" Let children know that it's okay not to like all products equally well; producing them is the really important part of the activity, anyway.

What do you say when he shows you what he's made?

Sometimes the product really is meaningful to the adult; in this case it is natural and appropriate to respond with positive comments. Sometimes it seems apparent that the process alone has been the important thing, and this, too, should merit adult response.

"My goodness, you worked hard on that."
"You were really able to get that to stand up. Fine."
"You had a great time mushing and squishing in that stuff, didn't you?"

Don't ask, "What is it?"

Avoid confronting the child with the perennial question, "What is it?" Not only does this question extend the expectation that there must be literal content, but it may seem deflating to the youngster for whom the answer to it is very, very clear. Sensitive adults have come to employ the questions: "Does it have a story?" or "Would you like to tell me about it?" They thus leave the issue of amplification and clarification in the hands of the maker and also provide an important base for language extension.

Don't always relate only to reality.

Many adults respond so much more enthusiastically to representational products than they do to nonobjective ones that children begin to feel that the former is more valid than the latter. Make certain that your comments don't make constant reference to how much "something looks like a dog . . . or a car, etc." or to the consistent interrelationship to storytelling. If children are to gain a sense of understanding about the physical, sensory, and visual aspects of art, it is important that they hear these dimensions articulated as well.

> "Look at how all these lines run together."
> "These colors are peppy . . . bouncy . . . ."
> 'That's a sleepy-looking shape over there."
> "It makes me feel like I want to stroke it."

Comments such as these help to communicate to the child the range of ways in which art can be considered yet do not reduce its existence to matters of representational accuracy.

If you're not certain, talk about some of the physical characteristics (colors, lines, shapes, etc.) of the child's work, but if the child persists with "What do you think it *is*?" be honest and say that you're not certain. What's important is extending the base of understanding regarding the ways in which people can respond to art; the child will provide the identification if he feels you're unable to do so, but it is vital that he gain a sense of the complexity of the visual process rather than just its literal communicative powers. **When it's something, only you don't know WHAT!**

Teachers of young children are often most attentive about making certain that children's paintings and other artwork are immediately labeled with the maker's name. Although this is reasonable for a variety of reasons (it increases the child's understanding of the written word; it reinforces a sense of self, etc.), it also can be overdone. One child was observed as she moved sequentially to each of three adults in her preschool classroom to share her just completed, much-loved painting. From each adult, the first response came automatically, "Did you put your name on it?" This mechanical issue dominated in each encounter, when attention might have been focused on feelings, aesthetics, or representational content. **Names on Artwork**

Children will approach art materials, as they do everything else, in a variety of ways, reflecting their own distinct personalities and modes of confronting the world. Some will investigate boldly—others will be most tentative; some will work systematically with consideration to detail—others will work in an offhand manner; some will have long attention spans and be capable of deep concentration—others will finish their involvement in a matter of moments. Developmental capabilities within a given group will run the gamut; individual differences will be pronounced. **INDIVIDUAL DIFFERENCES**

The teacher will want to be an acute observer, clarifying for herself exactly how each child is operating and whether or not his behavior is consistent with that revealed in other activities. She will want to know his level of conceptualization, his dexterity with various materials, and his concerns, preferences, and general reactions to the experience. In some cases, the teacher may feel that the child's approach is an immature one but that time and experience are all that are needed for him to grow. In other instances, she may feel that lack of maturation is not the whole issue and that there is need to structure the activity more firmly by clarifying expectations for the possible approaches to materials, **The teacher needs to observe.**

providing physical and verbal reinforcement, and helping the child to extend and persevere when it seems clear that it is difficult for him to do so.

One needs to exercise caution, however. Certainly the adult does not want to be controlling or overly manipulative within the art experience, but sensitive, aware teachers come to know the distinction between this approach and providing a somewhat fragmented child with the necessary supports to attend a task in a more deliberate manner.

This is not to imply that teacher intervention should assume the role of showing the child what to make or providing partially executed things for him to complete, etc. On the contrary, conceptualization should always rest with the child. But the teacher can help immeasurably just by her presence, by diverting distractions, and by simple supportive statements like the following:

> "It's getting so tall. It might just get taller and taller."
>
> "Now you have two funny shapes. How many more are you going to have?"
>
> "Tell me what you're going to do next."

. . . and by building in certain expectations (i.e., giving individual children a specific number of elements that they can utilize in any manner they choose, providing all of them are used—for example, ten small gummed reinforcements, short lengths of string, paper, or a base of Styrofoam with six twigs and ten Popsicle sticks.)

Or after having had frequent initial experiences with printing, the teacher can divide long strips of paper (perhaps three inches wide) into eight to ten equal boxes and establish the expectation that once a print is put into the first box, the same thing will go into the sequential boxes.

Again, the adult would present these goals as general provocations but would not be coercive in her insistence that the goals be honored.

When a Child Shows Excessive Frustration

Is he doing this in all of his activity? Or does his frustration seem to evidence itself only in his art experiences? If it is occurring within a child who is generally self-confident and productive, give consideration to the following possibilities:

1. Are adults drawing and producing things for him in abundance at home?

2. Is an older sibling or classmate ridiculing his work? Children can be injurious to one another and often hurl insults related to developmental capabilities and skills. "That's no good; it doesn't look like a truck!" "He's just a dopey scribbler!" are frequently heard impertinences in classrooms with young children. Teachers can communicate a great deal about art as well as social behavior by clarifying the individual's rights in regard to his production of artwork and reinforcing the values of "each person's doing his own work in his own way."

3. Are the materials frustrating in and of themselves (i.e., scissors that don't cut; collage scraps that need alteration when no appropriate tool is present; paint so thin that it runs down the paper no matter how much one attempts to control it; glue applicator is a Q-tip when the surface to be covered is vast)?

When children are frequently confronted with situations such as these, their creative attention is diverted—sometimes to the extent of utter frustration.

4. Are the materials or the expectations too advanced for this child's level of development?

5. Are too many children working with too few materials in an area that does not allow for adequate space and sharing? Not only is crowding at a given table problematic but also not having sufficient room in which to place a much-loved production can generate a sense of frustration. Watch to see whether or not children are unintentionally damaging each other's work.

6. Is too much pushing coming from adults within the classroom? Is the child being goaded beyond his legitimate interest and capability? Would he honestly rather be doing something else? Have you considered the range of ways in which his interests and preoccupations could have been joined with a particular art activity?

It is only natural that children have clear preferences for those ac- *When a Child Never* tivities that interest them most. The sensitive teacher will accept this and *Selects the Art* protect the child's right to pursue in depth what is ultimately exciting and *Activity* meaningful for him. On the other hand, children often avoid certain activities for reasons that are complex: insecurity about competence, peer identification, parental pressures, negative associations with the activity, and general lack of awareness and familiarity. Again, diagnosis is important in assessing what is really operative. The adult needs to determine:

Does Robert avoid all activities that require fine motor skills?
Do Anne and George prefer two-dimensional things to three-dimensional ones?
Do children indicate a location preference within the room and tend to go to the same area all the time?
Are there attitudes about some activities being "male" and others "female?"

The resourceful teacher will find a variety of methods for intervening once she is certain what the nature of the problem is.

What happens if cloth scraps, felt-tip markers, and strips of fabric tape **Try relocating** are set up on a small platform near the block area? How about having **certain activities.** painting on the floor instead of at the easel . . . on an enormous sheet of cardboard or on remnants of window shades unrolled to their full length?

Try placing interesting hardware items (springs, nuts and bolts, small gears, washers, etc.) on the table where coloring or pasting is usually done. Include some hunks of Styrofoam, wood scraps, and staplers as well.

Place paint in large coffee cans, each with an individual wide brush (two to three inches wide). Place these outside or on a large expanse of floor. Remnant sheets of cardboard, old billboards, or mural paper also can be utilized as surfaces. Limiting the paint to one or two infrequently utilized colors may add to the stimulation.

Again, the element of novelty is important. All too frequently, established attitudes about space and activities prevent children from approaching them objectively. Relocations and new juxtapositions encourage fresh considerations of the usual.

A FEW IMPORTANT THINGS TO KEEP IN MIND ABOUT ART EDUCATION

Motivation is tied intimately to individual differences. Try not to indicate a definite preference for work that "looks like something specific" over work that is nonobjective. Children rapidly pick up this attitude. Representationalism is *not a requisite* of art experience.

No matter how minimal the growth may seem, such comments as "You really did a fine job making that stick—all by yourself" and "I like the way you make trucks" are enormously meaningful in terms of developing self-confidence and providing incentive. This is not to imply that the teacher should offer praise when it is unwarranted; rather, her expectations for growth should be realistic.

Keep competition out of the picture—literally! Art is a personal, individual thing. Don't hang up "only the good ones." All attempts should be acknowledged.

Provide a variety of materials to sustain interest and offer maximum opportunities for growth.

When a material is new and exciting, don't impose a specific limitation about how it should be used. Let the children investigate it on their own. Specifically, this means that if you're introducing tissue paper for the first time, don't suggest that everyone make flowers!

Art is a personal, individual thing.

Remember that the highly creative child is the one who is more likely to deviate from what *you* expect him to do. Give him, as well as all children, the opportunity to express his *own* ideas. Don't subtly elicit the kind of work you prefer.

Show children reproductions and pictures of adult art and hang some of these pictures about the classroom. Slides are another excellent way of introducing adult art to very young children. Include many of the modernists and encourage discussion of feelings and responses. Help children to identify colors, shapes, lines, and objects that they find personally exciting. Communicate that there is no one way that is *right* when making a picture and that different people feel differently about the same thing.

Don't use patterns, mimeographed forms to fill in, or demonstrations that must be imitated exactly in teaching art to children. Such aids are in opposition to all the values that are inherent in a program founded on notions of self-expression.

Remember that organizing one's ideas with materials is an integral part of intellectual activity and that through art experiences children are extending their perceptual and cognitive capabilities.

And, in addition, have a wonderful time! Art is an exciting aspect of working with children. It offers the adult the opportunity to share the child's feelings and reactions to the world about him in a most poignant and revealing manner.

SELECTED REFERENCE MATERIALS IN ART EDUCATION FOR YOUNG CHILDREN

Brittain, W. Lambert. *Creativity, Art, and the Young Child.* New York: The Macmillan Co., 1979.

Davis Publications. 50 Portland Street, Worcester, Massachusetts 01608.
This company is a source of a wealth of additional materials relevant to art education. They specialize in this area. A complete listing of art publications can be obtained by writing to them. They also publish an excellent periodical, *School Arts.* Although this publication is not intended primarily for the preschool level, it provides the resourceful teacher with ideas and stimulation for challenging lessons.

DiLeo, Joseph H., M.D. *Young Children and Their Drawings.* New York: Bruner/Mazel, 1970.

Gardner, Howard. *The Arts and Human Development.* New York: John Wiley & Sons, 1973.

Jameson, Kenneth. *Art and the Young Child.* New York: The Viking Press, 1968.

Kellogg, Rhoda. *Analyzing Children's Art.* Palo Alto, Calif.: National Press, 1969.

Lark-Horowitz, Lewis, and Lark-Horowitz, Luca. *Understanding Children's Art for Better Teaching.* Columbus, Ohio: Charles E. Merrill Publishing Co., 1967.

Linderman, Earl W., and Herberholz, Donald W. *Developing Artistic and Perceptual Awareness.* Dubuque, Iowa: William C. Brown Co., 1964.

Lowenfeld, Viktor, and Brittain, W. Lambert. *Creative and Mental Growth,* 6th ed. New York: The Macmillan Co., 1975.

Montgomery, Chandler. *Art for Teachers of Children,* 2d ed. Columbus, Ohio: Charles E. Merrill Publishing Co., 1973.

Wankelman, Willard; Wigg, Philip; and Wigg, Marietta. *A Handbook of Arts and Crafts.* Dubuque, Iowa: William C. Brown Co., 1961.

Three

Music for Young Children

Everyone who has worked with young children knows that at the pre-school level "music is better caught than taught." It is best caught from the person for whom the child feels the most admiration. It may be a mother who sings gospel songs or a brother who plays drums or guitar. Whoever that special person may be, the child will follow his lead.

The link between home and school is an important one. In a small community, a teacher may be invited to make an occasional family visit. With an understanding of people and a love of music, she can make such a visit a rewarding experience. Particularly if music results from such a visit, a valuable link between home and school can be forged.

The teacher herself should be able to play the children's instruments and sing the songs they sing. She should also have had enough experience in teaching to quickly become aware of the level at which each willing performer might be approached.

People from other countries and from different parts of our own all speak the common language of music, but each speaks it in a slightly different way; these differences add color and life to a preschool program—a dance from Puerto Rico, a boat song from Sicily, a lullaby from Ireland.

Somewhere in the group, there may be buried a forgotten song or dance which would link the past with the present and the home with the school.

More than one parent would like to become familiar with the songs his or her child sings in school. Some may be a little more shy, but they might be persuaded to come to a parents' meeting and help with the making of a tom-tom for their own child. Yes, parents are important people!

We can hope that the first music a baby hears is his mother's soft **LEARNING TO LISTEN** singing. Unfortunately, if a mother sings at all, her voice, in many homes, is soon drowned out by the impersonal and often raucous voice of a radio or television performer.

We can set a good example in nursery school and kindergarten by being fully aware of the quantity and quality of the music we offer. A

45

child needs a quiet environment part of the time, indeed, during quite a large part of his day, if he is to become an attentive listener. This world needs good listeners as much as the child himself needs to learn to listen.

When children are noisy and restless at the beginning of rest period, have you tried sitting quietly at the piano (or whatever instrument you have) and playing one tone slowly and softly? Try it. Let the children drift on the tone and feel its vibrations. When all is peaceful, play, softly sing, or offer a recording of a gentle, simple, and beautiful melody. The even vibrations of the tone and the beauty of the melody may help to soothe the child and free him from some of his tenseness so he can rest, listen, and, perhaps, even sleep.

TIME FOR SINGING

The school's program should plan for periods of activity and for quiet periods. One of the quiet periods could involve music, and often this is a time when a group can be assembled. Sometimes this time occurs after juice and crackers, sometimes before or after a rest period.

Simple songs that utilize children's names are good for this period. An excellent one is an old Southern song, "Shake Hands Mary" (30).* Instead of "Shake hands Mary," children can sing "Wake up Mary," "Sit up Mary," or "Hello Mary, dum-a-la-lum," calling each child's name. Musically, this is a good song. The intervals are a little difficult for the youngest children, but the number of names which must be called gives the teacher an opportunity for many repetitions. After every child's name has been mentioned, the song ends with:

> Lum, lum, lum, lum
> Dum-a-lum-lum
> Lum, lum, lum, lum
> Dum-a-lum-lum.

—easy syllables to remember, and pleasant to say.

Action Songs

But time spent with music must not be regarded as just a quiet, listening time. Music is also good for action.

When a child listens, it is often with the expectation of responding actively to what he hears. His first response to a rhythmic beat is movement. He also begins, early, to experiment with vocal sounds. By the time he enters nursery school, he may be ready to sing his own little chantlike tunes or move to the directions of the words of a simple song like "The Wheels of the Bus."

Slightly older beginners might enjoy singing "London Hill" (30) with its accompanying action. The name of a familiar local hill might be substituted for the English title if this makes the song more real to the child.

Introducing the Songs

It is much better if the teacher can introduce the songs herself. A record player is impersonal and, therefore, not a good substitute. Much of the pleasure of singing is derived from the shared personal experience.

The songs should be sung slowly and distinctly, and the younger the child, the more slowly they should be introduced, provided, of course, that the teacher does not lose the feeling of the rhythmic progression, the thread of the musical thought.

---

* Numbers in parentheses refer to entries in the bibliography at the end of this chapter.

The teacher should not expect a response on the first day or the second. It takes time for a young child to understand and remember the words and longer still to gain a clear conception of a melody. Listening ability and vocal control come more slowly with some children than with others, but they will come if a child is exposed to music and no one worries about him. A loss of self-confidence is usually the stumbling block. Encourage him to sing, even if he isn't singing your tune. Vocal chords need exercise, and he needs vocal expression. Drill on either words or music is harmful for preschool children. Sing the song straight through and let him catch what he can, even if it is only the last note. Pitch will come on the wave of the rhythm.

Personal Songs

Two examples of songs about the child's clothes or what he is doing are:

"Toodala"
"Mary Wore Her Red Dress"

Transition Songs

Two examples of songs which take you from where you are to where you want to be are:

"Jim-along Josie"
"Hey, Betty Martin"

Songs of Dramatic Play

"Whoopie Ti-Yi-Yo"
"Night Herding Song"

Humorous Songs

"Aiken Drum"
"Pumpkin, Pumpkin"

Songs with Appealing Melodies and Warmth of Sentiment

"There's a Little Wheel A-Turning in My Heart"
"Lavender's Blue"

Singing Games

"Ringel, Ringel, Ring-o"
"Punchinello"
"Tideo"

Encouraging Participation

You could call on someone to come up and whisper in your ear the name of a song he would like to sing. ("Johnny, how about you?")
Play a familiar song and ask, "Who can guess the name of this song?"
Strum the chords which are appropriate for a familiar tune on the Autoharp. Play them in the rhythm of the melody. Ask, "Who can guess what song the Autoharp is playing?"

Original Calls and Chants

Calls and chants use melodic intervals freely and can be sung by one or more children. The time pattern is simple and rhythmic. It seems to come when the children are happy and unrestrained.

Original Songs

These songs are produced when a child is quiet and thoughtful, perhaps while playing in the doll corner and singing to a doll. On one occasion, a four year old arrived in school after a snowstorm. His footsteps were the first to break the crust of the new snow on that cold morning. He came up the path very slowly, turned to look at the unbroken whiteness of the fields, and sang to himself. "See how white it is! See how white it is!"

Often songs are sung without words. The child seems to be experimenting with his own voice and ways in which he could shape a melody.

Narrative Songs

Sometimes a child likes an audience when he sings his own story. Occasionally a teacher may ask, "Who would like to sing his own song?" In this case, a folded piece of colored construction paper will serve as music. You will be surprised to hear what endlessly long songs are "written" on that plain piece of paper! Sometimes you have to say, "Thank you, Bobby, you may sing some more another day," for one child cannot monopolize the period.

MUSICAL INSTRUMENTS

Tom-toms and Drums

The Indian tribes of the American Southwest make good-toned, durable tom-toms from hollow logs and wild-animal skins. There are also interesting drums from Africa and the Orient which find their way to our gift and artisans' shops. Latin America sends us bongo drums with durable goatskin heads. Be sure to purchase one large enough to produce a good tone.

Always listen for the quantity and quality of the sound when purchasing a drum or tom-tom. Think of the size of your room and the striking power of the children. A percussion instrument should be both pleasant-toned and durable to be acceptable in nursery school or kindergarten.

Mallets should be selected with care. Padded heads, or those made of rubber or lamb's wool, are best for most tom-toms. (The Indians pad theirs until each one is just right for a particular tom-tom.) Experiment with different mallets until you find the one which produces the best tone; when you find it, tie it to the instrument—nothing is more easily lost than a mallet, especially if it is a good one.

The Chinese once made a beautiful large drum similar to a kettle drum. You may still find some shipped from Hong Kong.

A tympani drum is large. The child stands when he plays it and thereby gains much freedom of movement. The mallet head is usually made of lamb's wool.

Hand Drum

This drum may be used by the teacher as an accompaniment for rhythmic dance movement.

Small Hand Drum

This one is for the children and is used for marching or during dramatic play.

A Sample Presentation

The teacher says to the children, "Try playing on different parts of the drum head. Where does it make the best sound?" The older children may be able to tell you in what part of the drum the tone is highest and where the lowest.

"Which mallet are you going to use, the one with the wooden or the one with the rubber head? Try them both and see which one makes the better sound."

"Do you want to play a game called 'Copy Cat'? I'll be the teacher, and you be the copy cat. I'll play ♫ |♩:‖ and see if you can play the same music. Try this; it is a long, long one: ♩ ♩ ♩ ♩ |𝅝: ‖ ."

The kindergarten child may become the teacher, occasionally.

See *Pocket Songs*, published by Cooperation Recreation Society (23). Pages 19, 34, 50, 53, 60, 62, 65, 67, 69 contain rhythmic folk tunes.   **Tom-tom Accompanying the Piano**

The triangle produces a pleasant sound but is difficult for a young child to hold and manipulate. If the triangle is used, the teacher may say: "Hold it with your hand. Hit it with the metal beater. Now hold it with the triangle holder and hit it again. Which sounds nicer?" "Put your finger against the triangle when it is singing and see how it feels." Suggested music: *Pocket Songs* (23), pp. 47, 52, 54, 69, 72, 79.   **Triangle**

"How do you think you could make a sound with these? Try them this way (edge to edge). Try them again like this (brush them across each other). Which way shall we play them for this music?" *Pocket Songs* (23), pp. 50, 51, 58, 68, 80.   **Finger Cymbals**

Suspend the large cymbal from a cymbal stand. To produce the best tone, strike it with a soft-headed mallet. Try it with a harder mallet. Ask, "Which makes the pleasanter sound?"   **A Large Cymbal**

"Listen. Isn't it beautiful?" Pass the mallet to the child, saying nothing. Wait! While he touches the gong, enjoy the sound together. Let him experiment for a while. Later, develop the experience: "Shall we see how long the tone can sing?" Sound one tone. Tell the child, "Hold up your hand when the sound is all gone."   **Dinner Gong**

Again: "Can you find the highest tone? The lowest tone?" Do not expect all the children to be able to do this.

The metal bars which produce the tone must be in good tune.   **Chromatic Single-Unit Resonator Bars**

It is preferable to have the lowest note four tones, G, below the key note, C. Many nursery songs begin with the interval five-one—e.g., "The Farmer in the Dell." This instrument offers the intuitive and musically trained teacher an opportunity to introduce the child gradually to the fundamentals of music—rhythm, melody, and harmony on a horizontal plane.

This is a melodic stringed instrument. Only diatonic melodies in the key of C can be played on it. The tone is made by plucking the strings with a shell plectrum. Playing this instrument adds another experience in soundmaking and in learning to listen for various qualities of tone.   **Psaltery**

This is the only instrument on which an untrained person can accompany himself or his friends with a minimum of practice. Even a young child can sweep across the strings with his felt plectrum while the teacher presses down the chord-selecting bars. It is the child's in-   **Autoharp** troduction to harmony, harmony which he can make himself and which he therefore finds increasingly satisfying.

The modern Autoharp holds its tune quite well, but the weather does affect the pitch a little so purchase a full-scaled chromatic pitch pipe (Hohner's True Tone) when you buy your Autoharp.

A carrying case is useful.

The softest and most beautiful tone is produced by a three-cornered felt plectrum.

RHYTHMIC MOVEMENT AND DANCING

The Beginning of Dance (without a Horizon)

The beginning of dance exists in the child's response to:

Space
A hill
Muscles which crave action
An ocean with waves rolling up on a beach
A balloon
A piper's tune
The joy of anything

Running is there on the inside waiting for something to tell the feet to run.

In the Yard

Wait, watch, and listen.

A sensitive teacher knows when a struck cymbal will add something to the climax of a running jump or a drumbeat will give courage to the inhibited child waiting for his turn on the bouncing board.

Always have a musical instrument readily available because when someone feels like skipping, you haven't time to go inside to get your recorder, drums, or bells.

In School

The child first has to feel confident about the teacher, the other children, and the physical environment. The space in a room larger than any he has known at home is sometimes frightening.

Group activity with a young or new group is often conducted most successfully close to the floor. Have you played the game of "Mother Cat and Kittens"? The kittens creep away and hide. Mother looks for them.

When she finds one she says, "Meow." The kitten replies, "Meow," and follows her. When all the kittens have been found, she leads them home (to the piano). They come most willingly to a simple little tune, appropriate for creeping, improvised with eighth notes.

It is a good game. When you are on the floor, you are in a safe place. You cannot fall much farther. The idea of the mother cat and the group of kittens suggests security and so, too, does " coming home." The muscle activity used in creeping is excellent for the pelvic muscles, and the familiarity with space breeds confidence. For the child who does not yet carry a tune, what better tone matching could we have than the response to the mother cat?

There is a helpful introduction to rhythmic movement for the older preschool child who has confidence in his own physical ability on page 72 in *Nursery Kindergarten Education* by E. Leavitt (16).

Entering the Classroom

Mimi comes in hopping on one foot. Allen comes in galloping, flopping his hands as he circles the room. Chuck comes on all fours, kicking one foot to the side and calling out, "I'm a shoemaker." All want a musical accompaniment, and all want it at the same time. First, you had better get organized and have it understood that everyone takes turns or that everyone moves together—first in Mimi's and then in Allen's way.

This is the time when it is almost essential that a teacher be able to improvise on the piano. There isn't time to thumb through the pages in your music book. Of course, it is terrifying if you haven't tried it, but forget about yourself and first watch an individual child, identify with him, feel the quality of his movement. When you are aware of his basic metric beat, play it softly on one black key; add a second black key at regular intervals. Be sure to keep it going. All worthwhile tunes come on the wave of a steady rhythm. Soon you may be able to follow his rhythmic pattern, which becomes more and more dynamic as it is repeated. Gradually the pulse of the rhythm dominates the group, and more and more children will begin to participate. You cannot make a really bad tune on the black keys if you do not lose the rhythm. On which black key will your improvisation end? Try it and discover for yourself.

At some later date you may find yourself improvising on both black and white keys, with one hand perhaps, but with a good feeling of a phrase and the general structure of the music.

DRAMATIC PLAY AND MUSIC

Follow the seasons. They offer a wealth of suggestions for dramatic play.

Teacher: "When you wake up some morning and see the ground all covered with snow, what do you want to do? Don't tell me. Show me and let me guess."

"Did someone have another idea? Good. Let's watch Richard."

Sometimes dancing follows story time. Story time might end with a poem, a poem with tempting imagery like "The Squirrel," from *Writing for Young Children* by Claudia Lewis (18). The dancing time that follows might begin with: "Do I see some squirrels? All right, squirrels. Scamper around and find the nuts. When you find one, hurry back and bury it under your own tree."

Or the poem might be one about a train, followed by the ever-popular train dramatization.

DIRECTION AND CONTROL

When there is group participation, there must be organization. Keep your groups as small as possible and "organize for freedom."

If standards of attention and behavior are established when the children first meet, they will become easy to continue but hard to break.

Forethought should be given to the physical environment. The temperature of the room should be comfortable, not too warm for active children nor too cool for essential temporary rest.

Distracting objects like wheel-toys should be removed.

Everyone should be familiar with the surroundings; otherwise, children may just explore. At one "music" period, for example, the children, having been taken to an unfamiliar room, spent the whole twenty minutes climbing or hiding under steps!

If you yourself play for the dance movements, all music should be memorized. If you depend upon records, they should be filed in a way which makes them readily available.

All properties, such as scarves and jingle bells, should be in condition and order for immediate distribution—better leave them in readiness the night before.

Conduct the music period at a time when the children are rested and not excited. For the younger children, a varied program is best—a little singing, a little listening, and a little movement.

Watch the children's eyes for signs of interest or fatigue and stop the period before discord develops. A ten-minute program with undivided attention is better than a half-hour session of restlessness.

Plan your program ahead of time so you will know exactly what you expect to do but don't carry on with your own program if original ideas come from the children. Yet you must not depend upon the children's creativeness to direct your thinking in class—that surely will be the day when no one has an idea!

Never exploit a talented child. If he is made self-conscious, he may never try again.

Do not allow a few children to monopolize a situation.

Treat all musical instruments with respect. If they do not possess some element of beauty, they should not be there.

Examine your own attitude toward a child who is disturbing. Fun should be an integral part of each day's experience.

THE SELECTION OF MUSIC

Gradually, the child progresses from the cradle-rocking, knee-riding stage of musical development and the enjoyment of tonal vibration for its own sake to the realization that music itself has meaning. Its pulsating, undulating flow and emotional content stir the feeling side of the child's nature. He wants to show himself and you what music means to him, so he sings and dances.

It is here that the teacher's role becomes increasingly important. She must select the music and see that it is artistically performed. This is no small task. A good beginning is the reading of Leonard Bernstein's *Young People's Concerts* (4). "Program One" and "Program Five" are particularly rewarding. The accompanying music is too complex for any but the exceptionally gifted preschool child, but Bernstein's explanation of the meaning of music will help a teacher greatly in the selection of music for her own group.

Folk songs are usually better for rhythmic movement than folk dances. Folk dances are often too stimulating or too formal for very young children. The music shops are now filled with folk songs from all over the world. If you can hear the music in your imagination when you look at a page of printed notes, all the better. If not, write to your radio stations—the educational ones or those which present only music—and ask them to offer a program of the best available music suitable for preschool children. It need not be a children's program, but it should be one from which parents and teachers could select the music they wish to present to young children.

Recent publications are few. Music publishing for children has been taken over by textbook publishers and presented in series.

A library may help you with your selection. Try the music room, the teachers' room, the children's room, and the periodical room.

The audio department may be able to assist in the selection of recorded music. If it cannot, write to the New York Library Association, Children's and Young Adults' Service Section, 20 West Fifty-third Street, New York, N.Y. 10019.

Good recordings are even more difficult to find than printed music. One cannot judge the sound of a record by its jacket; the cellophane wrappers are removable only after purchase, and there are few available machines or booths for listening.

Unlike picture books, recordings for young children seem to have no permanence. Perhaps it is because they are still regarded as mere entertainment. Catalog listings and record reviews of music for children do appear though in November or early December. Watch for reviews in the following:

New York Times
Saturday Review/World
Horn Book
Parents' Magazine
Library Journal

The reviewers' opinions may not always be yours, but the reviewers are intelligent people and will at least give you a choice within a choice.

A recent innovation in book publishing seems to be the inclusion of a small music record with textbooks. This is especially helpful for those who wish their children to hear an authentic interpretation of children's songs or native instrumental music from another land. Three such music books have recently been published:

Folks Songs of China, Japan and Korea by Betty Warner Dietz and Thomas Park (8)
Musical Instruments of Africa by Betty Warner Dietz and M.B. Olatunji (7)
Builder Buch für Kinder, music by Béla Bartók (3)

Folk Ballads for Young Actors (22), collected by John Jacob Niles, offers dramatizations for children beyond the preschool age, but the folk tunes are charming and very well performed.

It is a great privilege to be permitted to search for the meaning of music **THE SEARCH** in the company of a little child. If you find even a fragment of this meaning, it will add an area of beauty to your life as well as his.

Do you know this lovely song by Eleanor Farjeon from *Sing High, Sing Low*? It really sums up the experience of both teacher and child in approaching music.

> Walk, shepherdess, walk
> And I'll walk, too,
> To find the ram with the ebony horn,
> And the gold footed ewe,
> The lamb with the fleece of silver,
> Like summer sea foam
> And the wether with the crystal bell,
> That leads them all home.
> Walk, shepherdess, walk,
> And I'll walk, too,
> And if we never find them
> I shan't mind, shall you?*

SELECTED REFERENCE MATERIALS IN MUSIC AND DANCE

Books

Bartenieff, Irmgard. "How Is the Teacher Equipped to Do Dance Therapy?" *American Dance Therapy Association Monogram I*. Columbia, Md.: American Dance Therapy Assn., 1971

Boorman, J. *Creative Dance in the First Three Grades*. New York: David McKay Co., 1969.

Canner, Norma, and Klebanoff, Harriet. *And a Time to Dance*. Boston: Plays, Inc., 1974.

Cole, Natalie. *Children's Arts from Deep Down Inside*. New York: The John Day Co., 1966.

Davis, Bruce. *The Magical Child Within You*. Millbrae, Calif.: Celestial Arts, 1977.

Davis, Martha. *Understanding Body Movement: An Annotated Bibliography*. New York: Arno Press, 1972.

Ellfeldt, Lois. *Dance from Magic to Art*. Dubuque, Iowa: Wm. C. Brown, 1976.

Gerhardt, Lydia. *Moving and Knowing, The Young Child Orients Himself in Space*. Englewood Cliffs, N.J.: Prentice-Hall, Inc., 1973.

Mettler, Barbara. *Creative Dance in Kindergarten*. Tucson, Ariz.: Mettler Studios, 1976.

_____. Materials of Dance as a Creative Art Activity. Tucson, Ariz.: Mettler Studios, 1966.

_____. Basic Movement Exercises. Tucson, Ariz.: Mettler Studios, 1972.

Steiner, Rudolf. *Eurythmy and the Impulse of Dance*. New York: Rudolf Steiner Press, 1974.

Catalogues, Records, Song Books, and Musical Activities for Young Children

Association for Childhood Education International
3615 Wisconsin Avenue, N.W.
Washington, D.C. 20016

---

*Eleanor Farjeon, "Walk, Shepherdess, Walk," in *Sing High, Sing Low*, ed. L. Zeddies et al. (St. Louis: Concordia Publishing House, 1946). Reprinted by permission of Ober Associates.

Bank Street College of Education
610 West 112th Street
New York, New York 10025

Children's Music Center
5373 West Pico Boulevard
Los Angeles, California 90019

Children's Record Guild
27 Thompson Street
New York, New York 10013

Educational Resources for Information Center
4936 Fairmont Avenue
Bethesda, Maryland 20014

Folkways/Scholastic Records
906 Sylvan Avenue
Englewood Cliffs, New Jersey 07632

BIBLIOGRAPHY

1. Andrews, Gladys. *Creative Rhythmic Movement For Children*. Englewood Cliffs, N.J.: Prentice-Hall, Inc., 1954.

2. Aranoff, Frances W. *Music and Young Children*. New York: Holt, Rinehart & Winston, Inc., 1969.

3. Bartók, Béla. *Builder Buch für Kinder*. Mainz and Leipzig, Germany: Scott's Söhne, 1964.

4. Bernstein, Leonard. *Young People's Concerts for Reading and Listening*. New York: Simon & Schuster, 1962.

5. *Building Children's Personalities with Creative Dancing*. Color film available from Dailey Films, Inc., 6509 DeLongpre Ave., Hollywood, California 90028; Indiana University Audio-Visual Center; Pennsylvania State University Audio-Visual Aids Library; and Syracuse University Educational Film Library.

6. Cherry, Clare. *Creative Movement for the Developing Child*. Palo Alto, Calif.: Fearon Publishers, 1968.

7. Dietz, Betty Warner, and Olatunji, M.B. *Music Instruments of Africa—Their Nature, Use, and Place in the Life of a Deeply Musical People*. New York: John Wiley & Sons, 1965.

8. Dietz, Betty Warner, and Park, Thomas. *Folk Songs of China, Japan, and Korea*. New York: The John Day Co., 1964.

9. Heffernan, H., and Todd, V. *The Kindergarten Teacher*. Boston: D.C. Heath & Co., 1960.

10. Landeck, B. *Children and Music*. New York: William Sloan Assn., 1952.

11. _____. *More Songs to Grow On*. New York: Edward Marks Music Corp., 1954.

12. _____. *Songs to Grow On*. New York: Edward Marks Music Corp., 1950.

13. Langstaff, John. *Frog Went A-Courtin'*. New York: Harcourt Brace Jovanovich, 1973.

14. _____. *Jim-along Josie: A Collection of Folk Songs and Singing Games for Young Children*. New York: Harcourt Brace Jovanovich, 1973.

15. _____. *Over in the Meadow*, illustrated by F. Rojanovsky. New York: Harcourt Brace Jovanovich, 1973.

16. Leavitt, J.E. *Nursery Kindergarten Education*. New York: McGraw-Hill Book Co., 1958.

17. Leddies, L. *Sing High, Sing Low*. St. Louis: Concordia Publishing House, 1946.

18. Lewis, Claudia. *Writing for Young Children*. New York: Simon & Schuster, 1954.

19. Millan, Nina. *Children's Games from Many Lands.* New York: Friendship Press, 1952.

20. Moorhead, G.E., and Pond, D. *Music for Young Children: General Observations,* Book II. Santa Barbara, Calif.: Pillsbury Foundation Studies, 1942.

21. Music Educators National Conference. *Music for Fours and Fives.* Washington, D.C.: National Education Association, 1958.

22. Niles, John Jacob, collector. *Folk Ballads for Young Actors.* New York: Holt, Rinehart & Winston, Inc., 1962.

23. *Pocket Songs.* Delaware, Ohio: Cooperative Recreation Services, Inc. (Small booklets containing hundreds of folk tunes from around the world.)

24. *Recordings for Children.* New York Library Association, Children's and Young Adults' Service Section. 20 West 53rd Street, New York, N.Y. 10019

25. Richards, Mary. *Threshold to Music.* Palo Alto, Calif.: Fearon Publishing Co., 1965.

26. Rosenberg, Martha. *It's Fun to Teach Creative Music.* New York: Play Schools Association, 1963.

27. Smith, Robert. *Music in the Child's Education.* New York: The Ronald Press, 1970.

28. Steiner, Violette, and Pond, R.E. *Finger Play Fun Book.* Columbus, Ohio: Charles E. Merrill Publishing Co., 1970.

29. Sur, William R. et al. *This Is Music.* Boston: Allyn & Bacon, 1963.

30. Trent-Johns, Altona. *Plays of the Deep South.* Washington, D.C.: Associated Publishers, Inc., 1944.

31. Watters, Lorraine E. *The Magic of Music.* Boston;: Ginn & Co., 1965.

32. Wilder, Alec, and Engvick, William, eds. *Lullabies and Night Songs.* New York: Harper & Row, Publishers, 1965.

Four

Literature for Children: General Considerations

Literature for young children leads the child to a variety of learnings and **WHY DO WE READ** feelings, to personal and emotional involvements through the percep- **BOOKS TO YOUNG** tions and narrations of the literary artist which add dimensions quite **CHILDREN?** apart from the intellectual ones. In many instances, books are capable of deepening and enriching both the real and imaginative life of the child. Books can bring the excitement and pleasure of a good story which pits opposing forces or situations and the suspense of how it will all turn out. They can bring new information, understandings of things, processes, places, and people, aesthetic delight in beauty perceived and communicated, language aptly expressed. Through fantasy, they provide avenues for handling concerns and ways of exploring possibilities in our sensuous and sensual natures. Books, in acquainting us with the strange and unfamiliar, allow us to evaluate reality without fear. In presenting the common humanity of people or the universal child in all children, they help us relate to other people without prejudice.

Good literature for children is no different *qualitatively* from that for **HOW DO WE** adults. Selma Lanes, in an excellent book about children's literature, **RECOGNIZE A GOOD** *Down the Rabbit hole* (5),* calls attention to her belief that superior **BOOK?** quality involves "honesty and wholeheartedness of experience . . . the deep experience of the world intelligently digested and sensitively transformed."

Books that have become classics provide guidelines to this honest, sensitive quality: the personal-animal integrity in the creatures created by Beatrix Potter, the sensitive awareness of a child's feelings at night in *Good-Night, Moon* by Margaret Wise Brown. Maurice Sendak captures true feelings of rebellion, fantasy, and resolution of anger in *Where the Wild Things Are*. Helen Buckley reflects the child's universal experience with quietness and the satisfaction of a warm adult-child relationship in *Grandfather and I.*

---

*Numbers in parentheses refer to entries in the bibliography at the end of this chapter.

In general, young children cannot select their own books, so adults have a great responsibility to find the best available literature and to provide a wide variety of it. A bibliography beginning on page 76 presents a selection of what we consider to be good books in a number of different categories. But we cannot possibly include all categories or all books. Teachers must look constantly for new books. They need to consult librarians and recommended reviews, such as those in *The Horn Book* or the Sunday *New York Times* book review supplement. They will also be guided by the interest aroused in children themselves.

IT IS NOT ENOUGH JUST TO FIND A GOOD BOOK!

Presentation is important.

The presentation is also important. The setting should be comfortable and relatively quiet. Some books are good to present to a large group, if pictures are clear and vivid and the story or message exciting or compelling. Others, quieter or more intimate in nature, are better for one or two children.

The tale will be enhanced if the adult is both sensitive to and enthusiastic about the book. When a teacher reads a book to a group, she should know the story well. Words should be made clear and possible ambiguities explained. Young children, for example, sometimes miss the dramatic ending in Marjorie Flack's book *Ask Mr. Bear* because they do not know the meaning of a "bear hug." In this case, the teacher can clarify the term with a demonstration of a hug. And even such seemingly simple words as "deck" and "curious" in the favorite *Curious George* series by H. Rey may need to be explained, although the story itself should not be interrupted to explain the words.

Pauses must be strategically planned and contrasts in moods and words heightened. The teacher needs to be a bit of a "ham" to bring forth dramatic implications or sensitive nuances.

When a book, for any reason, does not "go well," the teacher should be prepared to stop, try another book, or move on to another activity.

Too often, teachers plough relentlessly through a presentation of a book of their choice even though it obviously is not holding the interest of the listeners. New teachers often read the story aloud to themselves first or tape their readings of a story in order to learn to evaluate the impact of their presentation.

When adults know the book well, they avoid the danger of looking down at the printed page at the moment of climax. They can draw attention to details in the illustrations that embellish the text. They can invite discussion from the children at appropriate points without allowing such discussion to interfere with the logical sequence of the story. They can judiciously add the use of puppets, flannel boards, costumes, filmstrips, and records.

Because we so often tend to condition children to believe there is no message without visual props, teachers should sometimes just tell a story simply for a more personal involvement. On one occasion, when a teacher told a story to a group of children without using a book, there was, at first, stunned incredulity. "Where is the picture? Show me the book," they demanded. When the teacher protested that no book existed, one persistent child left the group and came to circle around the teacher's back trying to find if the book was not in some way visible from behind the teacher. Such an incident brings questions about our usual overabundance of visual stimuli.

Obviously books for children are different from other books because they *are* written for children and therefore *reflect* some of our basic knowledge about the young children's language, thinking, feelings, and concerns.

Knowing child development makes a difference.

Language in children's books is relatively simple in quantity and quality; illustrations are abundant. Authors depend upon artists' creations to advance the narration and define images and ideas more clearly. In the best books, art and text blend in such perfect harmony that illustrations become an integral part of the story. We are aware of the young child's limited language ability and quite rightly rely in large measure on visual stimuli to convey meaning. With very young children, other sensory aids are used, such as those found in *Pat the Bunny* by D. Kunhardt or *Who Lives Here* by Pat and Eve Witte.

Children need more than words to bring understanding.

Such books invite active participation of the child through fuzzy patches or sandpaper to feel, holes to look through, flaps to lift and peek under. Other good books in this category are *Zoo City* by Stephen Lewis, *The Circus in the Mist* by Bruno Munari, and *The Secret Birthday Message* by Eric Carle.

The younger the child, the more he experiences the world as an extension of his own sensations. Past events are quite personal; the future is difficult to comprehend. Therefore, books for young children often have their setting in a generalized place and time rather than in a specifically identifiable era or location.

Children do not have a clear sense of past and future.

Children walk in and out of fantasy and reality; it is a flexible doorway for them. Authors of children's books thus are freer to present, without distinguishing between them, realistic and unrealistic scenes, characters, and episodes. In a sense, it could be said that at first everything is real to a child; only later does he learn to discriminate between what is real externally and what is real in his thoughts.

Children find it difficult to distinguish between fantasy and reality.

To a minimal extent, caution may be in order in choosing certain books for certain children, lest fantasy—particularly of a potentially frightening nature—is perceived by the child as a dangerous reality. But, in general, fantasy is congenial to children. In fact, it is through fantasy that many children practice their ability to handle their anxiety. They get a satisfaction from first being frightened and then feeling, "But I am not really scared. I am really safe."

Children cannot appreciate complicated personalities.

In general, characters in children's books are "flat" by adult standards because children themselves are not sufficiently aware of inner differentiation of psychological traits to appreciate the complexity of the psyche.

Children enjoy themes that reflect their own concerns with aggression, hurt, and insecurity.

Although stories for children sometimes present themes that seemingly are suitable and popular in adult literature, such as war and death and various aspects of ethics or morality, it is unlikely that the themes have the same import for children as for their elders. Death and warfare are forms of aggression and, as such, are favorite themes for children's books because aggression is something every child feels and must cope with. Hurt, misfortune, and various kinds of injury are alluring when we realize how insecure children are, how mysterious and threatening the world outside their families can be, and how important their own physical intactness is. Children have an avid interest in stories in which characters are hurt and bandages applied or doctors summoned.

Children are fascinated by what is good and what is bad, and they seek constant interpretation of these values. Yet they really come to grips with morality in simple black and white terms, and they are not likely to achieve true understanding of ethics or justice until they are ten years old.

A book commands complete attention.

Sensitivity to social issues takes a long time to develop.

Increasingly, children's books reflect contemporary social concerns; the isolation of minority groups, the problems of urban life, of environmental pollution, of one-parent families, and the changing views of male and female roles find their way into children's literature more and more often. Although we will treat this important matter in greater detail later, it is necessary to consider in the context of child development how difficult it is for children to incorporate the social understandings of values such books promote. The baby is at first almost pure *id*, caring only for the satisfaction of his own needs, indifferent to the physical or emotional well-being of his parents. Compassionate sensitivity to others' feelings is not a universal attribute of childhood. We must realize that attitudes about complex issues are not a one-shot deal. They come from consistent, long-time, cumulative exposure, from personal examples, and from sensitive interpretations in many ways and times. Children's literature has a role to play in this process.

Children need to take for granted that black and white, rural and urban, poor and rich are part of a common world, experiencing understandable happiness and sadness, participating in life's adventures. Repeated exposure to such variety makes for its acceptance and works against attitudes of prejudice. Nancy Larrick, in a compelling article in *The Saturday Review of Literature*, "The All White World of Children's Books" (6), documents to what extent a deplorable imbalance in children's literature existed in the past and, to a major degree, still does exist. Teachers must be especially alert to seeing the new literature coming in this field.

In a sense, the education of teachers in social issues is a prerequisite to the development of sound attitudes in children. As teachers are exposed to such learnings, it is to be hoped that they will also incorporate the messages within their own persons. We, as adults, make most progress in forming a child by first forming ourselves.

AGE DIFFERENCES

Age classifications in children's books are deceptive; the child who is unusually verbal or the mature child who has had many experiences is not confined in reading interests to his chronological age group. Many other individual differences in children make age grouping unworkable with literature, just as it often is with other activities. One general guideline is that children respond most easily and readily to those books that relate to their own experience, understanding, and feelings and thus have personal meaning and significance for them.

But age grouping is helpful in providing some sort of structure from which the adult can begin to make choices; after initial choices, she can move up or down as the child's interests or developmental changes suggest. Several general guidelines seem to operate: older children can enjoy a book written for younger children more easily than the younger child can appreciate a tale that is too long or complicated. Books that have become "classics" have withstood the test of time because of their excellence and are popular across wide spans of ages. Two such books are *Millions of Cats* by Wanda Gag and *The Little Engine That Could* by Watty Piper. Teachers who have made the wrong initial choice of a book to read can switch confidently to one of the classics, even though it may already be familiar to the children. Teachers may need to modify presentations slightly for different ages, but the classic books usually guarantee interest in most children.

The Child of Two

The two year old's first interest is in identifying single pictures and in matching visual presentation to spoken word and object. Almost any

*He identifies simple pic-
tures and enjoys repeated
words and phrases.*

book with clear, simple pictures lends itself to this stage of development. *The Giant Nursery Book of Things That Go* by George Zaffo, Richard Scarry's *Best Word Book Ever,* and Brian Wildsmith's books on *Birds* and *Fishes* heighten the young child's awareness of the world and help him to look more closely at the things around him.

It is exciting to find the two year old moving from his earlier interest in simple identification to the following of sequential events in a story. The child responds favorably to large, clear pictures with few details, a situation with minimum complexity, simple language with no abstract words or ideas, and ideas and words repeated over and over.

Often books for two year olds are called "lap books," reflecting the belief that two is an excellent age for the adult to hold the young child and, with book in front of both, foster a priceless togetherness, a shared value of mutual enjoyment of the world of books. This is the age at which to introduce Mother Goose—no child should be deprived of this extraordinary heritage. Although the two year old may not comprehend meanings, he will be fascinated by the rhythmic, repeated words, the action, and the compelling illustrations. There are many fine editions of this classic. Two new collections are commendable: Brian Aldersons's *Cakes and Custard* and Arthur Rorkham's *Mother Goose Nursery Rhymes.* Alphabet books are also good to use with young children, not to teach them the alphabet as such but to engage their identifying familiar objects, which in these books are usually presented in strong, clear colors and sharp outlines. This is a time, also, to sing to the young child—either Mother Goose rhymes or songs from such collections as William Engvik's *Lullabies and Night Songs* or Elizabeth Paston's *The Baby's Song Book.* Both of these books have excellent illustrations, so that sight, sound, and words can be utilized to reach the child in his sensorimotor stage of development.

He likes the here-and-now of home.

The child's limited experiences center on the here-and-now. Thus, he enjoys books which depict sights he commonly sees and days he usually experiences. *The Bundle Book* by Ruth Krauss is an intimate book, not designed for showing to too many children at once yet close to the two year old's experience. *The Moon in My Room* by U. Shulevitz and both *A Child's Good Night Book* and *Good Night, Moon* by M. Wise Brown are close to the daily experience and concern of the toddler and are gentle, quiet books which potentially can help the child accept the coming of night. Simple stories that tell of typical events of a child's day are *The Very Little Girl* and *The Very Little Boy* by P. Krasilovsky; *Good Morning Danny; Good Morning, Hannah* by Dale and Al Carson; *The Little Family* and *Papa Small* by Lois Lenski; and *Robin in Red Boots* by H. Herzka. Thus, we can say that successful books for two year olds deal in a most elemental way with events and people that children know something about.

The Child of Three

He enjoys seasonal experiences and people at work.

The three year old continues to like many of the same books he enjoyed at two although his range of experience is greater; for example, he now enjoys books dealing with seasonal experiences of which he may not have been aware before, such as *The Day Daddy Stayed Home* by Ethel and Leonard Kessler, *Surprise for Davy* by Lois Lenski, and *Josie and the Snow* by Helen Buckley.

His expanding interest includes men and machines; consequently, *The Man in the Manhole* and *The Fix-It Men* by J. Sage and Bill Ballatine are good for him. The repetition in this book is more of a general idea than that of the identical scene which the two year old so enjoyed. The repetitious chant in *Caps for Sale* by Esphyr Slobodkina is appealing. The disappearance of the peddler's caps into a tree is a slightly more complicated rendition of the same kind of surprise so amusing to a two year old in a game like Peek-a-Boo.

He also enjoys the expanded family and repetitious ideas.

Grandfather and I by Helen E. Buckley tells of a delightful relationship between child and grandfather. Although many grandfathers are more dapper and youthful looking than the one depicted in this book, the child is able to identify with *his* grandfather or his father in a tale where pictures and words go together beautifully, and the ending brings a sense of comfort and belonging. The repetition and contrasts in language as well as the simplicity of the pictures are so good that it would be difficult for this book to be unappealing to any young child.

In the Forest by M. H. Ets, with repetition and chanting, utilizes the child's growing interests in fantasy. The fantasy world becomes more distinctly appealing as the child moves toward his fourth birthday.

Excellent books that utilize his interest in animal persons are *A Birthday for Frances* by R. Hoban and *The Tale of Peter Rabbit* by Beatrix Potter, a classic which can be introduced even at this early age.

Although many of Grimm's fairy tales have shocked a few sensitive children and many sensitive parents and although the social messages in the tales are highly questionable, most three year olds show great enjoyment of the old favorites—"Little Red Riding Hood," "Three Bears," and "The Three Billy Goats Gruff." As was mentioned earlier, it seems that the average child can handle these themes with equanimity and enjoy the story for the story's sake as adults might a popular "thriller." However, groups should be screened so that the overly fearful child is not subjected to the tales except in a one-to-one relationship with an adult who can assess and interpret his concerns immediately, personally, and properly. Young children enjoy aggression, wickedness, and imminent disaster with bears, wolves, and foxes as villains. They seem to enjoy hearing about the threat to security, while remaining personally secure, unthreatened in the belief that good will triumph and evil get its due reward.

He needs to be secure while he experiences fantasies of aggression and wickedness.

The four year old is a humorous, dramatic, expansive creature. He has a voracious appetite for the dramatic and loves exaggeration and humor; no situation seems too fantastic or overtaxing for his constantly inventive imagination.

The Child of Four

The kind of dramatic appeal afforded by *Cecily G. and the Nine Monkeys* by H. A. Rey and *Katy No-Pocket* by E. Payne can be elaborately and almost excessively exploited. The child also may like the foolishness of *The Backward Day* by R. Kraus. Dr. Seuss is also a master of fancy and humor; he adds to his books a quality particularly delightful, an experimentation with words as well as ideas. It seems quite essential, however, that the teacher reading a Dr. Seuss book *also* appreciate the particular kind of word play and fancy; the humor is con-

Dramatic appeal and expansive humor are congenial.

tagious when the teacher really feels it. An undramatic, unsympathetic presentation of Dr. Seuss can leave children completely "turned off." *Horton Hatches the Egg, The Cat in the Hat, And to Think that I Saw It on Mulberry Street* are long-time Dr. Seuss favorites.

Selma Lanes sees in the books by Dr. Seuss more than the zany hyperboles or situational absurdities. Over and over again, they present a flouting of parental or societal authority. The child, through the Seuss books, is enabled to identify with the anxieties *he* experiences when he engages in activities forbidden by adults, such as messing up the kitchen in *Scrambled Eggs Super!*

Humor is one of the most neglected and difficult themes to present in children's books, since a child's humor is different from that of an adult. The adult must be responsive to the child's humor before he can transmit it to a child. Incongruous situations *are* funny to a child *providing* he can grasp their nature, novelty, timing (a sudden surprise) and provided a certain intellectual challenge is involved. The poems of Edward Lear, first published in 1846, can send four year olds into spasms of laughter, but they are better received when a teacher has memorized them and presents the amusing jingles at appropriate moments. Reading from the illustrated text is not so successful. Children can become rambunctious with laughter over *One Snail and Me* by E. McLeod, a story of a girl who takes a bath and invites two turtles, three ducks, four seals, five whales, and six kangaroos to join her in the tub. (The absurdity of this book can be heightened with a flannel board or chalkboard presentation.) *The House on 88th Street* by Bernard Waber is also funny, with its "whoosh, whoosh" sounds and crocodile in the bathtub. *The Gillygoofang* by George Mendoza contains delightful nonsense about a fish who swims backward to keep water out of his eyes.

Good stories with real plots hold interest.

Good stories with real plots, such as *Thumbelina* by Hans Christian Anderson, *The Diverting Adventure of Tom Thumb* by B. Wilkenson, and *The Shoemaker and the Elves* by J. Grimm, are favorites. The animated machine that has real adventures is an appealing theme in Virginia Burton's *Mike Mulligan and His Steam Shovel* and *Katy and the Big Snow.*

The Child of Five

Fantasy can be longer and more elaborate.

Five year olds are ready for longer and more complicated fare. They respond with fervor to stunning fantasy, such as that in *The Five Hundred Hats of Bartholomew Cubbins* by Dr. Seuss, or outrageous reality testing, as in *The Five Chinese Brothers* by Claire Bishop. They are not likely to be fearful of the fantastic events in these books. They accept the dream creatures in *Where the Wild Things Are* by Maurice Sendak, perhaps because there is a happy resolution. In response to his anger with his mother, Max has his anger grow like the pictures on the page. When his anger passes, he returns to mother, to home, to where he belongs, to where he wants to be.

Children of five can appreciate the ingenuity of clever animals in such tales as *Swimmy* and *Fish is Fish* by Leo Leonni. Beatrix Potter's *The Tale of the Faithful Dove* is a story they will enjoy for several years.

They respond to beauty in nature and in poetry.

Five year olds seem to have no trouble in the flight of imagination that sees life in nonlife, people in animals, reality in dreams. If adults share the child's views of the world and take time to stretch young minds about natural phenomena, the children will pick up silent lessons that lead to constructive wondering and symbolic resolving.

Things by Phoebe Dunn is a simple book that is good for younger children, too, with beautiful colored photographs portraying children feeding a worm to a chick, examining a spider, a seedling, an autumn leaf, and a starfish.

Look Again by Tana Hoban is a similar type of wondering book of exciting photographs. A square cut in the page before each photograph is an unusual format and reveals only a portion of a picture of a dandelion, zebra, snail, turtle, peacock. Surprise, as well as rich visual experience, is provided.

Words and images in poetry have power and beauty. In *In a Spring Garden*, edited by Richard Lewis, the child can enjoy a lovely collection of Japanese haiku and can be encouraged to express his own poems. Robert Louis Stevenson's *A Child's Garden of Verses* should not be forgotten. Noteworthy newcomers to the same field are Aileen Fisher's *Sing Little Mouse* and *Far and Few: Rhymes of the Never Was and Always Is* by David McCord.

The five year old appreciates tales about going to school, such as *New Boy in School* by May Justus and *Welcome Roberto!* by Mary Serfazo. The Bank Street preprimers, with their urban settings and simple vocabularies, as well as *Little Bear* by E. Minarik from the *I Can Read* series are good for encouraging new reading skills. An appeal to humor comes in a set of cards prepared for the early reader: *An Animal Shufflebook* by Richard Hefler and M. Miskof. One side of the card has an animal, the other side, an action; both sides are vividly portrayed. Children match picture and legend and apparently love to try to read or have the teacher read such incongruities as "And the deer . . . meowed."

They are school conscious and some may be able to read.

It is not necessary, however, to give the reading child just preprimers or reading cards. Once he unlocks the mystery of decoding written symbols, he can be encouraged to read all the books suitable for both his age and for children younger than he.

The appropriateness of teaching reading to kindergarten children is perennial. We believe that young children, from the time they are born, are developing reading "readiness" as they explore and understand the world, grow in visual and auditory perception, develop the ability to use and comprehend language, and utilize the rules and strategies of grammar. There is, however, no exclusive, magical method and no magical time for teaching reading that will be good for all children (4). But in this chapter considering children's books, it seems important to reiterate that the best way to start to teach reading is to read to a child.

Should we teach reading to five year olds?

Growth in both reading and writing can be promoted by the children making their own books. Children can cut out magazine pictures that deal with a certain theme—football, a party, a shopping trip. The teacher can help the child arrange the pictures in a left-to-right sequence that tells a story and then have the child paste the pictures on poster paper. She can then encourage the child to tell a story about the pictures;

Growth in reading and writing occurs as children make their own books.

the teacher can print the text under the pictures. Thus the child has made a book and may be encouraged to identify some of the words he has used.

Some children can make their own books.

The same technique can be used in various kinds of book making. One teacher in a kindergarten, regardless of what other activities were going on, always had a "book table." This table—equipped with paper, Magic Markers, crayons, pencils, and staplers—was an ongoing area where children could always go to make their own books. The productions were, for the most part, illustrations that were stapled together. From time to time, the teacher sat down with a child and elicited a story about these pictures, which she then printed in the child's book. Sometimes children could number their own pages; sometimes they could print a few words or even write all of the text. Finished productions were shared with the group, with the teacher or child reading the text.

Children can create their own spellings when they write.

Carol Chomsky brings up another intriguing dimension to the potential of the book-making child (3). She writes that "children of four and five who do not yet read, but who know the letters of the alphabet and their sounds, show themselves able to compose words and messages on their own, creating their own spellings as they go along." Children can use a set of plastic letters, alphabet blocks, or a crayon to put together words with their own invented spellings. She feels that the ability to write precedes the ability to read but that through such an activity as inventing spelling the "word is, in a very real sense, born of the creative effort of the learner." She does not believe that misspellings should be corrected or that children should necessarily be expected to read what they write.

"The spelling appears to share some of the aspects of the activity of drawing a picture. The child who draws, say, a person is not trying to match an arbitrary pattern, or to represent what someone else will deem correct or accurate. He works from his own perceptions and chooses to put down on paper those features which in some sense strike him as worthy of representation. As he matures, he represents increasingly many of these features and may organize them somewhat differently. The development from early productions to later ones is clearly visible."

Another congenial method, which is now fairly well known to teachers of young children, is that proposed by Sylvia Ashton-Warner in *Teacher* (1). In this instance, the teacher encourages children to make files of words which are useful and meaningful to them. Her thesis is that such words are charged with meaning or emotion and are more likely to be recognized and used in reading and writing than bland, unfamiliar words.

Because these children are approaching the psychosocial issue described as "industry" by Erikson, they like books that promote knowledge and build skills. *Hailstones and Halibut Bones* by Mary O'Neil enables children to make observations of their own concerning texture, color, consistency, and smells. Similarly, *What Happens at the Circus* by Arthur Shay is one of a series with real photographs that shows the setting up, performing, and tearing down of a circus. Other books in the same series show scenes from a car factory, newspaper, zoo, hospital, and airplane. Nature and science are areas of continuous interest: *A Book of Outer Space for You* by Franklin Branley; *I Caught a Lizard* by Gladys Conklin; and *What Makes Day and Night* by Branley are examples from an enormous list of possibilities. Five year olds are ready to learn about historical figures from such books as *Abraham Lincoln* by Ingri and Edgar d'Aulaire and are alert to festivals and holidays: *Chanuko* by Sophia Cedarbaum, *The Thanksgiving Story* by Alice Dalgliesh, *Christmas in Noisy Village* by Astrid Lindgren and I. Wikland, and *Erik and the Christmas Horse* by Hans Peterson all appeal to this aspect of their developing personalities. Stories of children in other cultures are comprehensible; American Indians appear in *Nanabah's Friend* by Mark Perrine, and Eskimos are the characters in *Ootah's Lucky Day* by Peggy Parish. This is an especially good age for introducing books dealing with social issues of all kinds.

Children acquire knowledge and skills of all kinds.

Because he is refining his number sense and beginning to identify letters and words even when he still cannot read, the five year old enjoys books which isolate and refine certain perceptual and cognitive skills. Since he likes to consult "reference" books in order to expand his ever-widening interests, books or films on dinosaurs, shells, bones, eggs, nests, ballet, Eskimos, and Indians should be part of every kindergarten class. The teacher correlates these books with the children's activities; she displays books on science, math, and social studies together with matching objects of related interest. She reads selected bits of information or points to pictures that clarify ideas. Insofar as she attempts to help the children gain new information and to order that which is already known, she can provide books dealing with central themes and can move from general to concise levels of presentation. (A more extensive discussion of developing specific topics is presented in chapter eight.)

Reference books are consulted.

The following list suggests some nonfiction books which might be assembled for a project on incubating eggs:

Bosinger, E., and Guilcher, J. M. *A Bird Is Born.* New York: Sterling Publishing Co., 1960

The chick is shown pecking its way through its shell, being fed by the mother, and then learning to fly.

Cosgrove, M. *Eggs—And What Happens inside Them.* New York: Dodd, Mead & Co., 1966.

This is a good reference work containing drawings and text explaining embryology.

Darby, Gene. *What Is a Frog?* Westchester, Illinois: Beuetic Press, 1957.

This book discusses the life cycle and anatomy of a frog.

Flanagan, G. *Window into an Egg.* New York: Young Scott Books, 1969.

This is a reference book dealing with the day-by-day development of a chick from a single cell.

Schloat, G. Warren. *The Wonderful Egg.* New York: Charles Scribner's Sons, 1952

This book concerns incubation, growth, production, storage, and marketing.

Three books of fiction that might be of help in this project are:

Kumin, M., and Sexton, Anne. *Eggs of Things.* New York: G. P. Putnam's Sons, 1963.

Buzz and Skippy get "eggs of things" from a pond. The eggs turn out to be tadpoles, and the boys form a frog club.

Milhaus, K. *The Egg Tree.* New York: Charles Scribner's Sons, 1950.

Easter on a farm brings an egg hunt. Children find decorated hollow eggs in the attic and make an Easter egg tree with decorated eggs.

Tresselt, A. *The World of the Candy Egg.* New York: Lothrop, Lee, & Shephard, 1969.

This book concerns a fantasy in a toy shop.

SPECIAL CONCERNS

Books Dealing with Special Issues: Minority Groups

Thus far, we have provided generalized guidelines for selecting books suitable for children of different ages. Because of their timely importance, we will now consider separately books that address current or special concerns.

Although there was almost a complete absence of books with black characters in typical black environments before the mid 1960s, literature, which has always responded to contemporary social issues, has responded with a proliferation of such books in the past decade (6). We are increasingly aware of the rights of minority groups and the essentially pluralistic nature of our society.

Goals

We believe that white children need to respect other life styles; we also believe that minority groups need to see children like themselves in skin color and life style, with whom they can more easily identify and thereby enhance their self-awareness and self-esteem. It is to be hoped that heterogeneous racial groupings in school and in play will accompany what children see in books. This will allow children to respect an essential common humanity and to enjoy play with another child whatever his racial background so that those who are different will no longer seem strange or unreal. Unquestionably, the black child has needs we have already underlined. He will relate more easily to books portraying what is familiar to him; he will respond to characters in books as they reflect what he is or could be or as they represent important persons he knows. He must learn that people of his own color and culture have worth in the eyes of others.

To provide respect for other life styles; to promote identification and self-esteem

Interracial books attempt to present society and people as they really are—or could be. They are most successful when they adhere to the definitions already established for good literature and when they avoid the danger inherent in too zealous teaching. We do not want didactic sociological tracts. The import of the message of these books also needs to be scrutinized in terms of the theoretical postulations already set forth: the age of the child; his capability of understanding the social implications of the message; the climate of tolerance or acceptance previously established by his parents, his teacher, and his play environment. As we have already stated, this climate of tolerance is basic to the import of the message.

The effectiveness of even the best books depends greatly on the wisdom of the adults who read them.

Two simple stories by Ezra Jack Keats have distinguished, beautiful illustrations and present a little black boy as he plays in the snow and as he tries to whistle (*The Snowy Day* and *Whistle for Willie*); in another book, he copes with the arrival of a new baby in his home (*Peter's Chair.*) There has been some adverse criticism of these books as being too simplistic and too middle-class oriented. One critic feels that the fat mother with the colorful bandana in *The Snowy Day* represents a stereotyped image. The books seem to be good ones, however, when we consider the age of the child to whom they are directed and the natural, childlike experiences they capture.

Black children appear with familiar, natural experiences.

Two books show black and white children in friendly encounters. In *Steffie and Me* by Phyllis Hoffman, two girls of different colors are best friends, and the white girl goes home to the black girl's mother. In *Will I Have a Friend?* by M. Cohen, both black and white children are in the school, and the teacher is black. In *What Mary Jo Shared* by Janice Udry, the little black girl takes her father to school to share at the "Show-and-Tell" period. *Benjie* by J. Lexau shows an inner-city black child who lives with his grandmother in a tenement building. Suspense comes when grandmother loses an earring and Benjie finds it. *Sam* by Herbert Scott is a beautifully illustrated book about a little black boy who has no one to play with him. It tells a sensitive and familiar story of a child at loose ends; in this case, his family realizes his predicament and lovingly helps him find something interesting to do in the house to help his mother.

Black and white children appear as friends in school, in the city, at home.

Some of the Days of Everett Anderson by E. Ness presents, in a delightful, poetic form reminiscent of A. A. Milne, some basic truths about black children—showing them as intelligent, responsible, sensitive. *Stevie* and *Uptown* by John Steptoe present recognizable *human* figures. Stevie has the same feelings of annoyance and sibling rivalry any

Some books are written in "black language."

child would have when encumbered with a small brother. *Uptown* tells about life in a black slum as it really is—with Black Panthers, drug addicts, etc. These books add a new dimension for they are written in a current street style of "black" language, with new, different uses of language forms. *Skimmy Skimmy Coke-Ca-Pop!: A Collection of City Children's Street Games and Rhymes* by John Langstaff intends to help children from American minorities discover their own, very different backgrounds. Blacks, American Indians, Puerto Ricans, Armenians, and Chinese groups are represented.

Angelita by W. Kesselman is a book with beautiful photographs which shows a child in her native Puerto Rico who then moves to New York. It is a long, drawn-out book which weaves a story around a lost doll and is more suitable for five year olds than for younger children. It serves a good purpose in bringing vivid awareness of another child's background to children in New York.

Other Minority Groups

Nanabah's Friend by Mark Perrine shows modern children living in an Indian way; family relationships and characterization of children are real and delightful. *Joanjo: A Portuguese Tale* by J. Balet presents a more international picture. Children in the fishing village bring credibility to the fact that there are other, different children doing things in their own way. I think we all will agree that such books are a far and better cry from Robert L. Stevenson's sentiment in a former time (9):

> Little Indian, Sioux or Crow,
> Little frosty Eskimo
> Little Turk or Japanee
> Don't you wish that you were me!

Sex-Role Typing in Books

Another issue is that of the stereotyped female image presented in children's books. A group known as "Feminists on Children's Media" is publishing articles and pamphlets and presenting slide shows attesting that books about boys outnumber those about girls, that girls are depicted as passive and foolish and boys as active and intelligent, that men are shown in a variety of occupational roles, while women are seen almost exclusively as housewives. Too often books portray ferocious daddy tigers and gentle mommy pussycats, and books about cars, trucks, trains show only men at the wheels.

Once one is alerted to this fact in children's literature, there is no denying its pervasiveness; it becomes a disturbing game to look for its subtle and blatant manifestations everywhere—in advertising, on television, among school and business personnel and their practices, in jokes, in songs. It begins as early as Mother Goose rhymes—"What are little girls made of?" "Georgie Porgie . . . kissed the girls and made them cry," "Bobbie Shaftoe went to sea . . . he'll come back and marry me," "Bye-baby-bunting, father's gone a-hunting." Even Jill comes tumbling down the hill *after* Jack.

Very young children are already sex typed.

If we agree with Freud that biology is destiny, perhaps feminists are fighting a losing battle. It is an impressive fact that when one analyzes stories of children between the ages of two to five, one recognizes that children are bound by the same sex stereotypes we see in adult authors. Girls are more likely to talk about people or themselves in a home situation, to see females in nurturing, passive roles; boys tend to like themes of action which present males or objects as aggressive protagonists; and they show little interest in female roles (8). Parents talk to boys and girls differently (even in terms of tone of voice), dress them differently, have different expectations for their behavior (7). Thus, whether it be basically biological or purely cultural in origin, the circular process of societal expectation leading to personal incorporation and returning to societal expectation has shown a powerful self-sustaining mechanism.

If one assumes that the tendency to passivity or activity is inherent in different degrees in the male-female biology and anatomy, it is not surprising that across a broad spectrum of society and over a long passage of time, training for girls has been stronger in responsibility and nurture, while for boys, it has been in self-reliance and achievement. Such differences have not been just arbitrary customs but also adjustments to the social implications of the biological differences between the sexes.

But an imperative call for societal change in attitudes toward sex differences has been sounded. We acknowledge that a stereotyped role for any individual is *limiting*, not liberalizing. We are encouraged to open opportunities for boys that are more receptive and to encourage girls to assume more aggressive or *penetrating* roles. There is a strong belief that more productive options in living will be available to both sexes if options in roles are opened up more.

New awareness exists of the limiting effect of a stereotyped role.

In the past decade, there has been a commendable effort to convert the image of the stereotyped female, as is evident in such titles as *Girls Can Be Anything* by Norma Klein, *Mothers Can Do Anything* by Joe Lasker, *What Can She Be? A Musician* by Gloria Goldreich, and *Mommies at Work* by Eve Merriam. In *Tommy Goes to the Doctor* by Wolde, the doctor is a woman. Charlotte Zolotow, in *It's Not Fair*, presents the adult character as a loving grandmother and busy lawyer. Adventuresome, active girls are the heroines in such books as *Tell Me A Mitzi* by G. Segal, as well as in *Mitzi Takes a Taxi, Mitzi Sneezes,* and *Mitzi and the President.* The female is far from passive in Lystad's *Jennifer Takes Over,* Terris's *Amanda the Panda and Redhead,* and Bonsall's *And I Mean It, Stanley.* In Delton's *Rabbit Finds a Way,* Squirrel hammers and saws to build a porch for her house. In Surowiecki's *Joshua's Day,* Joshua's friend, Maria, shows how to make a truck zoom and joins the boys in building a great superhighway. Joshua's favorite friend is Vanessa, who makes him laugh when she makes monster faces on the seesaw. We need more books in which girl *children* engage in activities more commonly associated with male-dominated interests or territories. Such books will be ultimately more influential than books depicting *adult* females in roles that have been typically male.

Good books are increasingly available.

We also applaud those books that focus on male sex stereotyping, such as *William's Doll* by Charlotte Zolotow, Wickland's *I Can Help, Too* and Delton's *Two Good Friends.* In the first book, a little boy wants a doll, but his parents won't buy it for him. Everyone tries to discourage him, but finally his grandmother gratifies his wish and explains that having a doll is necessary practice for being a good father some day. In the second, a boy does domestic tasks, scrubbing floors, washing dishes, sewing. And in the third, bear and duck are both males. Duck is a superb housekeeper and Bear an excellent cook.

Still another useful approach can be found in books that deliberately show cross-sex play or friendships, such as Viorst's *Rosie and Michael*, Merriam's *Boys and Girls, Girls and Boys*, and *He Bear, She Bear* by Berenstein, with the explicit teaching, "We can do all these things you see, Whether we are he or she."

Books Dealing with Psychologically Relevant Themes

Increasingly, there are types of books that address themselves to a special kind of teaching calculated to improve children's mental health. These books are often advertised as addressing "psychologically relevant themes" and are frequently sponsored by medical schools and mental health institutes. In general, the books of this nature are not meant for every child but only for the child asking questions or dealing with problems; their advertising often is directed to adults rather than to children: "One could wish that this book were required reading for all parents" or "I would recommend it very highly for church libraries . . . and for teachers/parents working with this age group." As is true with the other books dealing with issues, most of these publications do not qualify as good "literature." They can serve a purpose, however, when they are used judiciously. In many instances, the advertising for the books is appropriate: they are best utilized when the adult does not directly read them to the child but incorporates the intent of the book and presents it to the child in a personalized way.

Two Psychological Issues

Even though it would be impossible to deal with all the issues or the many publications in this area, a consideration of two issues may be helpful—the home without a father and the experience of death in relation to the child.

The home without a father

A Father Like That by Charlotte Zolotow and *The Man in the House* by J. Fassler deal with the same theme. The first is a relatively good book to read to an individual child. One of its best aspects is the implication that the mother and boy have enough confidence in each other for him to talk and for her to listen—a good point for the mother, especially. The second book is an example of one that goes wrong when a theoretical position dominates the story. When David's father leaves, he engages in violent imaginings—he'll shoot a crocodile, stamp down wolves that enter the house, burn a monster to bits. The intention apparently is to show that the child who feels deserted can express his hostility. A companion book that also goes wrong is *All Alone With Daddy* by J. Fassler in which Ellen takes her mother's place in the house by putting on make-up and jewelry, going for walks with her father, even getting into her parents' bed on Mommy's side. When her mother returns, she dreams of little girls "who really did grow up to marry their daddies—and had boy babies. . . . " We submit that the pernicious Freudian messages here expressed are more likely to create problems than solve them.

Books about death

There has been a great change in our society's attitude toward death in the last ten years, possibly triggered by our national viewing and involvement in the death of President Kennedy and intensified by the coverage of the deaths of Martin Luther King and Robert Kennedy. But when we consider books dealing with this theme, we must once again be aware of children's limitations of understanding and potency of feeling. It seems highly probable that stronger feelings of loss and personal concern about death are more likely to develop in children who have experienced abandonment or separation anxiety, especially if they have been exposed to grief and loss in connection with the word "death."

The best books on this subject are simple, direct, and draw as much as possible from a child's own experience. The young child tends to think concretely; presentations which are too complicated or abstract can disturb his thinking. An adult can be helped by asking the child, "Tell me what you think," and start from there. Such an approach also allows an adult to clarify gross misunderstandings or feelings of guilt or anxiety.

Books on the subject of death should be presented individually, sometimes only in part, sometimes retold by the adult in his own terms. The adult would be wise to hold or touch the child as she reads and also be prepared to give time to respond to questions or reactions during and after the reading. We are aware that body touch is very vital to human beings who experience anxieties and that verbal reassurances, even when not fully understood, are somehow able to be reassuring when the tone is right. *What* is said must be chosen carefully, but *how* it is said can have even greater bearing on whether a child develops or clings to anxiety.

The Dead Bird by Margaret Wise Brown is a simple, concrete presentation suitable for very young children. *Cock Robin* by Barbara Cooney is another story told matter of factly and reassuringly. *The Tenth Good Thing about Barney* by Judith Viorst is a matter-of-fact yet sensitive book for a somewhat older child, which recollects all the pleasant things about the cat who has died. Barney is buried, and his presence under the ground helps the flowers grow on top of the earth. *The Dead Tree* by Alvin Tresselt tells that nothing in nature is ever wasted; even in death the tree helps other new life to grow in the forest. *Sir Ribbeck of Ribbeck of Havelland* by Theodore Fontane tells of the productive old age of Sir Ribbeck and how, on his death, his good deeds live on after him. Telling about the life cycle of the salmon is also a positive way to show death as a part of life. *Charlotte's Web* is a book which deals poignantly with the life-death theme in this way. Although it was written for older children than the group we are considering, the message could be simplified and adapted to the younger child.

A guide for parents and teachers but a book not suited for reading to young children is *Talking About Death* by Earl H. Grollman.

An example of a book that does not succeed—because it is too didactic—is *My Grandpa Died Today* by Joan Fassler. As is abundantly clear from previous remarks, we have misgivings about the effectiveness of a book which seems to be manufacturing a story to prove a moral or a point. Such books lack both feeling and art form. Possibly children learn much more from a tale that is not consciously trying to teach them anything.

Such tales are to be found among folk and fairy tales. Bettleheim, in *The Uses of Enchantment*, beautifully conveys how fairy tales, subtly and by implication, deal with psychological problems of growing up: sibling rivalries, advantages of moral behavior, oedipal dilemmas, feelings of self-worth, and separation anxiety. A child, seeing the world subjectively, finds his own solutions to basic human predicaments in this type of literature. The tales always deal with good and evil, and evil always loses out. The compelling stories serve to clarify emotions and provide solutions to inner problems; they are truly classics.

CONCLUSION   Children's books can provide countless hours of pleasurable experience for teachers and children. Chosen judiciously and presented well, books can dramatize or enliven an event, quiet a group of children or a single child, extend a child's world and excite and enliven his imagination, teach specific concepts, and help in isolating and refining certain perceptual and cognitive skills. Books amuse and delight and involve children in the spoken and written word; they develop self-esteem and give help in dealing sensitively with problems and fears many children experience.

BIBLIOGRAPHY

1.   Ashton-Warner, Sylvia. *Teacher*. New York: Simon & Schuster, 1963.

2.   Bettleheim, B. *The Uses of Enchantment*. New York: Alfred A. Knopf, 1976.

3.   Chomsky, Carol. "Write First, Read Later." *Childhood Education* 47 (March 1971): 296–99.

4.   Goodacre, K. *Children and Learning to Read*. London: Rutledge and Kegan Paul, Ltd., 1971.

5.   Lanes, Selma. *Down the Rabbit Hole*. New York: Atheneum Publishers, 1972.

6.   Larrick, Nancy. "The All White World of Children's Books." *Saturday Review of Literature* 48 (September 1965): 63–65.

7.   Pitcher, E. "Male and Female." *Atlantic Monthly* 211 (March 1963): 87–92.

8.   Pitcher, E., and Prelinger, E. *Children Tell Stories: An Analysis of Fantasy*. New York: International Universities Press, 1963.

9.   Stevenson, Robert Louis. *A Child's Garden of Verses*. Baltimore: Penguin Books, 1963.

Five

Literature for Children:
A Bibliography

The following bibliography, as well as the categories, was first published by the Eliot-Pearson Alumni Association of Tufts University in 1970. It is reprinted in an adapted form here by permission of the publisher. The selections were made by Martha H. Chandler with the assistance of Evelyn G. Pitcher, by teachers at the Eliot-Pearson Children's School at Tufts University, and by Marie Cotter, Librarian of Wheelock College.

The categories included in the bibliography are:

Animals and Creatures
Bibliographies of Multiethnic Books
Books about Children's Literature
Children in School
Children's Concerns, Fears, and Special Needs
Close Relationships: Family and Friends
Concepts and Academic Preliminaries
Good Stories with Real Plots
Humor and Nonsense
International Friends
Minority Groups
Nature and Science
Poetry, Songs, and Verse
Religions and Holidays
Sex Role Diversity
The Urban Community
Sources for Locating Media Books
Sources for Reviews, Lists, and Evaluations of Good Children's Books

The bibliography is intended merely to suggest possibilities and is limited by the date of the publication of this volume. Each category could be enlarged, and others might be added under different circumstances. Where one book in a series is mentioned, the reader can assume that the others in that series are also of value. We have attempted to choose books with lasting qualities of literary and artistic merit and valid appeal to young children.

Animals and Creatures

Author and Title	Illustrator	Publisher	Date	Age
Birnbaum, A. *Green Eyes*	author	14*	1953	3–5
Brown, M. W. *The Golden Bunny*	L. Weisgard	38	1953	3–6
Brown, M. W. *Sleepy Little Lion*	L. Weisgard	44	1947	3–6
Brown, M. W. *Wait till the Moon Is Full*	G. Williams	44	1948	4–6
deBrunhoff, J. *The Story of Babar, the Little Elephant*	author	77	1933	4–5
Conklin, G. *I Like Butterflies*	B. Latham	50	1960	4–7
Conklin, G. *Lucky Ladybugs*	G. Rounds	50	1968	4–7
Conklin, G. *We Like Bugs*	A. Marokvia	50	1962	4–7
Duvoisin, R. *Veronica*	author	57	1961	4–6
Ets, M. H. *Another Day*	author	94	1953	3–4
Ets, M. H. *In the Forest*	author	94	1944	3–4
Ets, M. H. *Just Me*	author	94	1965	3–4
Ets, M. H. *Play with Me*	author	94	1955	3–4
Fatio, L. *The Happy Lion*	R. Duvoisin	63	1954	4–6
Feilen, J. *Squirrels* (Just Beginning Science Series)	T. Dolan	34	1967	3–7
Flack, M. *Angus and the Cat*	author	28	1931	2–3
Flack, M. *Angus and the Ducks*	author	28	1930	2–3
Flack, M. *The Restless Robin*	author	53	1937	4–6
Flack, M. *Tim Tadpole and Great Bullfrog*	author	28	1934	4–6
Freschet, B. *Bear Mouse*	author	82	1973	3–5
Fresnet, B. *The Web in the Grass*	R. Duvoisin	82	1972	4–7
Galdone, P. *The Hare and the Tortoise* (an Aesop Fable)	author	63	1962	4–6
Garelik, M. *Just Suppose*	B. Turkle	79	1969	3–5
Ginsburg, M. *The Chick and the Ducklings*	author	64	1972	3–5
Ginsburg, M. *The Three Kittens*	author	21	1973	3–5
Godden, R. *Mouse House*	A. Adams	94	1957	5–7
Green, M. M. *Everybody Eats*	L. Klein	80	1940	3–5
Green, M. M. *Everybody Has a House*	L. Klein	80	1944	3–5
Hader, B., and Hader, E. *The Big Snow*	authors	64	1948	3–6
Hazen, B. *Where Do Bears Sleep?*	I. Staunton	3	1970	4–7
Hoban, R. *A Birthday for Frances* (and others)	L. Hoban	44	1968	3–5
Hodges, E. *Free as a Frog*	P. Giovanopoulus	3	1969	4–7
Keats, E. J. *Pet Show!*	author	64	1972	5–7

*Publishers have been identified by numbers. See key at the end of the chapter for the list of publishers.

Author and Title	Illustrator	Publisher	Date	Age
Kepes, J. *Frogs Merry*	author	71	1961	3–6
Kepes, J. *Lady Bird Quickly*	author	60	1964	4–6
Krauss, R. *Bears*	P. Rowand	44	1948	3–5
Krauss, R. *The Happy Day*	M. Simont	44	1949	4–5
Kuskin, K. *The Bear Who Saw the Spring*	author	44	1961	4–6
Langstaff, J. *Over in the Meadow*	F. Rojankovsky	42	1957	3–5
Lawson, R. *Rabbit Hill*	author	94	1954	4–6
Lionni, L. *Fish Is Fish*	author	71	1970	4–6
Lionni, L. *Frederick*	author	71	1967	4–6
Lionni, L. *Swimmy*	author	71	1963	4–6
Lobel, A. *Frog and Toad Are Friends*	author	44	1970	5–7
Maestro, G. *The Tortoise's Tug of War*	author	12	1971	4–6
Marshall, J. *George and Martha*	author	53	1972	3–5
May, J. *Living Things and Their Young* (Follett Family Life Education Program)	(photographs)	34	1969	5–7
Minarik, E. *A Kiss for Little Bear* (Series)	M. Sendak	44	1968	4–7
Minarik, E. *Little Bear*	M. Sendak	44	1957	4–7
Munari, B. *Bruno Munari's Zoo*	author	106	1963	3–6
Peet, B. *Farewell to Shady Green*	author	53	1966	4–6
Petersham, M., and Petersham, M. *The Box with Red Wheels*	authors	64	1949	2–4
Potter, B. *The Tale of the Faithful Dove*	M. Angel	99	1970	4–7
Potter, B. *The Tale of Peter Rabbit* (and all the others in their original format)	author	99	1903	3–5
Rey, H. A. *Cecily G. and the Nine Monkeys*	author	53	1942	4–6
Schatz, L. *Whiskers My Cat*	P. Galdone	63	1967	3–5
Scher, P. *The Brownstone*	author	71	1973	3–6
Skaar, G. *All About Dogs*	author	108	1966	2–5
Skaar, G. *What Do the Animals Say?*	author	108	1968	2–5
Spier, P. *Gobble, Growl, Grunt*	author	28	1971	2–4
Stevens, C. *The Birth of Sunset's Kittens*	L. Stevens (photographs)	108	1969	5–7
Tensan, R. *Come to the Zoo*	(photographs)	78	1948	3–6
Tresselt, A. *The Beaver Pond*	R. Duvoisin	62	1940	5–7
Tresselt, A. *Wake Up Farm*	R. Duvoisin	62	1957	3–5
Ward, L. *The Biggest Bear*	author	53	1952	5–7
Wildsmith, B. *Wild Animals*	author	100	1967	4–6
Williams, G. *Baby Animals*	author	84	1952	3–5

Bibliographies of Multiethnic Books

Author and Title	Illustrator	Publisher	Date	Age
Carlson, R. *Multi-Ethnic Literature for Children and Adolescents*	L. N. Gray and E. Jaco	13	1972	
Griffin, L. *Multi-Ethnic Books for Young Children: Annotated Bibliography for Parents and Children*		67	1970	
Information Center on Childrens' Cultures Africa: A List of Printed Materials for Children		91	1968	
White, D. *Multi-Ethnic Books for Head Start Children, Parts 1 and 2*		31	1969	
Wolfe, A. S. *About 100 Books . . . A Gateway to Better Intergroup Understanding*		4	1972	

Books about Children's Literature

Author and Title	Illustrator	Publisher	Date	Age
Anderson, W., and Groff, P. *A New Look at Children's Literature*		96	1972	
Arbuthnot, M. H., and Sutherland, Z. *Children and Books, 4th ed.*		80	1972	
Arbuthnot, M. H., and Root, S. *Time for Poetry*		80	1968	
Bauer, C. F. *Handbook for Storytellers*		5	1970	
Bettelheim, B. *The Uses of Enchantment*		57	1976	
Cameron, E. *The Green and Burning Tree*		60	1969	
Carlson, R. K. *Literature for Children: Enrichment Ideas, 2d ed., Literature Series*		13	1976	
Cattersen, J.H., editor. *Children and Literature*		54	1970	
Chukovsky, K. *From Two to Five: A Critical Approach to Children's Literature*		92	1963	

Author and Title	Illustrator	Publisher	Date	Age
Cianciolo, P. *Picture Books for Children*		5	1973	
Coody, B. *Using Literature with Young Children*		13	1973	
Cullinan, B., and Carmichael, C. *Literature and Young Children*		68	1977	
Dagliesh, A. *First Experiences with Literature*		82	1932	
Danoff, J.; Bratbart, V.; and Barr, E. *Open for Children*		63	1977	
Duff, A. *Bequest of Wings: A Family's Pleasure with Books*		94	1946	
Egoff, Sheila; Stubbs, G. T.; and Ashley, L. F., editors *Only Connect, Readings on Children's Literature*		70	1969	
Favat, F. H. *Child and Tale: The Origins of Interest*		68	1977	
Gillespie, M. C. *History and Trends*		13	1970	
Gillespie, M. C., and Connor, J. W. *Creative Growth through Literature for Children and Adolescents*		65	1975	
Handel, R., and Siegelman, M. *The Reader in the Kitchen*		30	1976	
Hazard, P. *Books, Children and Men*		52	1960	
Hennings, D. G. *Smiles, Nods and Pauses, Activities to Enrich Children's Communication Skills*		15	1974	
Hopkins, L.B., editor. *Pass the Poetry Please*		15	1972	
Huck, C. *Children's Literature*		51	1976	
Karl, J. *From Childhood to Childhood*		94	1970	
Kingston, C. F. *The Tragic Mode in Children's Literature*		88	1974	
Kock, K. *Wishes, Lies and Dreams*		95	1970	
Lanes, S. *Down the Rabbit Hole*		6	1972	
Landan, E. D.; Epstein, S. Landan; and Stone, A., editors. *Child Development through Literature*		75	1972	
Lapate, P. *Being with Children*		28	1975	
Larrick, N. *Parents Guide to Children's Reading*		7	1975	

Author and Title	Illustrator	Publisher	Date	Age
Lickteig, M. J. *An Introduction to Children's Literature*		65	1975	
Livingston, M. *When You Are Alone It Keeps you Capone*		6	1973	
Pitcher, E. G., and Prelinger, E. *Children Tell Stories: An Analysis of Fantasy*		55	1963	
Reasoner, C. *Releasing Children to Literature*		24	1976	
Reasoner, C. *When Children Read*		24	1975	
Reasoner, C. *Where the Readers Are*		24	1972	
Root, S. *Adventuring with Books*		15	1973	
Rudman, M. K. *Children's Literature: An Issues Approach*		48	1976	
Simmons, B. *Paperback Books for Children*		15	1972	
Smith, D. V. *Fifty Years of Children's Books*		68	1963	
Smith, L. H. *The Unreluctant Years*		94	1971	
Viguers, R. H. *Margin for Surprise*		60	1964	
White, M. L. *Children's Literature: Criticism and Response*		65	1976	
Yolen, J. *Writing Books for Children*		107	1973	

Children in School

Author and Title	Illustrator	Publisher	Date	Age
Alexander, M. *Sabrina*	author	25	1971	3–6
Beim, J. *Andy and the School Bus*	L. Shortall	66	1947	4–6
Brown, M. *My Daddy's Visiting Our School Today*	P. Bolian	100	1961	3–5
Buckler, P., and Jones, H. *Five Friends at School* (Holt Urban Social Studies)	authors (photographs)	51	1966	5–7
Caudill, R. *A Pocketful of Cricket*	E. Ness	51	1964	5–6
Caudill, R. *Did You Carry the Flag Today, Charlie?*	N. Grossman	51	1966	5–8
Cohen, M. *The New Teacher*	L. Hoban	64	1972	4–6
Cohen, M. *Will I Have a Friend?*	L. Hoban	64	1967	3–4
Justus, M. *New Boy in School*	J. Payne	46	1963	5–7
Mannheim, G. *The Two Friends*	author (photographs)	57	1968	3–6
Marino, D. *Where Are the Mothers?*	author	59	1959	3–5
Meshover, L. *The Guinea Pigs That Went to School*	E. Hoffman (photographs)	34	1968	4–7

Author and Title	Illustrator	Publisher	Date	Age
Pope, B., and Emmons, R. *Your World: Let's Go to School*	authors	87	1967	5–7
Serfozo, M. *Welcome Roberto!*	J. Serfozo	34	1969	5–7
Udry, J. *What Mary Jo Shared*	E. Mill	104	1966	5–6

Children's Concerns, Fears, and Special Needs

Author and Title	Illustrator	Publisher	Date	Age
Adams, F. *Mushy Eggs*	M. Hirsh	76	1973	3–7
Alexander, M. *And My Mean Old Mother Will be Sorry, Blackboard Bear*	author	25	1969	5–7
Alexander M. *Nobody Asked Me if I Wanted a Baby Sister*	author	25	1971	4–6
Andry, A. C., and Schepp, S. *How Babies Are Made*	B. Hampton	89	1968	3–8
Ardizzone, E. *The Wrong Side of the Bed*	author	28	1970	4–6
Bartoli, J. *Nonna*	author	45	1975	5–7
Bendick, J. *What Made You You?*		63	1971	5–7
Brightman, A. *Like Me*	(photographs)	60	1976	5–7
Brown, M. B. *The First Night Away From Home*	D. Marino	100	1960	4–6
Brown, M. W. *A Child's Goodnight Book*	J. Charlot	81	1950	2–3
Brown, M. W. *The Dead Bird*	R. Charlip	81	1958	4–6
Brown, M. W. *Goodnight Moon*	C. Hurd	44	1947	2–4
Brown, M. W. *The Runaway Bunny*	C. Hurd	44	1972	3–5
Buckley, H. *Too Many Crackers*	T. Chen	62	1966	3–5
Clifton, L. *Everett Anderson's Year*	A. Grifalconi	51	1974	4–8
Cooney, B. *Cock Robin*	author	82	1965	3–6
DePaola, T. *Nana Upstairs and Nana Downstairs*	author	76	1973	5–7
Fassler, J. *All Alone With Daddy*	S. Kranz	9	1972	5–7
Fassler, J. *My Grandfather Died Today*	S. Kranz	9	1972	6–7
Fassler, J. *The Man in the House*	S. Kranz	9	1972	5–7
Fisher, A. *My Mother and I*	K. Mizumura	20	1967	4–6
Fontane, T. *Sir Ribbeck of Ribbeck of Havelland*	H. Hogrogian	64	1969	5–7
Gordon, S. *Girls are Girls and Boys are Boys*	F. Smith	22	1975	5–8
Greenfield, E. *She Came Bringing Me that Little Baby Girl*	J. Steptoe	59	1974	5–7

Author and Title	Illustrator	Publisher	Date	Age
Grollman, E. *Talking about Death*	G. Heau	8	1970	6–7
Hitte, K. *Boy Was I Mad!*	M. Mayer	72	1969	4–6
Hoban, R. *A Baby Sister for Frances*	L. Hoban	44	1964	3–5
Hoban, R. *Bedtime for Frances*	G. Williams	44	1960	3–5
Howell, R. *Everything Changes*	A. Strong (photographs)	6	1968	4–5
Hutchins, P. *Titch*	author	64	1971	4–5
Jarrell, M. *The Knee-Baby*	S. Shimin	32	1973	3–5
Kantorowitz, M. *When Violet Died*	E. A. McCully	72	1973	5–8
Keats, E. *Pete's Chair*	author	44	1967	3–5
Keller, B. *Fiona's Bee*	author	18	1975	5–7
Krasilovsky, P. *Scaredy Cat*	Ninon	64	1959	3–5
Krasilovsky, P. *The Shy Little Girl*	T. Schart-Hyman	60	1970	5–7
Krasilovsky, P. *The Very Tall Little Girl*	O. H. H. Cole	28	1969	4–8
Kraus, R. *Leo the Late Bloomer*	J. Aruego	105	1971	4–6
Kraus, R. *Whose Mouse Are You?*	J. Aruego	64	1970	3–5
Lasker, J. *He's My Brother*	author	104	1974	6–8
Mayer, M. *There's a Nightmare in My Closet*	author	25	1968	4–6
Mayer, M. *You're the Scaredy Cat*	author	72	1974	4–6
Memling, C. *What's in the Dark?*	author	72	1971	3–4
Miller, A. *Jane's Blanket*	E. A. McCully	94	1972	5–7
Minarik, E. *No Fighting, No Biting*	M. Sendak	44	1958	4–6
Ness, E. *Sam, Bangs, and Moonshine*	author	51	1966	5–7
Nicklaus, C. *Katy Rose Is Mad*	author	74	1975	5–7
Peterson, H. *The New House*	Y. Kallstrom	63	1964	4–7
Peterson, J. *I Have a Sister, My Sister Is Deaf*	author	104	1976	6–8
Raskin, E. *And It Rained!*	author	6	1969	4–7
Raskin, E. *Spectacles*	author	6	1968	5–7
Rey, M., and Rey, H. A. *Curious George Goes to the Hospital*	authors	53	1966	3–7
Robinson, B. *The Fattest Bear in the First Grade*	C. Szekeves	77	1969	5–7
Rockwell, H. *My Dentist*	author	39	1975	4–6
Schick, E. *City in Winter*	author	64	1970	5–8
Schweintz, K. *Growing Up*	author	64	1968	5–7
Sendak, M. *In the Night Kitchen*	author	44	1970	4–7
Sendak, M. *Where the Wild Things Are*	author	44	1963	4–6
Shay, A. *What Happens When You Go to the Hospital*	(photographs)	78	1969	4–6

Author and Title	Illustrator	Publisher	Date	Age
Showers, P., and Showers, K. P. *Before You Were a Baby*	P. Galdone	20	1968	4–5
Shulevitz, I. *The Moon in My Room*	author	44	1963	2–3
Sobol, H. L. *My Brother Steven Is Retarded*	Agre (photographs)	64	1977	6–8
Stein, S. B. *About Dying*	D. Frank	98	1974	4–8
Steptoe, J. *My Special Best Words*	author	94	1974	3–7
Stevens, C. *The Birth of Sunset's Kittens*	L. Stevens (photographs)	108	1969	5–7
Stull, E. G. *My Turtle Died Today*	author	51	1964	5–8
Tresselt, A. *The Dead Tree*	R. Duvoisin	72	1972	5–7
Udry, J. *Let's Be Enemies*	Sindak	44	1961	5–8
Viorst, J. *Alexander and the Terrible, Horrible, No Good, Very Bad Day*	R. Cruz	6	1972	4–6
Viorst, J. *My Mamma Says There Aren't Any Zombies, Ghosts, Vampires, Creatures, Demons, Monsters, Fiends, Goblins or Things*	K. Chovao	6	1973	4–6
Viorst, J. *The Tenth Good Thing about Barney*	E. Bieguad	6	1971	5–7
Waber, B. *Ira Sleeps Over*	author	53	1972	4–8
Warburg, S. S. *Growing Time*	L. Weisgard	53	1969	5–8
Webber, R. *The Train*	D. Ray	71	1972	4–7
Weber, A. *Elizabeth Gets Well*	J. Bliss	20	1969	3–7
White, E. B. *Charlotte's Web*	G. Williams	24	1952	6–7
Zolotow, C. *A Father Like That*	B. Schester	44	1952	4–6
Zolotow, C. *My Grandson Lew*	W. Pene DuBois	44	1974	4–7
Zolotow, C. *The Hating Book*	B. Scheiter	44	1969	3–8
Zolotow, C. *The Quarreling Book*	A. Lobel	44	1963	4–6

Close Relationships: Family and Friends

Author and Title	Illustrator	Publisher	Date	Age
Alexander, M. *Babies Are Like That*	author	38	1967	3–6
Anglund, J. *A Friend Is Someone Who Likes You*	author	42	1958	3–6
Borack, B. *Grandpa*	B. Shecter	44	1967	4–6
Borea, P. *First Thing in the Morning*	R. Borea (photographs)	19	1970	4–7
Brown, M. *Best Friends*	D. Freeman	38	1967	4–6
Brown, M. W. *The Runaway Bunny*	C. Hurd	44	1972	3–5
Buckley, H. *Grandfather and I*	P. Galdone	62	1959	3–5
Buckley, H. *Grandmother and I*	P. Galdone	62	1967	3–5
Buckley, H. *Josie and the Snow*	E. Ness	62	1964	3–5

Author and Title	Illustrator	Publisher	Date	Age
Buckley, H. *The Little Boy and the Birthdays*	P. Galdone	62	1965	3–6
Buckley, H. *My Sister and I*	P. Galdone	62	1963	3–6
Buckley, H. *The Wonderful Little Boy*	R. Howard	62	1970	5–7
Byars, B. *Go and Hush the Baby*	E. A. McCully	94	1971	3–5
Carlson, D. *Good Morning, Danny; Good Morning, Hannah*	authors	6	1972	2–3
Ets, M. *Just Me*	author	94	1965	3–5
Fisher, A. *My Mother and I*	K. Mizumura	20	1967	4–6
Goffstein, M.B. *Fish for Supper*	author	25	1976	4–6
Guilfoile, E. *Have You Seen My Brother?*	M. Stevens	34	1962	4–6
Herzka, H. *Robin in Red Boots*	author	42	1970	2–3
Hoban, R. *Best Friends*	L. Hoban	44	1969	3–5
Hoban, R. *A Birthday for Frances* (Series)	L. Hoban	44	1968	3–5
Hoffman, P. *Steffie and Me*	E. McCully	44	1970	4–7
Horvath, B. *Be Nice to Josephine*	P. Porter	100	1970	5–8
Jackson, L. A. *Grandpa Had a Windmill, Grandma Had a Churn*	G. Ancona	72	1977	4–6
Kay, H. *One Mitten Lewis*	K. Werth	62	1955	3–5
Keeping, C. *Charley, Charlotte and and the Golden Canary*	author	100	1967	5–7
Kessler, E., and Kessler, L. *The Day Daddy Stayed Home*	authors	28	1959	3–5
Kessler, E., and Kessler, L. *Kim and Me*	authors	28	1960	3–5
Krasilovsky, O. *The Very Little Boy*	Ninon	28	1962	2–4
Krasilovsky, P. *The Very Little Girl*	Ninon	28	1953	2–4
Krauss, R. *The Bundle Book*	H. Stone	44	1951	2–4
Kruss, J. *Our Favorite Things*	E. Witt	74	1970	3–5
Kunhardt, D. *Pat the Bunny*	author	102	1940	1–2
Langstaff, N. *A Tiny Baby for You*	S. Szasz	42	1955	2–5
Lasky, K. *I Have Four Names for My Grandfather*	C. G. Knight (photographs)	60	1976	4–6
Lenski, L. *Debbie and Her Family*	author	97	1969	3–4
Lenski, L. *The Little Family*	author	70	1932	3–4
Lenski, L. *Papa Small*	author	70	1951	3–4
Lenski, L. *Surprise for Davy*	author	70	1947	3–4
Lundgren, M. *Matt's Grandfather*	F. Halel	25	1974	5–7
Marino, D. *Where Are the Mothers?*	author	59	1959	3–5
McCloskey, R. *Blueberries for Sale*	author	94	1948	3–5
McCloskey, R. *One Morning in Maine*	author	94	1952	4–5

Author and Title	Illustrator	Publisher	Date	Age
McCloskey, R. *Time of Wonder*	author	94	1957	5–7
Meeks, E., and Bagwell, E. *Families Live Together* (Follett Family Life Education Program)	authors (photographs)	34	1969	5–7
Miles, B. *Having a Friend*	E. Blevad	57	1959	3–5
Minarik, E. *Little Bear* (Series)	M. Sendak	44	1957	3–5
Mizumura, K. *If I Were a Mother*	author	20	1968	3–5
Pincus, H. *Mina and Pippin*	author	32	1972	3–5
Puner, H. *Daddies: What They Do All Day*	R. Duvoisin	62	1946	3–5
Schick, E. *5A and 7B*	author	64	1967	5–7
Scott, A. *Sam*	S. Shimin	63	1967	4–7
Shimin, S. *I Wish There Were Two of Me*	author	99	1976	5–7
Skorpen, L. M. *Mandy's Grandmother*	M. Alexander	25	1975	5–7
Turkel, B. *Thy Friend, Obediah*	author	94	1969	4–7
Udry, J. *What Mary Jo Shared*	E. Mill	104	1966	4–7
Wright, E. *Saturday Walk*	R. Rose	80	1954	3–5
Zolotow, C. *Big Sister and Little Sister*	M. Alexander	44	1966	5–7
Zolotow, C. *My Friend John*	B. Shecter	44	1968	4–6
Zolotow, C. *The New Friend*	A. Stewart	1	1968	4–7
Zolotow, C. *The Sky Was Blue*	G. Williams	44	1963	4–7

Concepts and Academic Preliminaries

Author and Title	Illustrator	Publisher	Date	Age
COLOR				
Brooks, R. *Annie's Rainbow*	author	16	1975	4–6
Carle, E. *My Very First Book of Colors*	author	64	1971	4–5
Emberly, E. *Green Says "Go!"*	author	60	1963	4–7
Lionni, L. *A Color of His Own*	author	71	1975	4–6
Lobel, A. *The Great Blueness and Other Predicaments*	author	44	1968	5–7
McGovern, A. *Black Is Beautiful*	(photographs)	35	1969	4–6
McKee, D. *Elmer*	author	26	1961	3–6
O'Neill, M. *Hailstones and Halibut Bones*	L. Weisgard	28	1961	3–7
Provenson, A., and Provenson, M. *What Is Color?*	authors	38	1967	3–7
Reiss, J. *Colors*	author	12	1969	3–7

Author and Title	*Illustrator*	*Publisher*	*Date*	*Age*
Rossetti, C. *What Is Pink?*	Aruego	64	1971	4–6
Showers, P. *Your Skin and Mine*	P. Galdone	20	1965	3–5
Steiner, C. *My Slippers Are Red*	author	57	1957	2–3
Zolotow, C. *Mr. Rabbit and the Lovely Present*	M. Sendak	44	1962	3–5

COMPARISONS

Carle, E. *The Secret Birthday Message*	author	20	1971	5–7
Green, M. *Is It Hard? Is It Easy?*	L. Gittleman	81	1960	3–5
Hoban, T. *Big Ones, Little Ones*	(photographs)	39	1976	3–5
Hoban, T. *Over, Under and Through*	(photographs)	64	1973	4–6
Hoban, T. *Push-Pull, Empty-Full*	author (photographs)	64	1972	2–4
Martin, J. *Fast and Slow* (Fun to Read Series)	P. Thomas	74	1965	4-7
Schlein, M. *Fast Is Not a Ladybug*	L. Kessler	80	1953	4-7
Schlein, M. *Heavy Is a Hippopotamus*	L. Kessler	80	1954	3-7

ECOLOGY

Mizumura, K. *If I Built a Village*	author	20	1971	4-6
Peet, B. *Farewell to Shady Glade*	author	53	1966	4-6

INFORMATION

Aliki. *My Five Senses*	author	20	1962	4-6
Charlip, R., and Surpree, B. *Harlequin and the Gift of Many Colors*	author	72	1973	5-7
Cole, J. *My Puppy Is Born*	J. Wexler, (photographs)	66	1973	4-6
DePaola, T. *Charlie Needs a Cloak*	author	64	1973	4-6
Spilka, A. *Paint All Kinds of Pictures*	author	97	1963	4-6
White, R. *All Kinds of Trains*	J. Young	40	1972	3-5
Wildsmith, B. *Circus*	author	100	1970	3-5

LETTERS AND WORDS

Anno, M. *Anno's Alphabet: Adventure in Imagination*	author	20	1975	3-6
Cathy, Marly, and Wendy. *A Is for Alphabet*	G. Suyeoka	80	1968	4-6
DePaola, T. *Andy, That's My Name*	author	75	1973	6-8
Dugan, W. *The Sign Book*	author	38	1968	2-5
Ets, M. *Talking without Words*	author	94	1968	3-6

Author and Title	Illustrator	Publisher	Date	Age
Fife, D. *Adam's ABC*	D. Robertson	18	1971	3–6
Hefter, R., and Mishop, M. *An Animal Shufflebook*	authors	38	1971	5–6
Nolan, D. *Alphrabutes*	author	75	1977	4–6
Rojankovsky, F. *Rojankovsky's ABC*	author	38	1970	4–7
Scarry, R. *Best Word Book Ever*	author	77	1963	2–4
Wildsmith, B. *Brian Wildsmith's ABC*	author	100	1963	3–7

NUMBERS

Baum, A., and Baum, J. *One Bright Monday Morning*	authors	77	1962	4–6
Bright, R. *My Red Umbrella*	author	66	1959	3–4
Brown, M. *One, Two, Three: An Animal Counting Book*	author	60	1976	4–6
Ehrlich, A. *The Everyday Train*	M. Alexander	25	1977	3–5
Hefter, R., and Moskof, M. *Everything*	author	72	1971	3–6
Hoban, T. *Count and See*	author	64	1972	4–6
Holl, A. *Let's Count*	author	3	1976	4–6
Ipcar, D. *Brown Cow Farm*	author	28	1959	4–7
Keats, E. J. *Over in the Meadow*	author	35	1972	5–7
Nolan, D. *Monster Bubbles*	author	75	1976	4–6
Oxenbury, H. *Numbers of Things*	author	100	1968	3–7
Ziner, F. *Counting Carnival*	P. Galdone	18	1962	3–7

SHAPES

Emberly, E. *The Wing on a Flea*	author	60	1961	4–6
Martin, J. *Round and Square*	P. Thomas	74	1965	4–7
Schlein, M. *Shapes*	S. Berman	80	1952	4–7

SOUNDS

Brown, M. W. *The Noisy Book* (Series)	L. Weisgard	44	1939	2–4
Engvick, W., editor. *Lullabies and Night Songs*	M. Sendak	44	1965	1–5
Poston, E., compiler and arranger. *The Baby's Song Book*	W. Stobbs	20	1972	1–3
Shay, A. *What Happens at the Circus*	(photographs)	78	1972	5–7
Victor, J. *Sh-h! Listen Again!*	author	106	1969	4–7

TOUCH

Carle, E. *The Secret Birthday Message*	author	20	1972	2–3
Kunhardt, D. *Pat the Bunny*	author	102	1940	1–2

Author and Title	Illustrator	Publisher	Date	Age
Lewis, S. *Zoo City*	author	39	1976	2–3
Munari, B. *The Circus in the Mist*	author	16	1975	2–3
Witte, E., and Witte, P. *The Touch Me Book*	author	38	1961	2–3
Witte, E., and Witte, P. *Who Lives Here*	author	39	1976	2–3

Good Stories with Real Plots

Author and Title	Illustrator	Publisher	Date	Age
Alexander, M. *No Ducks in Our Bathtub*	author	25	1973	4–6
Anderson, H. (R. Keigwin, translator) *Thumbelina*	A. Adams	82	1961	5–7
Arkin, A. *Tony's Hard Work Day*	author	44	1972	4–6
Asbjnsen, P. C., and Jorgen, E. M. *The Three Billy Goats Gruff*	M. Brown	42	1957	3–5
Bemelmans, L. *Madeline*	author	84	1939	4–7
Bishop, C. *The Five Chinese Brothers*	K. Wiese	18	1938	5–7
Burton, V. L. *Katy and the Big Snow*	author	53	1943	4–6
Burton, V. L. *The Little House*	author	53	1942	4–6
Burton, V. L. *Mike Mulligan and His Steam Shovel*	author	53	1939	4–6
Flack, M. *Angus and the Cats*	author	28	1931	2–3
Flack, M. *Angus and the Ducks*	author	28	1930	2–3
Flack, M. *Ask Mr. Bear*	author	64	1932	2–3
Flack, M. *Story about Ping*	K. Wiese	94	1933	4–5
Gag, W. *Millions of Cats*	author	18	1928	4–5
Galdone, P. *The Frog Prince*	author	63	1975	4–6
Galdone, P. *The Gingerbread Boy*	author	83	1975	3–5
Galdone, P. *The Three Bears*	author	83	1972	3–5
Garrison, C. *Little Pieces of the West Wind*	D. Goode	12	1975	5–7
Grimm Brothers (C. Scribner, Jr., translator) *Hansel and Gretel*	A. Adams	82	1975	5–7
Grimm, J. *Rumplestilskin*	J. Ayer	42	1967	5–7
Grimm, J. *The Shoemaker and the Elves*	A. Adams	82	1960	4–6
Grimm, J. *Snow White and Rose Red*	A. Adams	82	1964	5–7
Hogrogian, N. *One Fine Day*	author	64	1971	5–7
Keats, E. J. *Louie*	author	39	1975	5–7

Author and Title	Illustrator	Publisher	Date	Age
Lowrey, J. *The Poky Little Puppy*	C. Tenggren	38	1942	3–4
McCloskey, R. *Make Way for Ducklings*	author	94	1941	3–6
Mosel, A. *Tikki, Tikki, Tembo*	B. Lent	51	1968	5–7
Payne, E. *Katy-No-Pocket*	H. A. Rey	53	1944	4–5
Piper, W. *The Little Engine That Could*	G. Hauman and D. Hauman	74	1954	3–4
Potter, B. *The Faithful Dove*	M. Angel	99	1970	4–7
Potter, B. *Peter Rabbit* (Series)	author	99	1903	3–5
Rey, H. A. *Curious George* (Series)	author	53	1941	4–6
Ryan, C. *Hildidid's Night*	A. Lobel	64	1971	4–6
Seuss, Dr. (T. Geisel) *The Five Hundred Hats of Bartholomew Cubbins*	author	93	1938	5–7
Steig, W. *Amos and Boris*	author	32	1971	5–7
Turkle, B. *Sky Dog*	author	94	1969	5–7
Turska, K. *The Woodcutter's Duck*	author	64	1972	5–7
Watts, B. *Rapunzel*	author	20	1974-75	4–6
White, E. B. *Charlotte's Web*	G. Williams	24	1952	6–7
Zemach, H. *Duffy and the Devil*	author	32	1973	5–7

Humor and Nonsense

Author and Title	Illustrator	Publisher	Date	Age
Adoff, A. *Ma na Da la*	E. McCully	44	1971	4–6
Aliki. *Keep Your Mouth Closed, Dear*	author	25	1966	4–8
Barrett, J. *Animals Should Definitely Not Wear Clothes*	author	6	1970	3–6
Bodecker, N. *It's Raining said John Twaining*	author	6	1973	5–7
Brown, M. W. *Shhhhhh..Bang!*	R. DeVeyrac	44	1943	4–6
Carle, E. *Do You Want to Be My Friend?*	author	20	1971	3–6
Cole, W. *The Book of Giggles*	T. Ungerer	106	1970	4–7
Copp, J. *Martha Matilde O'Toole*	S. Kellogg	12	1969	3–6
DeRegniers, B. *May I Bring A Friend?*	B. Montressor	6	1964	4–6
Duvoisin, R. *Our Veronica Goes to Petunia's Farm*	author	57	1962	4–6
Eichenberg, F. *Ape in a Cape*	author	42	1952	4–6

Author and Title	Illustrator	Publisher	Date	Age
Freeman, D. *Dandelion*	author	94	1964	4–6
Guilfoile, E. *Nobody Listens to Andrew*	M. Stevens	34	1957	4–7
Kessler, E. *Do Baby Bears Sit on Chairs?*	author	28	1961	3–4
Knight, H. *Where's Wallace?*	author	44	1964	4–6
Krasilovsky, P. *The Man Who Didn't Wash*	B. Cooney	28	1950	4–6
Kraus, R. *A Very Special House*	M. Sendak	44	1953	4–6
Krauss, R. *The Backward Day*	M. Simont	44	1950	3–4
Krauss, R. *Bears*	P. Rowand	44	1948	3–4
Leaf, M. *The Story of Ferdinand*	R. Lawson	94	1938	4–7
Lear, E. *The Complete Nonsense Book*	author	27	1948	4–7
Levarie, N. *I Had a Little _____*	R. Wright	77	1961	5–7
McGovern, A. *Too Much Noise*	S. Tabach	53	1967	4–6
McLeod, E. *One Snail and Me*	W. Lorraine	60	1961	4–5
Mendoza, G. *The Gillygoofang*	M. Mayer	25	1968	4–6
Mordello, G. *The Damp and Daffy Doings of a Daring Pirate Ship*	author	43	1971	5–6
Parish, P. *Amelin Bedelin and the Surprise Shower*	F. Siebel	44	1966	4–6
Raskin, E. *Who, said Sue, said Whooo?*	author	6	1973	4–6
Scheer, J. *Rain Makes Applesauce*	M. Bileck	50	1964	4–7
Segal, L. *Tell Me a Mitzi*	H. Pincus	32	1970	5–7
Shulevitz, U. *One Monday Morning*	author	82	1967	4–6
Seuss, Dr. (T. Geisel) *And to Think I Saw It on Mulberry Street*	author	93	1937	4–7
Seuss, Dr. (T. Geisel) *The Cat in the Hat* (and others)	author	53	1957	4–7
Seuss, Dr. (T. Geisel) *Horton Hatches the Egg*	author	77	1940	4–6
Waber, B. *An Anteater Named Arthur*	author	53	1967	4–8

International Friends

Author and Title	Illustrator	Publisher	Date	Age
AFRICA				
Aardena, V. *Why Mosquitoes Buzz in People's Ears*	L. Dillon and D. Dillon	25	1976	4–7

Author and Title	Illustrator	Publisher	Date	Age
Bernheim, M., and Bernheim, E. *A Week in Aya's World: The Ivory Coast* (Face to Face Series)	authors (photographs)	20	1969	5–7
Brown, M. *Once a Mouse*	author	82	1961	5–7
Dayrell, E. *Why the Sun and the Moon Live in the Sky*	B. Lent	53	1968	5–7
Langner, N. *Rafiki*	author	94	1977	5–7
McKee, D. *The Day the Tide Went Out . . . and out . . . and out . . . and out . . .*	author	1	1975	5–7
Steptoe, J. *Birthday*	author	51	1972	5–8
Sutherland, E. *Playtime in Africa*	author	6	1962	4–6

AUSTRALIA

Rockwell, A. *Tuhurahura and the Whale*	author	72	1971	5–8

CHINA

Flack, M. *Story about Ping*	K. Wiese	94	1933	4–5
Handforth, T. *MeiLi*	author	28	1938	5–7
Martin, P. *The Dog and the Boat Boy*	E. Hollander	76	1969	5–7
Mosel, A. *Tikki, Tikki Tembo*	B. Lent	51	1968	5–7
Williams, J. *Everyone Knows What a Dragon Looks Like*	M. Mayer	35	1976	5–7
Wolkstein, D. *8,000 Stones*	E. Young	28	1972	5–7
Wright, M. W. *Sky Full of Dragons*	C. Dolezal	85	1969	4–7
Yolen, J. *The Emperor and the Kite*	E. Young	106	1967	5–7
Yolen, J. *The Seventh Mandarin*	E. Young	83	1970	5–7

FRANCE

Bemelmans, L. *Madeline*	author	84	1939	4–7
Francoise. *Springtime for Jeanne-Marie*	author	82	1955	4–6
LaFontaine. *The Miller, the Boy, and the Donkey*	B. Wildsmith	100	1969	5–7
Weiss, H. *A Week in Daniel's World: France*	S. Weiss (photographs)	20	1969	5–7

GREECE

Sasek, M. *This Is Greece* (Series)	author	64	1966	5–7
Zolotow, C. *A Week in Yani's World: Greece*	D. Getsug	20	1969	5–7

Author and Title	Illustrator	Publisher	Date	Age
INDIA				
Gobhai, M. *Lakshmi, The Water Buffalo Who Wouldn't*	author	47	1969	5–7
McDermott, G. *Arrow to the Sun*	author	94	1974	5–7
ISRAEL				
Aleichem, S. (A. Harlaf, translator; D. Spicehandler, editor) *Tevye; Oh, a Miracle*	K. Kerman	33	1972	6–8
Lisowski, G. *How Tevya Became a Milkman*	author	51	1976	5–8
Reit, S. *A Week in Hagar's World: Israel*	L. Goldman (photographs)	20	1969	5–7
ITALY				
Sasek, M. *This Is Rome* (Series)	author	64	1960	5–7
JAPAN				
Bannon, L. *The Other Side of the World*	author	53	1960	4–7
Hodges, M. *The Wave*	B. Lent	53	1964	5–7
Matsuno, M. *A Pair of Red Clogs*	K. Mizumara	106	1960	4–6
Mosel, A. *The Funny Little Woman*	B. Lent	29	1972	5–7
Nakatani, C. *The Day Chiro Was Lost*	author	106	1969	4–7
Yashima, T. *Crow Boy*	author	94	1955	3–6
Yosniko, S. (adaptation) *Twelve Years, Twelve Animals*	M. Locke	2	1972	5–7
MEXICO				
Ets, M., and Labastida, A. *Nine Days to Christmas*	authors	94	1959	5–7
Schweitzer, B. *Amigo*	G. Williams	64	1963	5–7
NORWAY				
d'Aulaire, I., and d'Aulaire, E. *Ola*	authors	28	1932	5–7
PHILIPPINES				
Aruego, J. *A Crocodile's Tale: A Philippine Folk Story*	J. Aruego and A. Aruego	82	1972	3–8
PORTUGAL				
Balet, J. *Joanjo: A Portuguese Tale*	author	24	1967	4–7

Author and Title	Illustrator	Publisher	Date	Age
PUERTO RICO				
Barry, R. *The Musical Palm Tree: A Story of Puerto Rico*	author	63	1965	5–8
Belpre, P. *Dance of the Animals*	P. Galone	99	1972	6–8
RUSSIAN				
Ransome, A. *The Fool of the World and the Flying Ship*	U. Shulevitz	32	1968	5–7
Tolstoy, A. *The Great Big Enormous Turnip*	H. Oxenbury	100	1968	5–7
SWEDEN				
Beskow, E. *Pelle's New Suit*	author	44	1929	4–7
Lindgren, A. *The Tomten*	H. Wiberg	18	1961	4–6
Lindgren, A., and Wikland, I. *Christmas in Noisy Village*	authors	94	1964	5–7
Lindman, M. *Flicka, Ricka, Dicka and Their New Friend* (Series)	author	104	1942	4–5
Lindman, M. *Snipp, Snapp, Snurr, and the Red Shoes* (Series)	author	104	1936	4–5
THAILAND				
Ayer, J. *The Paper Flower Tree*	author	42	1962	5–7
UKRAINE				
Rudolph, M. *How A Shirt Grew in the Field*	Yaroslava	63	1967	5–7
OTHER				
Raynor, D. *Grandparents Around the World*	(photographs)	104	1977	4–7

Minority Groups

Author and Title	Illustrator	Publisher	Date	Age
BLACK AMERICANS				
Adoff, A. *Black Is Brown Is Tan*	E. A. McCully	44	1973	3–8
Baldwin, A. *Sunflowers for Tina*	A. Grifalconi	35	1970	4–6
Bank Street College of Education. *The Bank Street Readers*	author	64	1965	4–7
Bourne, M. *Raccoons Are for Loving*	M. Morton	77	1968	5–7
Burch, R. *Joey's Cat*	D. Freeman	94	1969	3–6
Caines, J. *Abby*	S. Kellogg	44	1973	3–8
Cannon, C., and Wickens, E. *What I Like to Do*	author	18	1971	5–7

Author and Title	*Illustrator*	*Publisher*	*Date*	*Age*
Clifton, L. *The Black BC's*	D. Miller	29	1970	3–9
Clifton, L. *Some of the Days of Everett Anderson*	E. Ness	51	1970	3–5
Freeman, D. *Corduroy*	author	94	1968	3–5
Grifalconi, A. *City Rhythms*	author	11	1965	5–7
Haley, G. *A Story, A Story*	author	6	1970	5–7
Hill, E. *Evan's Corner*	N. Grossman	51	1967	5–7
Hoffman, P. *Steffie and Me*	author	44	1970	4–5
Horvath, B. *Hooray for Jasper!*	F. Rocker	100	1966	4–7
Horvath, B. *Jasper Makes Music*	F. Rocker	100	1967	5–7
Justus, M. *New Boy in School*	J. Payne	46	1963	5–7
Justus, M. *A New Home for Billy*	J. Payne	46	1966	5–7
Keats, E. J. *Goggles*	author	64	1969	5–7
Keats, E. J. *Hi Cat!*	author	64	1970	5–7
Keats, E. J. *Letter to Amy*	author	94	1968	4–6
Keats, E. J. *Peter's Chair*	author	44	1967	3–4
Keats, E. J. *The Snowy Day*	author	94	1962	3–5
Keats, E. J. *Whistle for Willie*	author	94	1964	3–5
Lewis, M. *Joey and the Fawn*	T. Hull	56	1967	4–6
Lexau, J. *Benjie*	D. Bolognese	25	1964	4–6
Lexau, J. *Benjie on His Own*	D. Bolognese	25	1970	4–6
McGovern, A. *Black Is Beautiful*	H. Wurmfeld	35	1969	4–7
Palmer, C. *A Rise on High*	H. Hall	59	1966	5–7
Roberts, N. *A Week in Robert's World: The South* (Face to Face Series)	B. Roberts	20	1969	5–7
Scott, A. *Big Cowboy Western*	R. Lewis	62	1965	3–5
Scott, A. *Sam*	S. Shimin	63	1967	4–7
Selsam, M. *Tony's Birds*	K. Werth	44	1961	4–7
Showers, P. *Look at Your Eyes*	P. Galdone	20	1962	4–7
Showers, P. *Your Skin and Mine*	P. Galdone	20	1965	4–7
Simon, N. *What Do I Say?*	J. Lasker	104	1967	3–5
Sonneborn, R. *Friday Night Is Papa Night*	D. Freeman	94	1970	4–6
Steptoe, J. *Birthday*	author	51	1972	5–7
Steptoe, J. *Stevie*	author	44	1969	4–6
Steptoe, J. *Uptown*	author	44	1970	5–7
Tarry, E., and Ets, M. *My Dog Rinty*	A. Alland and A. Alland	94	1946	5–7
Udry, J. *Mary Jo's Grandmother*	E. Mill	104	1970	5–8
Udry, J. *What Mary Jo Shared*	E. Mill	104	1966	4–6
Udry, J. *What Mary Jo Wanted*	E. Mill	104	1968	4–6
Vogel, I. M. *Hello Henry!*	author	72	1965	4–5

AMERICAN INDIANS

Baker, B. *Little Runner*	H. Lobel	44	1962	4–6

Author and Title	Illustrator	Publisher	Date	Age
Bierhorst, J. *The Ring in the Prairie: A Shawnee Legend*	L. Dillon and D. Dillon	25	1970	5–8
Clark, A. *Along Sandy Trails*	A. Cohn	94	1969	5–7
Clark, A. *This for That*	D. Freeman	38	1967	5–7
McDermott, G. *Arrow to the Sun*	author	94	1974	5–8
Perrine, M. *Nanabah's Friend*	L. Weisgard	53	1970	5–7
Perrine, M. *Salt Boy*	L. Weisgard	53	1968	4–9
CHINESE AMERICANS				
Martin, P. *The Rice Bowl Pet*	E. J. Keats	20	1962	5–7
Politi, L. *Moy Moy*	author	82	1960	4–6
ESKIMOS				
Glubok, S. *The Art of the Eskimo*	A. Tamarin (photographs)	44	1964	5–7
Hopkins, M. *The Three Visitors*	A. Rockwell	72	1967	4–7
Morrow, S. *Ingtuk's Friend*	E. Raskin	60	1968	5–7
Parish, P. *Ootah's Lucky Day*	M. Funai	44	1970	5–7
Rasmussen, K. *Beyond the High Hills: A Book of Eskimo Poems*	G. Mary Rousseliere (photographs)	106	1961	5–7
Scott, A. *On Mother's Lap*	G. Colson	63	1972	3–5
HAWAIIANS				
Bannon, L. *The Gift of Hawaii*	author	104	1961	4–6
Spilka, A. *Aloha from Bobby*	author	97	1962	4–6
JAPANESE AMERICANS				
Politi, L. *Mieko*	author	37	1969	4–6
Yashima, T. *Umbrella*	author	94	1958	3–4
Yashima, T. *Youngest One*	author	94	1962	3–4
MEXICAN AMERICANS				
Bolognese, D. *A New Day*	author	23	1970	5–7
Ets, M. *Gilberto and the Wind*	author	94	1963	2–4
Politi, L. *Song of the Swallows*	author	82	1949	4–6
PUERTO RICANS				
Keats, E. J., and Cheer, P. *My Dog Is Lost*	author	20	1959	4–6
Kesselman, W. *Angelita*	N. Holt (photographs)	49	1970	4–7
Lexau, J. *Maria*	E. Chrichlow	25	1964	5–7
Sonneborn, R. *Seven in a Bed*	D. Freeman	94	1968	5–7
OTHERS				
Buckler, P., et al. *Five Friends at School*	authors (photographs)	51	1966	5–7

Author and Title	Illustrator	Publisher	Date	Age
Buckler, P., et al. *Living as Neighbors* (Holt Urban Social Studies Series)	authors (photographs)	51	1966	5–7
Buckler, P., et al. *William Andy and Ramon*	authors (photographs)	51	1966	5–7
Hautzig, E. *In the Park: An Excursion in Four Languages*	E. J. Keats	64	1968	5–7
Langstaff, J. *Skimmy Skimmy Coke-Ca-Pop!* (a collection of city children's street games and rhymes)	F. Rojankorsty	28	1973	4–7
Pope, B., and Emmons, R. *Your World: Let's Build a House* (Series)	authors (photographs)	87	1966	5–7

Nature and Science

Author and Title	Illustrator	Publisher	Date	Age
Bancroft, H., and Van Gelder, R. *Animals in Winter*	G. DiPalma	20	1963	5–7
Birmingham, J. *Seasons*	author	11	1971	4–8
Bosinger, E., and Gulcher, J. *A Bird Is Born*	author	86	1960	5–7
Branley, F. *Big Tracks, Little Tracks*	L. Kessler	20	1960	5–7
Branley, F. *A Book of Astronauts for You*	L. Kessler	20	1963	5–7
Branley, F. *A Book of Outer Space for You*	L. Kessler	20	1970	5–7
Branley, F. *A Book of Stars for You*	L. Kessler	20	1967	5–7
Branley, F. *Flash, Crash, Rumble and Roll*	E. Emberley	20	1964	5–7
Branley, F. *Snow Is Falling*	H. Stone	20	1963	5–7
Branley, F. *What Makes Day and Night*	H. Borten	20	1961	4–7
Branley, F. *What the Moon Is Like*	Bobri	20	1963	5–7
Burton, V. L. *The Little House*	author	53	1942	4–6
Busch, P. *A Walk in the Snow*	M. Thatcher (photographs)	59	1971	5–8
Busch, P. *Puddles and Ponds: Living Things in Watery Places*	A. Strong (photographs)	106	1969	5–7
Carle, E. *The Tiny Seed*	author	20	1970	4–6
Carrick, C., and Carrick, D. *Swamp Spring*	authors	64	1969	5–6

Author and Title	Illustrator	Publisher	Date	Age
Cherney, J. *Wolfie*	M. Simont	44	1969	6–8
Conklin, G. *I Caught a Lizard*	A. Marokvia	50	1967	4–6
Conklin, G. *We Like Bugs*	A. Marokvia	50	1962	4–6
Cosgrove, G. *Eggs—And What Happens to Them*	(photographs)	27	1966	5–7
Darby, G. *What Is a Frog?*	author	10	1957	4–5
Davis, H., compiler *A January Fog Will Freeze a Hog* (verse)	author	21	1977	4–7
Dempsey, M., and Sheehan, A., editors. *Into Space* (The Starting Point Library)	authors	106	1970	4–7
Dunn, P.; Dunn, T.; and Dunn, J. *Things*	authors	28	1968	4–7
Exler, S. *Growing and Changing*	F. Exler	62	1957	3–6
Fisher, A. *Going Barefoot*	A. Adams	20	1960	4–6
Fisher, A. *I Like Weather*	J. Domanska	20	1963	4–6
Fisher, A. *In the Middle of the Night*	A. Adams	20	1965	4–6
Fisher, A. *Where Does Everyone Go?*	A. Adams	20	1961	4–6
Flanagan, G. *Window into an Egg*	(photographs)	108	1969	4–6
Freschet, B. *Turtle Pond*	author	82	1971	2–6
Gans, R. *It's Nesting Time*	K. Mizumura	20	1964	4–6
Giambarba, P. *The Lighthouse at Dangerfield*	author	60	1969	4–7
Ginsburg, M. *Mushrooms in the Rain*	J. Aruego and A. Dewey	64	1974	4–6
Goudy, A. *Butterfly Time*	A. Adams	82	1964	5–7
Goudy, A. *The Day We Saw the Sun Come Up*	A. Adams	82	1961	4–6
Goudy, A. *Houses from the Sea*	A. Adams	82	1959	4–6
Graham, M. *Be Nice to Spiders*	author	44	1967	5–7
Hoban, T. *Look Again*	author	64	1973	4–7
Hoff, S. *When Will It Snow?*	M. Chalmers	44	1971	3–6
Hogrogian, N. *Apples*	author	63	1969	4–6
Howell, R. *Everything Changes*	A. Strong	6	1958	4–7
Hutchins, P. *The Wind Blew*	author	64	1974	4–6
Krauss, R. *The Growing Story*	P. Rowand	44	1947	3–5
Mari, I., and Mari, E. *The Chicken and the Egg*	authors	71	1970	3–5
Mendoza, G. *And I Must Hurry for the Sea Is Coming In*	DeWayne Dalrynple	75	1970	4–6
Parnall, P. *Alfalfa Hill*	author	28	1975	5–6
Scarry, R. *The Great Big Air Book*	author	77	1971	4–7
Selsam, M. *Egg to Chick*	B. Wolff	44	1970	5–7
Wildsmith, B. *Birds*	author	100	1967	2–5
Wildsmith, B. *Fishes*	author	100	1967	2–5

Poetry, Songs, and Verse

Author and Title	Illustrator	Publisher	Date	Age
Adoff, A. *Black Is Brown Is Tan*	E. McCully	44	1973	5–7
Aiken, C. *Cats and Bats and Things with Wings*	M. Glaser	6	1965	6–7
Alderson, B. *Cakes and Custard*	author	66	1975	2–5
Aldis, D. *All Together*	J. Jameson M. Flack	76	1952	3–6
Aliki. *Go Tell Aunt Rhody*	author	64	1974	3–6
Allen, M. *A Pocketful of Poems*	S. Greenwald	44	1957	3–6
Behn, H. *The Golden Hive*	author	42	1966	4–7
Behn, H. *Windy Morning*	author	42	1953	4–7
Caudhill, R. *Come Along!*	E. Raskin	51	1959	4–7
Ciardi, J. *Reason for the Pelican*	M. Gekiere	59	1959	5–7
Cole, W. *I Went to the Animal Fair*	C. Rosselli	106	1958	4–7
Craig, M. J., compiler. *The Sand, the Sea and Me*	A. Newell	98	1972	5–7
DeAngeli, M. *Book of Nursery and Mother Goose Rhymes*	author	28	1954	2–5
DeForest, C. *The Prancing Pony: Nursery Rhymes from Japan*	K. Hilda	101	1968	3–5
Fisher, A. *Cricket in a Thicket*	F. Rojankovsky	82	1963	4–7
Fisher, A. *Sing Little Mouse*	S. Shumin	20	1969	4–7
Frank, J. *More Poems to Read to the Very Young*	D. Wilson	77	1968	2–4
Frank, J. *Poems to Read to the Very Young*	D. Wilson	77	1961	2–4
Geismer, B., and **Suter, A.** *Very Young Verses*	M. Bronson	53	1975	4–7
Jacobs, L. *Is Somewhere Always Far Away?*	J. Johnson	51	1967	4–6
Kerrigan, A., and **Reid, A.** *Mother Goose in Spanish*	B. Cooney	20	1968	4–7
Kuskin, K. *The Rose on My Cake*	author	44	1964	5–7
Kuskin, K. *Near the Window Tree*	author	44	1975	5–7
Larrick, N. *The Wheels of the Bus Go Round and Round*	G. Holton	37	1972	2–4
Lear, E. *The Complete Nonsense Book*	author	27	1946 (c) 1846	5–7
Lewis, C. *Poems of Earth and Space*	S. Shimin	29	1966	5–7
Lewis, R. *In a Spring Garden*	E. J. Keats	25	1965	3–7
McCord, D. *Far and Few: Rhymes of the Never Was and Always Is*	H. Kanes	24	1971	3–7
Milne, A. A. *Now We Are Six*	E. Shepard	29	1927	6

Author and Title	Illustrator	Publisher	Date	Age
Milne, A. A. *When We Were Very Young*	E. Shepard	29 24	1924	3–7
Moore, L. *See My Lovely Poison Ivy*	D. Dawson	6	1975	4–6
Poston, E., compiler and arranger. *The Baby's Song Book*	W. Stobbs	20	1972	2–4
Rasmussen, K. *Beyond the High Hills: A Book of Eskimo Poems*	G. Mary Rousseliere	106	1961	5–7
Rockman, A. *Mother Goose Nursery Rhymes*	author	94	1975	2–5
Seeger, R., editor. *American Folk Songs for Children*	B. Cooney	28	1948	3–6
Smith, W. *Laughing Time*	J. Kepes	60	1955	4–7
Stevenson, R. L. *A Child's Garden of Verses*	T. Tudor	97	1947	3–7
Thompson, B. *All the Silver Pennies*	U. Arndt	64	1967	3–7

Religion and Holidays

Author and Title	Illustrator	Publisher	Date	Age
Adams, A. *A Woggle of Witches*	author	82	1971	5–7
d'Aulaire, I., and d'Aulaire, E. *Abraham Lincoln*	authors	28	1939	5–7
Barrett, J. *Benjamin's 365 Birthdays*	R. Barrett	6	1974	5–7
Bolognese, D. *A New Day*	author	23	1970	4–8
Bornstein, R. *Little Gorilla*	author	83	1976	3–5
Brown, M. *Christmas in the Barn*	author	20	1952	3–5
Brown, M. *The Golden Egg Book*	L. Weisgard	38	1947	3–5
Brown, M. *The Little Fir Tree*	B. Cooney	20	1954	3–5
Cedarbaum, S. *Chanuko* (First Holiday Books Series)	C. Ross and J. Ross	90	1961	3–5
Clifton, L. *Everett Anderson's Christmas Coming*	author	51	1971	5–7
Dalgliesh, A. *The Columbus Story*	L. Politi	82	1955	5–7
Dalgliesh, A. *The Thanksgiving Story*	H. Sewell	82	1954	5–7
Ets, M., and Labastida, A. *Nine Days to Christmas*	authors	94	1959	5–7
Field, R. *Prayer for a Child*	E. Jones	64	1941	3–5
Fitch, F. *A Book about God*	L. Weisgard	62	1953	3–6
Fitch, F. *One God, the Ways We Worship Him*	B. Creighton (photographs)	62	1944	5–7

Author and Title	Illustrator	Publisher	Date	Age
Goodall, J. S. *Shrewbettina's Birthday*	author	42	1970	3–6
Hoban, L. *Birthday for Francis*	author	44	1968	6–8
Iwasaki, C. *The Birthday Wish*	author	63	1972	4–6
Jones, J., compiler. *Small Rain*	E. O. Jones	94	1944	3–6
Keats, E. J. *The Little Drummer Boy* (Christmas)	author	64	1968	4–7
Kellogg, S. *Won't Somebody Play With Me?*	author	25	1972	4–6
Lindgren, A., and Wikland, I. *Christmas in Noisy Village*	authors	94	1964	5–7
Massie, D. R. *A Birthday for Bird*	author	72	1966	4–6
Milhous, K. *The Egg Tree*	author	82	1950	4–6
Miller, E. *Mousekin's Golden House* (Halloween)	author	75	1964	4–6
Petersham, M., and Petersham, M. *The Christ Child as Told by Matthew and Luke*	authors	82	1931	2–7
Peterson, H. *Erik and the Christmas Tree* (first American edition)	I. Wikland	62	1970	4–7
Shimin, S. *A Special Birthday*	author	63	1976	3–5
Trent, R. *The First Christmas*	M. Simone	44	1948	2–3
Tresselt, A. *The World in the Candy Egg*	R. Duvoisin	62	1969	5–7
Tudor, T., Scripture compiler. *And It Was So*	author	103	1952	5–7
Wiese, K. *Happy Easter*	author	41	1952	3–5
Wolcott, C. *I Can See What God Does*	M. Locke	2	1969	3–7
Zolotow, C. *The Beautiful Christmas Tree*	R. Robins	73	1972	5–7
Zolotow, C. *The Bunny Who Found Easter*	B. Peterson	73	1959	4–6
Zolotow, C. *Over and Over*	G. Williams	44	1957	3–5

Sex Role Diversity

Author and Title	Illustrator	Publisher	Date	Age
Berenstain, S., and Berenstain, J. *He Bear, She Bear*	author	77	1974	3–6
Bonsall, C. *And I Mean It, Stanley*	author	44	1974	5–8
Clifton, L. *Don't You Remember?*	E. Ness	29	1973	3–7
Clifton, L. *Good, Says Jerome*	S. Douglas	29	1973	4–7
Delton, J. *Two Good Friends*	G. Maestro	21	1974	3–6
Delton, J. *Rabbit Finds A Way*	J. Lasker	21	1975	4–6

Author and Title	Illustrator	Publisher	Date	Age
Gaeddert, L. A. *Noisy Nancy Norris*	S. Fiammenghi	28	1970	4–6
Garber, N. *Amy's Long Night*	author	104	1970	5–6
Goffstein, M. B. *Goldie the Dollmaker*	author	32	1969	5–7
Goldreich, G., and Goldreich, E. *Who Can She Be? A Musician*	R. Spear (photographs)	62	1975	5–7
Gordon, S. *Girls are Girls and Boys are Boys*	F. Smith	22	1975	5–7
Heywood, D., and Zarssoni, M. *The Country Bunny and the Little Gold Shoes*	author	53	1939	5–8
Klein, N. *Girls Can Be Anything*	R. Doty	29	1973	3–6
Krasilovsky, P. *The Man Who Didn't Wash Dishes*	Ninon	28	1950	4–6
Lasker, J. *Mothers Can Do Anything*	author	104	1972	3–8
Lystod, M. *Jennifer Takes Over*	R. Cruz	76	1972	4–8
McCloskey, R. *One Morning in Maine*	author	94	1952	5–7
Merriam, E. *Boys and Girls, Girls and Boys*	author	51	1972	4–8
Merriam, E. *Mommies at Work*	B. Montresor	57	1961	3–5
Ness, E. *Sam, Bangs and Moonshine*	author	51	1966	5–7
Scott, A. H. *Sam*	S. Shimin	63	1967	3–8
Segal, G. *Tell Me a Mitzi*	H. Pincus	32	1970	4–6
Surowiecki, S. *Joshua's Day*	P. Lenthall	61	1977	3–5
Terris, S. *Amanda the Panda and Redhead*	E. McCully	28	1975	3–8
Viorst, J. *Rosie and Michael*	L. Tomei	6	1974	4–6
Webber, R. *The Winter Wedding*	author	71	1975	5–7
Wikland, I. *I Can Help Too*	author	77	1974	4–6
Williams, J. *The Practical Princess*	F. Henstra	72	1969	5–7
Wolde, G. *Tommy Goes to the Doctor*	author	53	1972	4–6
Young, M. *Jellybeans for Breakfast*	B. Komoda	72	1968	4–6
Zolotow, C. *It's Not Fair*	W. P. duBois	44	1976	5–7
Zolotow, C. *William's Doll*	G. Williams	44	1972	4–5

The Urban Community

Author and Title	Illustrator	Publisher	Date	Age
Baldwin, A. N. *Sunflowers for Tina*	A. Grifalconi	35	1972	4–6
Bank Street College of Education. *The Bank Street Readers*	authors	64	1965	4–7
Bate, N. *Who Built the Highway*	author	82	1953	4–7
Binzen, B. *Miguel's Mountain*	author	18	1968	4–7

Author and Title	Illustrator	Publisher	Date	Age
Brooks, R. *The Run, Jump, Bump Book*	D. McPhail	60	1971	3–5
Brown, M. W. *The Diggers*	C. Hurd	44	1960	3–5
Burton, V. *Katy And The Big Snow*	author	53	1943	3–5
Burton, V. *Mike Mulligan and His Steamshovel*	author	53	1939	3–5
Clifton, L. *The Boy Who Didn't Believe in Spring*	B. Turkle	29	1973	5–7
Collier, J. *A Visit to the Firehouse*	Y. Joel	69	1966	5–7
DeRegniers, B. *Circus*	A. Giese	94	1966	5–7
Greene, C. *Truck Drivers: What Do They Do?* (Series)	L. Kessler	44	1967	5–7
Greenfield, E. *She Came Bringing Me that Little Baby Girl*	J. Steptoe	59	1974	4–7
Hader, B., and Hader, E. *Snow in the City*	authors	64	1963	4–7
Hill, E. *Evan's Corner*	N. Grossman	51	1967	4–7
Hitte, K. *What Can You Do Without a Place to Play?*	C. Szekers	72	1971	4–6
Hoffman, H. *The Green Grass Grows All Around*	author	64	1968	4–6
Keats, E. J. *Apt. 3*	author	64	1971	4–6
Kessler, E., and Kessler, L. *All Aboard the Train*	author	28	1964	4–7
Kessler, E., and Kessler, L. *The Big Red Bus*	authors	28	1957	3–4
Lattin, A. *Peter's Policeman*	G. Espenshied (photographs)	34	1958	5–7
Liang, Y. *The Skyscraper*	author	59	1958	5–7
Merriam, E. *Project One, Two, Three*	author	63	1971	4–6
Miller, B. *Alphabet World*	author	64	1971	4–6
Pope, B., and Emmons, R. *Your World: Let's Build A House* (Series)	authors (photographs)	87	1966	5–7
Sage, J. *The Man in the Manhole and the Fix-It Man*	B. Ballantine	81	1955	3–5
Schick, E. *City in the Summer*	author	64	1969	4–6
Schick, E. *City in the Winter*	author	64	1970	5–7
Schick, E. *Neighborhood Knight*	author	60	1976	5–6
Shulevitz, U. *One Monday Morning*	author	82	1967	4–6
Slobodkin, L. *Read about the Policeman*	author	100	1966	5–7
Slobodkin, L. *Read about the Postman*	author	100	1966	5–7
Steptoe, J. *Train Ride*	author	44	1971	4–6

Author and Title	Illustrator	Publisher	Date	Age
Thomas, I. *My Street's a Morning Cool Street*	E. McCully	44	1976	5–7
Tresselt, A. *Wake Up City!*	R. Duvoisin	62	1957	4–6
Ventura, P. *Book of Cities*	author	77	1975	4–6
Zaffo, G. *Airplanes and Trucks and Trains, Fire Engines, Boats and Ships, and Building and Wrecking Machines*	author	40	1968	4–7

SOURCES FOR LOCATING MEDIA BOOKS

Brelowski, Joseph S. *Guide to Educational Technology; Early Childhood Education.* Westport, Conn.: Technomic Publishing, 1973.

Greene, Ellin, and Schoenfeld, Madelynne, eds. *A Multimedia Approach to Children's Literature.* Chicago: American Library Association, 1972.

Rice, Susan. *Films Kids Like.* Chicago: American Library Association Center for Understanding Media, 1973.

SOURCES FOR REVIEWS, LISTS, AND EVALUATIONS OF GOOD CHILDREN'S BOOKS

American Library Association, 50 E. Huron St., Chicago, Ill. 60611.

Association of Children's Libraries of Northern California, San Francisco Public Library, San Francisco, Calif.

Bulletin of the Center for Children's Books. University of Chicago, 5750 Ellis Avenue, Chicago, Ill. 60637.

The Child Study Association of America, Inc., 9 East 89th Street, New York, N.Y. 10028.

Council on Interracial Books, 1841 Broadway, New York, N.Y. 10023.

Eakin, Mary. *Good Books for Children.* Rev. ed. Chicago: The University of Chicago Press, 1962. (Based on books reviewed by the *Bulletin of the Center for Children's Books* from 1948 to 1961.)

Eaton, Anne Thaxter. *Treasure for the Taking.* Rev. ed. New York: Viking Press, 1957.

Horn Book (Bimonthly magazine). 585 Boylston Street, Boston, Mass.

National Foundation for the Improvement of Education Resource Center on Sex Roles in Education, Suite 918, 1156 15th St., N.W., Washington, D.C. 20005.

"Notable Children's Books." Children's Service Division of the American Library Association, 50 East Huron Street, Chicago, Ill. 60611. A short free list compiled annually.

Saturday Review/World, New York Times, and *Christian Science Monitor* all carry reviews of children's books in the spring and fall of the year.

United States Committee for UNICEF, 331 East 38th Street, New York, N.Y. 10016.

KEY TO PUBLISHERS

1	Abelard-Schuman, Ltd.	55	International Universities Press, Inc.
2	Abingdon Press	56	Ives Washburn, Inc.
3	Addison-Wesley Publishing Co.	57	Alfred A. Knopf, Inc.
4	American Jewish Committee	58	R. Lee
5	American Library Association	59	J.B. Lippincott Co.
6	Atheneum Publishers	60	Little, Brown & Co.
7	Bantam Books	61	Lollipop Power, Inc.
8	The Beacon Press	62	Lothrop, Lee & Shephard
9	Behavioral Publications, Inc.	63	McGraw-Hill Book Co.
10	Benefic Press	64	Macmillan Publishing Co.
11	Bobbs-Merrill Co.	65	Charles E. Merrill Publishing Co.
12	Bradbury Press	66	William Morrow & Co., Inc.
13	William C. Brown, Publishers	67	National Association for the Education of
14	Capitol Press		Young Children
15	Citation Press	68	National Council of Teachers of English
16	William Collins & World	69	W.W. Norton & Co., Inc.
	Publishing Co.	70	Oxford University Press, Inc.
17	Contemporary Books, Inc.	71	Pantheon Books, Inc.
18	Coward, McCann & Geoghegan, Inc.	72	Parents' Magazine Press
19	Cowles Book Co., Inc.	73	Parnassus Press
20	Thomas Y. Crowell Co.	74	Platt & Munk Publications
21	Crown Publishers	75	Prentice-Hall, Inc.
22	The John Day Co.	76	G.P. Putnam's Sons
23	Delacourte Press	77	Random House, Inc.
24	Dell Publishing Co.	78	Reilly & Lee Books
25	The Dial Press	79	Scholastic Book Services
26	Dobsen Books, Ltd.	80	Scott Foresman & Co.
27	Dodd, Mead & Co., Inc.	81	William R. Scott, Inc.
28	Doubleday & Co., Inc.	82	Charles Scribner's Sons
29	E.P. Dutton & Co., Inc.	83	Seabury Press
30	Educational Performance Associates	84	Simon & Schuster, Inc.
31	ERIC Clearinghouse	85	Steck-Vaughn Co.
32	Farrar, Straus & Giroux	86	Sterling Publishing Co.
33	Fleet Press Corp.	87	Taylor Publishing Co.
34	Follet Publishing Co.	88	Teachers College Press
35	Four Winds Press	89	Time-Life Books
36	Franklin Watts, Inc.	90	Union of American Hebrew Congregations
37	Golden Gate	91	US Committee for UNICEF
38	Golden Press, Inc.	92	University of California Press
39	Greenwillow Books	93	Vanguard Press
40	Grosset & Dunlap, Inc.	94	The Viking Press, Inc.
41	E.M. Hale & Co.	95	Vintage
42	Harcourt Brace Jovanovich	96	Wadsworth Publishing Co., Inc.
43	Harlin Quist Books (Dell)	97	Henry Z. Walck, Inc.
44	Harper & Row Publishers, Inc.	98	Walker & Co.
45	Harvey House (E.M. Hale & Co.)	99	Frederick Warne & Co.
46	Hastings House Publishers, Inc.	100	Franklin Watts, Inc.
47	Hawthorn Books, Inc.	101	John Weatherhill, Inc.
48	D.C. Heath & Co.	102	Western Publishing Co., Inc.
49	Hill & Wang	103	The Westminster Press
50	Holiday House	104	Albert Whitman & Co.
51	Holt, Rinehart & Winston, Inc.	105	Windmill Books
52	Horn Book, Inc.	106	The World Publishing Co.
53	Houghton Mifflin Co.	107	The Writer, Inc.
54	International Reading Association	108	Young Scott Books

Six

Important Activities in the Classroom

Where young children are concerned, *working* and *playing* are synony- **VARIETY IN THE** mous. While "fooling around" with blocks or in the housekeeping **CURRICULUM** corner, children freely experiment with materials and relationships. Most adults, other than scientists, designers, or actors, would have to create artificial situations in order to engage in a similar type of experimentation. For children it happens naturally and appropriately. The words *play* and *work* are therefore used interchangeably throughout this chapter.

In the "old days," children were members of large extended families in which grown-ups engaged in recognizable forms of work close to home. Children saw how crops were raised, how houses and furniture were made by hand, how goods were manufactured. As the society became more complex and more mechanized, more and more adults worked far from their homes performing distinct phases of work that were hard to relate to the end product that would be used or sold. Relatively few children now enjoy life styles that include witnessing and participating in the raising of food crops, the production of goods from raw materials, or the construction of dwellings. We must therefore work harder to create situations in which children can explore real materials and try out the roles of adults.

In this chapter, we have chosen to present a few curriculum areas that are particularly rich in work/play experiences, and we have left out others that can be equally enriching. We discuss in detail water play, cooking, block play, carpentry, and animals in the classroom. Each of these is an area that demands the personal interest and investment of the classroom teacher to be maximally productive. Each is an area that, without the teacher's personal concern, may cause supervision and discipline problems to the extent that the teacher may eventually choose to leave it out completely. For instance, poorly supervised carpentry, water play, or cooking activities may lead to lack of respect for the teacher and misuse of materials and may create conditions that are downright unsafe. Yet each area offers the opportunity for children to experiment with real-life situations in which their play approximates adults' real work.

The teacher should never feel obligated to include all of these activities at a given time in the classroom schedule. For younger children and those of any age who have not had a lot of prior experiences, one newer activity at a time is plenty. Beginning experiences with carpentry, cooking, or block play should be introduced for a few children at a time, in a protected part of the classroom, and only on days when the teacher can give relaxed attention to the activity. As children grow older and more experienced, the activity can be expanded, new props or materials can be added, and the children can be given increasing responsibility for conducting their own affairs. Any of these activities require the nearby presence of an adult who is genuinely interested in the particular materials to be used and who feels comfortable in letting children explore their properties.

An experimental attitude develops early when children have a chance to explore with real materials.

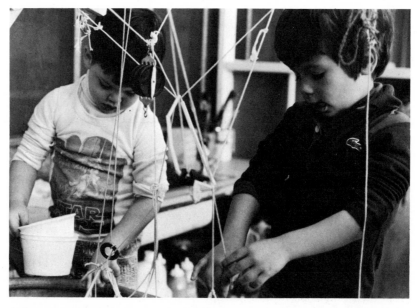

For organizational reasons, we discuss the various parts of the curriculum separately, but, in reality, they are woven together in such a way that each child and each group has a varied and balanced overall experience. The integrating element is the teacher herself. She brings each activity to children in ways which help them understand the relatedness to earlier experiences. Block play has connections with carpentry and wood scupture, with mathematics and science, and with social development when the child becomes involved in small-group projects. Cooking relates to housekeeping and dramatic play and leads to important learnings in science, mathematics, and language arts. Literature cuts across all the areas discussed in this book, as does art—if these are seen as possible ways of carrying out and expressing ideas grasped in other curriculum areas.

Any curriculum for young children should be "tailor-made" to the group for which it is planned. Ideas contributed by the children can be expanded by the teacher. She keeps pace with the children and their interests, but she also takes the lead in the sense of making the decision to

have certain materials and equipment available and arranged strategically to invite children's interest and use. In the very best classrooms, the
teacher is not the most active or most talkative person present, and yet
her presence and leadership are felt in subtle ways as she picks up cues
from children and facilitates expansion of ideas.

The kinds of materials which are of most value in the classroom lend
themselves to use in a variety of ways and at many levels. The wise
teacher allows them to be experienced fully at the simple levels so long as
the children's interest remains strong. But when interest fades, she takes
this—other things not contraindicating—as a signal that the time has
come to move her group on, to help them ask another sort of question, to
look at the material in a new way. Often children do this for
themselves—as when the solitary piling-up-and-knocking-down use of
blocks spontaneously evolves into block building by a group of children
in a true social situation, with dramatic play about city life, transportation, or airports and harbors going on, transforming a manipulative
exercise into a microcosm of the world seen through children's eyes.

Sometimes the teacher must introduce new ways of using materials
which will make them more challenging. For example, many
preschools have some version of a feeling game, composed of a group of
wooden plaques covered with different kinds of materials with various
textures (velvet, net, sandpaper, satin). At first, the simple tactual sen-
sation is sufficient to intrigue young children. They compare and contrast again and again—not consciously but inevitably—as they feel the
various substances. After a time, some children will realize that there are
two of each kind of material, and they begin to match. Later, they test
themselves, discovering whether they can find pairs with their eyes shut,
simply by touching. The same materials are being used yet, in many different ways, are being moved from easier to more difficult uses. The
teacher must be ready as needed to move in with a question when a child
is clearly unaware of what to do or how to vary a procedure which has
become boring: "Do you think any of these materials are the same?"
"Can you find two pieces of sandpaper?" "How would the satin feel with
your eyes shut?" Thus, the teacher, in countless ways, helps each child to
move, at his own pace, from "doing" to "thinking."

The "doing" stage is an essential part of the learning process, but it is
only part. For instance, children experimenting with magnets soon
realize that if you put the magnet near some things, it will pull them or
shove them away, while others are unaffected. Now the child has a
strong base for learning more about magnets, for he has experienced the
"how." At this point, he may well become fascinated in finding out what
things will react to the magnet and what will not. But in most cases, it
will take some query of the teacher to move him into an understanding
that there must be something alike, some general quality underlying the
similar behavior, of all the things that are attracted. He begins to ask a
"why" question. Eventually, he generalizes that iron responds to a
magnet, while things that are not iron lie inert. This realization may not
come for a long time, but it should not be hurried. The teacher should be
available to move the child on toward it when he is ready to make the
step.

The five areas discussed here will provide models for ways of thinking
about other possible kinds of activities. Start from the child's interest;

make manageable materials available; plan for simple and logical steps in a progression toward increasing complexity; plan for a maximum of successes and opportunities to experiment and verbalize one's wonderings and findings; plan for an atmosphere in which both the teacher and the children are free to ask questions and work together toward answers.

WATER PLAY

A discussion of water play is included in this section even though it belongs equally well under "science." We place it here because it is such a basic experience for children that it should not be put under an imposing heading which might cause it to be allocated for "special occasions only."

Water is probably the least expensive of all the materials available and one of the most readily obtained. It has a natural attraction for children, and if it is presented in interesting and expanding ways, it is one that is not outgrown. It is a natural medium for play as well as for relaxation in learning. When children are upset or tired, they will often choose repetitive water play. Many teachers dread water play because some children tend to go easily out of bounds in its use. This probably happens because the teaching and learning possibilities of water have not been fully exploited. (It is also true that some children have strong emotional needs which lead them to particular uses of water.) But children can learn a great deal from experimentation with the use and control of water, and the imaginative teacher can help to keep them reaching out for new things to explore and find out.

Making Arrangements for Successful Water Play

A classroom should have running water, but if yours doesn't, don't be defeated. You can "import" water—in large plastic dishpans, in a large metal wash tub, with a hose. Try a "bucket brigade" from kitchen or bathroom, with each child bringing a small amount in a pitcher or cup.

Avoid unnecessary spilling. Most sinks have control faucets, so the teacher can preset the volume the child will be able to obtain from the faucet. Setting the control faucet ahead of time avoids the necessity of saying no, giving constant reminders to turn the volume down, and having upset children and angry parents when clothing gets wet.

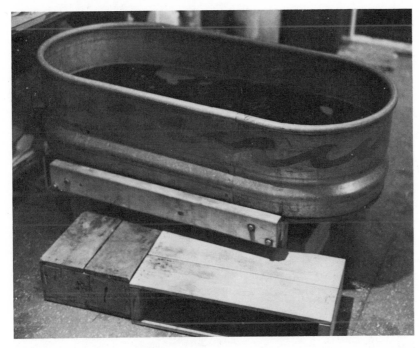

Plan carefully to make the water play area inviting.

It is also helpful to make a line with a felt-tip marker to help the child know when a container is full enough for play (half full or less is usually plenty if you want to stimulate really inventive water play and minimize the limitations you, as the teacher, will have to set during the play.) Helpful items are:

> Small cotton throw rugs on the floor under the water play area to help avoid puddles and to avoid slipperiness if there are puddles.
>
> If your classroom is carpeted, a large piece of plastic, vinyl fabric, or linoleum can be taped to the floor under the water play area, right over the carpet. It protects the carpet and also conveys the idea that "water stays here."
>
> Mops and large sponges which the children can get without help to encourage independence in taking care of spills.
>
> Plastic coverall aprons and extra changes of dry clothing to help both teacher and children feel more secure about allowing freedom in water play.

Children may turn other activities into water play. Cooking, painting, cleaning, housekeeping play—anything which provides a legitimate use of water or "messy" materials—can sometimes deteriorate into just plain play with water. This is the indication that some provision for legitimate water play is needed!

Provide water and simple materials for experimentation and let the child become an experimenter and discoverer.

Start out simply with small plastic cups as the only accessory.

Gradually add:

> Unbreakable cups and containers of other kinds and sizes (clear plastic if possible), plastic squeeze bottles, flexible plastic tubing of

several different diameters, short lengths of pipe and hose, plastic meat-basters, small eyedroppers (soft plastic disposable ones are safest), syringes, funnels of different sizes, small pieces of sponge, sieves, bottles with sprinkler tops, egg beaters.

and just about anything else that is fairly small, unbreakable, rustproof, transparent (if possible), and can either contain water or cause it to pour or move about in interesting ways.

Other things you will soon want:

Liquid soap (not detergent), food coloring, a variety of small wooden and metal objects.

As children gain experience in water play, more materials may be added.

Related Learnings in Water Play

If you, the teacher, bring an experimental and questioning attitude to your observations of what the child is doing, the learnings are endless. Ask a lot of open-ended questions: "What do you suppose made it do that?" "I wonder what would happen if . . . ."

Let the child find out about the relationship of air and water (bubbles, blowing to make water move, pressure, siphoning, evaporation, and drying).

Air and Water Pressure

What happens when you force water through a small opening? Pour it into different substances? Try to force it to stay in a confined space?

Volume and "Conservation"

Experiment with containers of different sizes and shapes to see how these are independent of or related to the actual volume of water.

Color Mixing

Work with food coloring or dry tempera paints to discover how they mix together or affect each other.

Help the children describe what they see and verbalize questions. But don't force them to have answers, don't give them too many answers, and don't feel obligated to teach them technical terms such as *evaporation* or *displacement*. Let them find their own operational ways of describing what they see. When a child has a question he can't answer (and perhaps you can't either), help him think of some way to get closer to the answer. This is really the beginning of the scientific attitude— accurate observation and description of what is happening; formulation of experiments to find out why something happened or what could happen next; expression of what did happen in a way that someone else can understand.

Some children have been prohibited from this kind of play at home. They may have concerns about getting wet and messy and may be afraid to try. Allow these children to approach slowly and just watch others. Limit the area and the amount of activity so they can feel safe at first.

Things to Keep in Mind

Let them use water in legitimate cleaning activities before they are free enough for real "play" with water.

Be sure they know where the mop, sponges, dry clothes, and aprons are and give them matter-of-fact help in taking care of the situation if they do get wet.

Splashing and aggressiveness with water are least likely to occur when children are challenged by intriguing equipment which they can really do things with. The teacher should be an interested observer and commenter and questioner who focuses on the constructive things that are happening and not just on the spills.

As in other activities, new equipment should be introduced slowly and in a sensible progression. One or two new things at a time are enough to keep the child challenged. Presenting things slowly rather than all at once will really help him discriminate between the different materials, think about them, and find out all the possible things he can do with them. Start each water play session with just one or two interesting accessories in the water play table. Supply a few others on request from the children. Before the area begins to look cluttered, remove a few toys that are not in use.

Decide in advance on a few "house rules." "Water stays here." "No water in the corn meal table." "No water play unless you wear an apron." "Clean up your own spills," for example. These rules, publicly announced and consistently enforced, will soon be repeated by the children who will help to remind each other.

The preparation of food is a meaningful activity for young children and one that is not difficult to provide for in a preschool program. Many types of food can be prepared right in your classroom even if you have no stove available. Preparation is fun, but it is also important work. Of all the activities one might provide in preschool, here is an area which is basic to life itself and with which every person has had daily, repeated experience. This is also an area where emotions have been intimately involved; children have had intense feelings about the people who feed them and the attitudes surrounding food. This is an area for education and sometimes also for emotional re-education.

COOKING WITH YOUNG CHILDREN

In spite of having repeated daily experience with being fed, children often have not had the realistic opportunity to help in preparing food. They need concrete experiences in understanding the magic that seems to take place in relating the package in the supermarket or the plateful on the dinner table to the raw product on the farm. City and suburban children are unfortunate in that it is much more difficult for them to

understand the origins of common agricultural products. A country child
has natural everyday experiences with growing things, changing seasons,
and the interrelationships of these. (For suggestions on ways to meet this
problem, see the chapter on science.)

By making cooking an important activity in preschool, we can help
children to gain some of these same understandings. For this reason, the
cooking activities should be planned with care to include meaningful, interrelated steps.

Using Natural Foods   In recent years, a great deal has been written and said about good
nutrition, natural foods, and the dangers of using too many refined and
artificial ingredients. Biologists, psychologists, and members of the
medical profession have explored the influence of maternal and infant
malnutrition upon intelligence, learning capacity, and children's general
health. A great controversy has sprung up. While some of the interest
may run to an extreme, much is valid. Teachers and parents have become seriously interested in educating children about good nutrition and
counteracting the strong influence of television commercials which "sell"
children sugar-coated cereals and all sorts of refined goodies with little or
no real food value. Snack times and cooking activities at school offer
numerous spontaneous as well as planned opportunities to discuss foods
and to introduce a variety of natural foods, flavors, and textures.
Whenever possible, natural ingredients can be used, and children can be
directly involved in the preparation of raw materials—shelling and chop-
ping nuts, grinding flour, preparing raw fruits and vegetables. Most large
supermarkets and the numerous health foods stores carry natural or
organically grown foods. Some parents may be interested in contributing
the raw ingredients for particular projects from such stores. In reading
the rest of this section, bear in mind the opportunities for good informal
nutrition education. Consider the substitution of natural ingredients
(such as honey for sugar) in some of your favorite recipes. Consult the
references at the end of the chapter for a few newer children's cookbooks
which reflect this new concern.

Food has special meaning to some children. Those who have come
from economically deprived circumstances, where there has been an actual hardship, have had a particular need to know what there is to eat

and that there is enough of it. These children will bring with them certain strong feelings about being sure everyone has a share and will probably be concerned about wasting food.

But, perhaps, even more important (regardless of the particular economic circumstances), children who have had any real or imagined reason to question the reliability of parental care will often have strong and sometimes distorted feelings about food and the people who provide it. For the very young child (and for many older people, too), food is closely equated with love. If the child has felt a lack of love, he may have developed an exaggerated concern for the availability of food. Becoming active in the preparation of food will be an important experience for such a child. Learning to cook something and discovering that he really knows how will be helpful. Learning to measure, count, and predict how much is needed will help him to feel less vulnerable to the whims of others. The teacher's matter-of-fact approach to the situation will be reassuring to him.

Children have observed adult activities at home and often have been told to stay out of the way or not to bother mother until she is finished. Cooking in school gives the child a chance to try out adult roles, and it may give parents a chance to see how they could include the child in their necessary activities at home.

Cooking is meaningful work, and the child can point to the product as something worthwhile which he has made or done. The group can enjoy the food at juice time at school, invite another group to a party, or take some home.

Besides these aspects of identification with adult activities and actual **Hidden Learnings** food preparation, there are various important learnings hidden not too far beneath the surface in well-planned cooking activities:

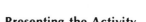

> Working together as a team with other children and the teacher
> Learning to follow and interpret a recipe
> Finding words that stand for things
> Following directions in a certain sequence
> Getting ideas from books
> Learning about quantity and weight and measure
> Developing new vocabulary
> Keeping time—watching a clock or timer
> Seeing changing forms of ingredients when combined or heated or cooled
> Learning basic principles of good nutrition

If one wanted to label them so, these are language arts, mathematics, and science learnings.

The first experiences should be of the simplest kind: one- or two- pro- **Presenting the Activity** cess activities which do not include hazardous steps with heat or dangerous implements. Consider making a simple icing to spread on graham crackers. This is a good first activity because several ingredients are needed, exact quantities are not too important, children can take turns adding things and stirring, and there is no waiting time.

The first time the icing is made, the teacher may measure the ingredients and simply say, "This is what we will need."

At subsequent times, she may encourage the children to help her look at a recipe, decide what is needed, walk to the store to buy the things, and measure out just the right amount.

If the teacher objects to using icing because of its sugar content, she may want to try a simple spread made from shredded tuna fish, mayonnaise, and finely chopped celery. Again, several processes are involved, and precise quantities aren't important. Younger children might even begin simply by spreading peanut butter or apple butter on a cracker or by placing a dab of peanut butter on a apple wedge or on a piece of celery cut by the teacher. Any one- or two-step process gets the children actively involved.

A Simple Progression of Steps

The teacher plans to have the children make a recipe several different times. Each time they repeat some already familiar steps and add something that's new, thus making it slightly more complex, which renews the challenge. This is like the "spiral curriculum" of the elementary school.

When an activity is presented more than once, the teacher may review with the children in discussion what they used, how they did it, what came first, what came next, etc. She may talk afterwards about what was needed and about each child's part, thus helping to retell the story of the activity and get the idea of the importance of a sequence of steps in achieving an end result. But she shouldn't feel it's necessary to push every activity to this conclusion—a lot should be done just for the sake of cooking itself and for the enjoyment of the food.

Auxiliary Activities

Gardening—growing vegetables. Even in a city classroom, a few radishes or a cocktail-tomato plant or some lettuce could be grown in a sunny window.

Discussion—where foods come from . . . how they are grown, prepared, packaged, transported, sold, and kept in the home.

Anticipating Problems

Many children have been taught never to touch a stove, never to interfere when mother is busy in the kitchen. We don't want to undo these habits in a way that would put the child in conflict with home standards. But it should be possible to develop the idea that, with reasonable precautions, things can be done safely. Explain to the parent that working with appropriate equipment at the child's height and under supervision is different from standing up on a chair and reaching to an adult stove. If parents are especially concerned about safety, invite them to help at school. They will see what can be done and may be able to relax home standards as well. Of course this presupposes all necessary safety precautions—e.g., protection from such a hazard as having too many children pushing to see.

The teacher should try the recipe first, before presenting it to the children. She should be aware of the number of steps involved and the subtle little things she does to make the end result successful. Then she will be able to anticipate the points at which the children might have trouble.

She should be sure the first experiences are successful ones. Afterwards, the children may be able to learn from failures as well as successes.

Not all children will like all foods. Some will enjoy the cooking process but won't even want to taste the product. If they've had fun in the doing, they shouldn't feel they must enjoy the eating; watching those who do may help them to try it the next time.

Parents may show legitimate concern if children eat too many sweet and filling things just before a mealtime. The activity should be planned so it is finished and eaten before the very end of the session. The activity of cooking is sufficient excitement; large quantities of food are unnecessary. A taste is plenty.

Besides the ingredients of the actual recipe, utensils such as these may be needed:

Needed Materials

> Measuring spoons, knives, bowls of several sizes, graduated measuring cups, a timer or "minute minder," an assortment of pans and cookie sheets.

Most schools do not have access to all of these at first but can gradually accumulate them. In the meantime, parents can be asked to lend the things needed for a particular project. Most schools don't have a real stove. A portable hot plate and a portable tabletop oven are really better because they can be placed at a safe, low height for children while in use and removed from the classroom when not in use.

If a refrigerator is not available, a portable cooler can be used or the ingredients can be brought just before they are to be used.

Other Things to Try, Some Requiring No Cooking

Flavors can be varied. For variety, add chocolate bits one time. Another time, add raisins or small pieces of peppermint candy or pieces of canned fruit or whipped cream prepared by the children; experiment with food coloring.

Pudding

For the children, the activity is peeling, cutting, taking out seeds. Fruits and vegetables can be tasted raw, and some can later be boiled or stewed. This can lead to a lot of related discussion about how different foods look when raw and when cooked and how they feel and taste as well.

Preparation of Raw Fruits and Vegetables

Make juice, starting with fresh oranges or lemons and limes. Let the children measure and add sugar and water.

Make butter, using either an old-fashioned churn or simply by shaking cream in a covered jar.

Special Projects

Make ice cream in an old-fashioned freezer.

Freeze ice cubes or "popsicles" of flavored or colored water or make ice cubes from real fruit juices.

For variation, add fresh fruit, tiny pieces of marshmallow, or whipped cream. Or, "Jell-O" can be made "from scratch" using plain gelatin and natural fruit juices.

Jell-O

Use a packaged dehydrated soup the first time. Later, start from "scratch" with a meat bone; prepare and add fresh vegetables or alphabet letters or all kinds of noodles and macaroni.

Soup

Making soup could be a full week's project if you begin with planning and walking to the store the first day and spend several days working on preparation of the vegetables.

You can stimulate good discussion of the differences in the vegetables, which leads to vocabulary development as the children find good words to describe each. Or play a guessing game to see if the children can identify the different vegetables they've been working on by touch, smell, taste, or word pictures given by the teacher.

On the final day of the project, the soup can be eaten in place of fruit juice at juice time. Some parents or another group of children could be invited.

Hamburgers

Let each child make his own small hamburger pattie.

Cookies, Cupcakes, Cake

There are endless variations in flavor and form. Some are quite simple—preparing a drop cookie from a mix or slicing ice-box dough made by the teacher in advance—or quite complex—making the entire recipe and finishing off with a fancy topping. It's good to have a reason for making something as special as a cake—a child's birthday or a school party, for instance. Individual cupcakes are easily handled by children; each can have his own to decorate or lèave plain.

Consult a natural foods cookbook for ways to make cookies and cakes with natural ingredients. Recipes that substitute honey or ground raisins for sugar can be found. There are also recipes that utilize vegetables such as zucchini or carrots to produce moist cakes and breads with rich, natural flavors.

Pancakes

Pancakes are interesting to measure and mix and to watch while cooking.

Children may need a fair amount of help in turning pancakes. Most children enjoy them, however. Try spreading them with a thin layer of jelly and rolling them up to eat with the fingers.

Candy

There are a few simple candy recipes which children will enjoy. Try crisped-cereal balls, for instance.

Things to Remember

Work out a sequence of steps in your own mind. Plan a series of cooking projects which gradually become more complex. Encourage children to talk about what they are doing and relate it to home experiences. Ask children and their mothers for ideas about things to make. Whenever you can begin your project by having a few of the children walk to the store for the supplies, you enrich the children's experience.

Encourage discussion of what's been done. As a teacher, keep in mind the number of different kinds of learnings involved in cooking—science, math, language arts, understanding more about community and home activities—but don't always feel that a lesson or a moral must be derived from the activity.

BLOCK PLAY

Blocks are in just about every preschool classroom. They have natural appeal for nearly all children. But in many classrooms they are "part of the furniture," there because every classroom has them, not because the teacher herself has selected them or chosen to make work with blocks a focal point in the curriculum.

Working with blocks provides children with experiences that combine visual and motor skills with the ability to plan ahead and execute one's ideas through a necessary sequence of steps. To reproduce something he has seen, the child needs to be able to analyze the component parts and visualize each in relationship to the others. Problems of relative size, volume, space, and weight must be resolved. Recognition of mathematical relationships and good descriptive vocabulary building are natural by-products when work with blocks is given attention in supervised play.

Table blocks, unit blocks, and hollow blocks are the most common kinds.

What kinds of blocks?

Table blocks are small enough to be packed in a large cardboard carton and are usually used by one or a few children seated around a play table. The basic unit in a table block set may be a cube that is one or one and one-half inches square. The largest block in the set will not be more than a few inches long. Often, sets of table blocks include some unique shapes, such as pyramids and chair leg turnings, which invite a child to imagine interesting kinds of structures such as ultramodern buildings or old-fashioned castles. Working with table blocks utilizes fine motor coordination skills. A child can make a tower of twelve or fifteen cubes, an ornate bridge for small cars or boats, or a bricklike pattern.

Table Blocks

Unit blocks are the most typical hard-wood blocks found in classrooms for young children. They are expensive to buy but almost indestructible; a well-made and well-cared for set will last for years. Handmade unit blocks, however, are rarely satisfactory. To produce real constructions, the individual blocks must be precisely measured and cut from hard wood. The basic unit is usually about three and one-half inches square and one and one-half inches thick. The dimensions of all the other blocks in the set are multiples or fractions of the basic unit. A complete set includes unit, double unit, and quadruple unit blocks as well as wedges, triangles, cylinders, half rounds, and others. Unit blocks lend themselves to construction of houses, garages, roads, railroad stations, airports, and anything else a child may have seen and wanted to better understand through real experimentation.

Unit Blocks

Hollow blocks are large wooden blocks that are hollow and often have open spaces or strips that make good handholds for carrying purposes. The basic unit is usually about twelve, or perhaps fifteen, inches square and five or six inches thick. Most sets of hollow blocks include single and double units as well as cleated boards three or four feet long. The cleated ends of the boards hook over the edges of the blocks to make secure structures that children can actually play in or climb upon. Hollow blocks are made of a softer and lighter wood than unit blocks. They need careful maintenance and periodic refinishing to be kept splinter free; shellac or waterproof spar varnish is good for refinishing if the blocks are used and stored outdoors. Hollow blocks take up a lot of space for storage, and a large open floor space is required for their use indoors. Children often use the blocks to build a large structure such as a playhouse, which may be left intact for days and weeks while various embellishments are added. The original intent of the structure, a playhouse in this case, may slowly evolve into something completely different as children's ideas and interests change.

Hollow Blocks

Adequate storage space for blocks, within reach of children, is essential if the blocks are to be well used. When looking at a classroom, a

Storage and Display

visitor can quickly tell whether the teacher values and plans for good block work and play. Each size and shape of block needs a designated space on a low shelf. The shelf should be arranged so one can immediately tell what shape is stored where. When blocks are jumbled together, a nonverbal message is communicated: "These are not important." "These can go any old way." Many teachers have found that a sketch or photo of each shape, pasted to the edge of the shelf where that shape belongs, helps inform children that each block has its special place and purpose. When clean-up time comes, a teacher stationed near the block area can help by handing children individual blocks and asking, "Can you find all the ones shaped like this?" or "Where do you see the picture of the blocks that are this size?" In this way, she helps children with classification skills and encourages them to observe the different properties of the various sizes and shapes, so that next time children build they will be more aware of selecting a particular size to do a particular building job.

Block play should take place in a protected area out of the way of traffic patterns in the room. A light portable room divider can be strategically placed during block play if there is no natural division of space in the classroom. Children usually enjoy building on a hard, bare floor where blocks can be placed firmly and levelly. If the room is carpeted, the block area should be covered with a densely woven industrial type of carpeting; the frustrations of building on a rough or soft surface will discourage most children before they get deeply involved in major constructions. In many classrooms, small wheel toys are stored near the blocks. Children naturally combine the toys and blocks to make streets, cities, railroads, airports, truck depots, and space-age creations.

Rules of the House

In classrooms where blocks are popular, some limits may be placed on the number of children who can use them at one time. The limit is determined by the space, the number of available blocks, and, more importantly, by the complexity of the children's buildings and their capacity to cooperate or respect each other's territory. Strips of masking tape can be placed on the rug or floor to define territory, leaving a common ground in the middle that suggests a cooperative effort is possible. The rule about how many children can play may be firm, "You know we never have more than three children in the big block corner," or flexible, "Today, John and Ginny and two other people may use big blocks." A flexible rule gives the teacher a chance to adjust the numbers according to the skills and needs of the particular children involved.

"You can build as high as your shoulders." "You can get inside your building but not on top." "If you build something to climb on, only two people can play." These are examples of rules teachers have established in particular situations. When impersonally stated as rules of the house, they will enable the teacher to remain a provider of ideas rather than someone who must constantly police the play and set limits.

Useful Props

Beginning block builders will be satisfied with making separate buildings and constructions as they experiment with the possibilities. More advanced builders may name their constructions and launch into more elaborate dramatic and cooperative play. When children seem to get stuck in their block play, a nearby teacher may casually begin to provide signs and labels. Some teachers keep, just for the block area, a box of materials that contains strips of cardboard or heavy paper, felt-tip

The teacher should establish ground rules about the number of children who may play.

markers, scissors, and masking tape. Sitting by the block area, the teacher can provide paper streets to go with small blocks, a small cut-out sketch of a window or door to add to a house, circles of red and green for traffic signals, badges and licenses to enhance transportation games, and all kinds of captions and labels to encourage children to differentiate and name the various parts of their constructions.

Where large blocks and boards are used, dramatic play props will be popular: special hats and dress-up clothes or shoes, grown-up handbags, an old mailbag or milk bottle carrier, a bus driver's coin holder, a ticket punch, a worker's lunch pail, a nurse's hat, a stethoscope, or a myriad of other things may be used over the course of a year. But more is not always better; a few props should be added at one time, and others in which the children have lost interest should be put away to reappear several months later.

Block work is ideal for building real experience with physical and mathematical relationships. Words for shapes may be learned: *square, cube, oblong, rectangle, cylinder, half round, triangle.* Contrasting words might be emphasized: *longer/shorter, wider/narrower, thinner/thicker, heavier/lighter, higher/lower, longest/shortest,* etc. **Building Vocabulary**

After younger children have had a chance to explore blocks on their own, the teacher might one morning place on the table or floor a large piece of brown wrapping paper on which she has traced the various **Building Visual Skills** shapes of blocks that are available. The children can then be encouraged to find each block and place it on top of the corresponding shape on the paper. Or the teacher may wait until children have made some block patterns and then trace around the outlines. Children can also be encouraged to build replicas of certain structures that the teacher provides. This exercise develops visual observational skills and is useful provided children also have an opportunity for free exploration.

The most important element is the teacher.

Teachers who do not personally enjoy block building or appreciate the potential in this kind of play may send children to the block area and provide supervision only when things get out of hand. Block play then becomes like recess time—listless or boisterous and, perhaps, even dangerous. To encourage the learning potential in block work, a grown-up who genuinely enjoys these materials should be present and actively aware of the play, able to make a subtle suggestion, provide props, encourage cooperative efforts, and assist with clean-up. Blocks themselves have inherent appeal, and an enthusiastic teacher adds to their magnetism.

CARPENTRY FOR YOUNG CHILDREN

Carpentry is a visual experience, a motor experience, a problem-solving experience.

The Values of Carpentry for Young Children

Construction of small and useful objects with scrap wood, tools, glue, and various accessories helps children gain knowledge of tools and their uses and a better idea of how familiar objects are made. This kind of awareness may encourage children to have more respect for materials and furniture and a greater appreciation of the roles of different workers in the community.

Woodworking also develops the ability to visualize a three-dimen- working toward a finished product.

Woodworking develops inventiveness.

Wood can be combined in all sorts of ways with other materials to achieve useful results as well as real art forms. Since most of the materials can be scrap ones, it can be especially helpful to children whose backgrounds do not include a plentiful supply of store-bought supplies and toys.

Woodworking also develops the ability to visualize a three-dimensional outcome and helps children gain specific physical skills in using tools.

Specific Skills to Be Learned in a Long-Range Carpentry Program

Ability to visualize and select the needed wood and accessories; working with all kinds of tools (hammer, saw, screwdriver, plane, chisel, jigsaw, vise, drill, clamp, file) and techniques, such as sandpapering, filing, drilling, gluing, clamping, planing, drawing a plan, measuring.

There is a progression from very simple one-step activities to more complex ones. Some of the above skills would be attempted only by older preschoolers who had already had a great deal of experience in handling tools and in planning projects. Others are simple enough so that even a three year old could have a meaningful experience.

Selection of Materials

The teacher sets the stage for inventiveness and safety.

Scrap wood is easy to find at almost any lumber yard, building supply store, carpenter's or cabinet-maker's shop. Disposing of the scraps is usually one of their problems! They will be willing to put scrap aside for you or to let you go through the scrap pile to find usable pieces. Find out when they usually clean out and dispose of their rubbish and plan to go just beforehand, when you will have the largest selection.

Select wood of all sizes and shapes, but be sure it is "clear" (with no knots or blemishes) and "finished" (planed down so there are no splinters). Although one-inch boards, if "finished," are actually only about three-fourths of an inch thick, they are still referred to as one-inch lumber.

Wood varies in hardness. In general, white pine and spruce are best. Just as a carpenter would select wood according to the qualities he needs for a particular job, you will want to do this for children, especially for their first efforts. If children are going to be doing some hammering and sawing, the best wood is usually one-inch clear finished pine. You will want as many scraps of this as you can find, in all shapes and sizes. Be sure there are no splinters, jagged edges, or knots. Some of the most useful dimensions to look for will probably be one inch by two inches, one by four, one by six, two by four, and two by two. When you order lumber, you must give three dimensions, in this order: thickness, width, and length.

All wood has a "grain." You can see the grain—it appears as light lines or shadings and usually runs the long way of the piece (floor boards are a good example). The grain is really the fiber of the wood, which produces its strength. (In hard wood, the fibers are much finer and denser, or closer together, than in soft wood.) Soft wood is best for children because it can be hammered and sawed with much less effort than hard wood. It is especially important when choosing scrap wood for children's use to choose pieces in which the grain runs lengthwise, like this:

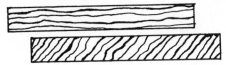

not like this:

This is because when you drive a nail into a piece of wood, it makes its way by forcing the fibers slightly apart. The nail may cause it to split, which is a common and unnecessary frustration in children's first efforts with woodworking. It's especially likely to be true in scrap wood, where the end of a board has been cut off and left in the scrap pile, with the grain, therefore, running the short way of the piece.

Other Useful Things

Pieces of dowling (long, very slender, and round, in various diameters), molding (such as quarter round, half round, and various decorative shapes), and mill turnings will all be very useful and will add to the variety of things which relatively unskilled carpenters can make. You will also find scraps of plywood. (Plywood is made by gluing several thin layers together with the grain of each piece going at right angles to the last. This increases strength and eliminates the possibility of splitting.) In a cabinet-maker's shop, you will find many other kinds of wood of various thicknesses and hardnesses which are useful when children are constructing with glue but which may be difficult to use when they are hammering and sawing. White pine is really the best for that. Some people recommend balsa wood for children's work (it is very light in weight, soft, and porous and is used for making models). Balsa seems to be of doubtful value for children because it is extremely expensive, hard to procure through the usual channels a teacher would have available, and is so soft and light that making really firm structures is not possible. However, tiny scraps of balsa are very good for wood sculpture and collage work with glue, where the lightness is an asset.

Collect these, too.   Scraps of floor tile, Masonite, pegboard, composition board, linoleum, Formica, aluminum stripping, cork, plastic, etc.

Choosing Tools   Children should be given real tools which are scaled down slightly in size but are of real tool quality and proportion. There is nothing more frustrating than trying to do a real piece of work with a tool that is only a toy. The kinds of toy tools which are given to children as gifts are often useless as real workers' implements.

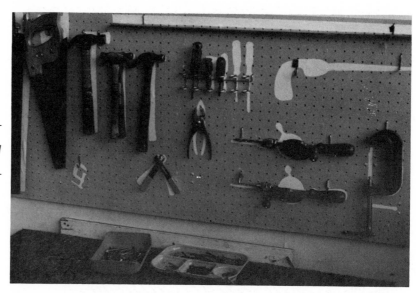

A good storage place for tools helps establish a good attitude about their care.

Storing Materials   The arrangement for storing and displaying carpentry materials will make a big difference in how they are used as well as in the general spirit of good workmanship and respect for the value of tools. If tools and materials are jumbled together without thought, children will not be motivated to think about their various properties and to choose the right things for the task at hand.

Store scrap wood by size in several different cardboard cartons or in the sort of stacking vegetable bins you can find in discount hardware and department stores. Keep the tiny scraps in one box, the long, thin pieces in another, the short, wide pieces in another, and so on. Discussion of these shapes develops vocabulary and general discrimination ability. Storing by size encourages the child to choose the best piece for the job he wants to do, rather than the first one he finds in the box.

Choosing Nails   Get several lengths and thicknesses; keep each in a separate container. Clear plastic food dishes are ideal for their see-through quality. Have a heavy-duty magnet handy, as it will immensely simplify the task of picking up spilled nails.

There are several varieties of nails. You will want the common wire ones which have flat heads, as these are the easiest for children to work with. "Finishing" nails don't have heads, and, therefore, are more difficult for children to hit. Roofing nails have especially large heads but are usually too short for many purposes, though they are useful for such things as holding wire on cages and for many decorative purposes. If children are building things which will be used outdoors or in water, consider using galvanized or rustproof nails for greater safety.

Nails come in different thicknesses in relation to their length. The more slender ones are best for children because they are less likely to split the wood, which is always a danger when unskilled hands use a hammer with sometimes crooked or uneven blows. Help the children to decide just what size nails they need for a particular task—again you are encouraging them to think ahead about the best way to solve a particular construction problem, and you are helping them to discriminate between the various materials available. These are skills with "transfer" value beyond the project at hand. A nail should be long enough to hold two surfaces together firmly (about three-fourths as long as the thicknesses of the two pieces of wood together). If the nail is shorter than this, the structure will pull apart when under any strain. If it is longer, there is danger of the nail's coming through on the other side, causing injury to the child or the working surface.

Nails can be used for making designs if the positions are arranged so that the heads make a pattern on the wood. Nails driven only part way into the wood can be used to simulate other things—door knobs, handles, switches; a series connected with string or wire can be a fence or a railing, etc.

Children need practice before they develop skill. It's a good idea to have a section of an old tree stump, a piece of railroad tie, or a very thick and firmly attached board, which can be reserved for times when a child just wants to hammer but doesn't really care about a finished product. This will provide needed practice and will prevent the use of a smaller piece of good scrap wood for random nailing without a particular goal.

Other Things You Need and Can Acquire Gradually

Assorted sizes of screws, hooks and eyes, cup hooks, all kinds of fastening devices, wire of varying lengths and thicknesses; string; sturdy wooden rulers and a long steel measuring tape; "kindergarten" pencils (large wooden pencils with very thick leads which do not break easily); Elmer's glue and quick-drying airplane cement; fabric scraps; all kinds of beautiful junk, such as bottle caps, molded cardboard, Styrofoam, tile, plastic, cellophane tape, and movie film rolls; "real" paint, varnish, and a supply of brushes; rags and old shirts or smocks for painting.

Arrangement of the Working Area

A very solid working surface is needed if any tools are to be used. Heavy children's workbenches can be purchased, but these are neither as big nor as solid as something you can make yourself by using very heavy two-inch planks to make a top for a sturdy table or a wooden packing crate. You can also rest heavy planks on two sawhorses. It is important to secure the top to the legs with slide bolts or other fasteners that will prevent it from moving. Children need a good deal of working space and "elbow room," especially when they are first learning to work with saws and hammers. The working surface should also be quite low to allow for greater leverage and use of body weight in applying necessary pressure in using tools.

Tools are best displayed on a pegboard equipped with a variety of hooks. You can paint the outlines of the particular tools on the pegboard, which will help children find the right places for putting things away. Displaying tools in this way will encourage the child to select the proper tool for the job he wants to do. If safety and supervision at other times is a problem, there might be a movable divider made of pegboard, with the tools displayed on one side. When not in use, it can be turned against the wall or against another piece of furniture.

First Experiences

Before real carpentry with real tools, plan for lots of spontaneous play with small bits of wood used as building blocks. This will sharpen the children's abilities to visualize and try shapes in different combinations, to plan what they want to do, to modify as they go along. When they need added challenge or are frustrated because things won't stay, glue can be introduced. When they make something they like, they can "save" it by holding it together with glue. Later, when they also know how to use other tools, this skill will still be useful.

The rich background in building with blocks and inventing with various shapes will enhance the ability to see a range of possibilities in ordinary shapes. If the teacher has selected wood in many shapes and has no preconceived ideas about what they are supposed to be, the children will be able to be even more inventive.

Working with glue will also lead to combining wood with all the other "found" materials previously mentioned.

If the child has a rich choice of materials and an imagination, he can easily create a "boat" (large block of wood with a smaller one on top for a cabin), an airplane (two narrow strips glued at right angles—small pieces could also be glued in place for a tail, motors, etc.), or many other objects. Other things a child could make with just wood and glue, without any tools: a small table and bench or chair for a doll, a small box for "treasures," and innumerable other things.

Even a school which is not equipped for any type of "real" carpentry can use this type of wood-with-glue-and-beautiful-junk activity as a variation during its art or work period.

**The First Simple
Use of Tools**

After the child has the idea that things can go together to make other things and has some experience in selecting shapes and sizes of wood, you can introduce some simple skills with tools: driving one nail into crossed pieces of wood to make an airplane, drilling one hole to insert a piece of dowling for a smokestack or a mast on a boat, making two cuts with a saw to produce a point for the bow of a boat.

Insuring Success

Help the child select a piece of wood which is almost the size he wants so that the remaining work is relatively simple. These first efforts take a great deal of coordination and persistence, and it is important to plan for a high likelihood of success for the first few times.

*Give help with tools
at first for safety and
encouragement.*

"Start" the nail so it is firm enough in the wood that it will not have to be held, thus reducing the likelihood that the child will bang his fingers. Also, make the beginning cut with the saw until there is enough of a groove so that the blade will not jump out, and encourage the child to keep his free hand away from the board and the saw. Show him the basic principles of use of hammer and saw. The beginning child's tendency is to hold the hammer close to the head and follow the hammer with his eye. He will have better luck and more strength if he holds the hammer at least midway on the handle and keeps his eye on the nail. With a saw, it is important to keep the blade straight. If it bends to one side or the other, it will "bind" instead of going easily through the wood. Friction may cause a saw blade to become very hot if it is not going exactly straight. If this happens, the saw should be removed from the wood and

Carpentry skills develop eye-hand coordination.

allowed to cool for a moment. The beginner's tendency is to make short, rapid strokes. A better way is to use long, slow ones. It helps, in both cases, if a child can listen to the rhythm of a good worker using the same tools and watch the motion used before trying to do it himself. These are skills that have to be learned in the muscles, like the reflexes in driving a car.

Older children may use a block plane and a drill. The block plane is used for smoothing the surface or reducing the thickness of wood. When the child is planing a piece of wood, be sure to put it in a vise and be sure he understands that the blade on the bottom of the tool is very sharp.

The drill has two handles, one held in the left hand to keep the tool in an upright position and the other in the right hand to turn the drill. The teacher probably will have to insert the drill or bit into the holder and tighten it for the child and remind him that it should be held straight and that the crank should be turned slowly and evenly.

Helping the child to think about the thing he wants to make will also insure that he is making *his* version of the thing—not the teacher's. You can ask questions which will help him elaborate what he wants to do, and these will also serve him as a model for solving future problems: "What's the most important thing about a boat?" "What do you need to start with?" "What else does it need?" "How could you make it look even more like a sailboat [only if you sense that he's not satisfied]?" "Do you like it just the way it is?" "Do you want it to have some other parts?"

Help the child to think first about the thing he wants to make.

Again, this kind of planning will encourage combinations of other processes and materials which can lead into other art forms and related activities: fabric scraps for a sail or to simulate windows; bottle caps or buttons for steering wheels, portholes, or doorknobs; nails and string for a railing, etc.

ANIMALS IN THE CLASSROOM

Classroom pets can supply wonderful experiences for children, provided the teacher has clearly thought out her reasons for having them there. If animals are just like more toys on the shelf—to be pushed and pulled and prodded and ignored—they had best not be there, since the attitudes being developed will not be helpful ones for the children. As with any other resource material provided in a preschool room, we should know why the animal is there and how it can be used. (Even if it's just for fun, that's something in itself!) Every object in a classroom introduces some kind of learning—positive and useful if understood and appreciated, negative if ignored or misused. What are we teaching when we have animals in the classroom, and is it worthwhile? If animals are a subject for observation and study and if children assume responsibility for their care, then they are useful additions to a total curriculum and a stimulus for developing many good attitudes which have high transfer value to other situations.

Animals have a natural appeal for most young children, with the exception of those who either have had specific traumatic experiences or have been exposed to adults who had unrealistic fears and fantasies. Nursery school, where things can be treated naturally and casually, is a good place to develop enjoyment or overcome fears.

Ways of Providing Experiences with Pets

The teacher can invite children in her group or members of the community to bring pets to visit for a short time, during which the focus of the group can be on talking about and getting to know the particular animal and its habits.

There are good books and resource materials about pet care. A local pet store, veterinarian, or animal-rescue shelter will usually be glad to provide information.

The school also may own some pets and the proper housing for them. It is usually not difficult to find a family that will be delighted to "borrow" a pet during a vacation. Most classroom pets, properly caged, can be left over a weekend without care. In fact, this probably should be a prime criterion in choosing pets for a school. If teachers are going to handle animals, it is important that they feel really comfortable in doing so, because their feelings and attitudes will be communicated quickly to the children. If the school is going to own some pets, there should be one person on the staff who knows about them and who takes the final responsibility for seeing that they receive the proper care. If the school has pets, children should participate in feeding and caring for them. Sharing in this responsibility will be helpful in their overall development and will give them an opportunity to carry out some important tasks in which another living creature is dependent on them. The teacher can make a schedule for feeding and cage cleaning. The discussion of this schedule will be a stimulus to academic learnings about days on the calendar, times of day, quantities of food, reading the names of children who have certain duties, etc.

These are some of the animals which have proved successful in groups **Suitable Animals**
of young children: guinea pigs, hamsters, gerbils, mice, rabbits, birds,
turtles, frogs, toads, snakes, fish. Create as comfortable and natural an
environment as possible for the animal. If the space is limited, choose a
small animal, and allot sufficient space so that it can be housed in a cage
which is large in relation to itself. It is probably not helpful for children
to have experience with animals kept under poor conditions. In discussion with the children, emphasize the things a particular animal needs in
order to be comfortable and healthy. The children can consult resource
books, with your help, and can contribute ideas and even cage materials.
Their powers of observation will be sharpened as they watch the animal,
notice its habits and needs, and decide on this basis how to keep it well.

Many groups appreciate an animal more if it arrives after they are well **Introducing an Animal**
established in school and the teacher has prepared them for it.

If the animal has always been there, it may seem too much like "part
of the furnishings," and many of the teaching possibilities may be over-
looked.

Children who are fearful of animals should be allowed to watch from a
distance for a long time. The teacher may make factual comments about
what the animal is doing, what another child is doing with it, and how
she thinks the animal might feel under certain conditions as a way of
focusing on the fact that it is another living creature with habits and
needs of its own. She can anticipate some of the reactions of the animal
which might be misinterpreted by the child as aggressive or frightening
behavior: a sudden move when an animal is frightened, running over to
the side of the cage if it is very friendly or very hungry, etc.

Some children who seem overly anxious to hold or care for animals
may actually be trying to answer some puzzling questions about the particular qualities which distinguish something that is alive: about how
their own behavior influences another creature, about sexual parts and
differences, or about reproduction. It's important for the teacher to
realize that extreme curiosity or possessiveness may have these and other
underlying causes and that the child sometimes may need reassurance
and protection from the possibility of hurting the animal and the guilty
feelings which would follow. (This child also needs other ways to express
the same wonderings!) If, because of the intensity of a child's curiosity, it
is not possible to keep a classroom animal safely and comfortably, it may
be best to remove it for a while.

Animals which are repeatedly teased or molested will usually become
nasty—or at least very unfriendly. A most important understanding for
children is that there can be no compromise in this area of respecting and
safeguarding the welfare of another living thing.

Dig a shovelful of moist earth; spread it on a sheet of white paper and **Other Ways to Make**
examine it carefully with a magnifying glass. Look at the components of **Use of Planned and**
the soil as well as the insects. **Spontaneous Experiences**

Look for bugs and worms under a rock or board that has been resting **with Animal Life**
on damp earth for some time. Catch a live insect and put it in a small
clear plastic or glass pill bottle. Look at it with a magnifying glass, and
study its parts and coloring carefully. Then let it go. Find some pictures
in books to help remember what it looked like. Encourage the children to
find descriptive words to tell how it looks.

Watch a beetle or caterpillar eating a plant leaf. If you find a caterpillar on a tree branch, break off part of that same branch and put it in a wire cage or a jar with holes in the top.

Watch ants eating aphids, which in turn have been eating plants.

Watch bees collecting pollen from flowers. Suck honey from honeysuckle blossoms as a way of finding out what insects get from plants.

Look very closely at the flowers of many different kinds of plants in the garden and see what insects you can find with a magnifying glass. Watch for a while to see what they are doing—eating, resting in the shade, escaping from an enemy. Do some flowers attract more insects than others do?

Put earthworms in a glass frame and observe how they stir up and aerate the soil. They make better conditions for plant growth.

Talk about observable differences between plants as a group and animals as a group.

Make a "vivarium"—a natural environment for a frog, toad, salamander, or a small snake. Observe and discuss such things as climatic conditions causing hibernation or protective coloration.

Worms can be fascinating to young children.

Discuss the differences between a frog (smooth, moist skin) and a toad (rough, dry skin).

Talk about ways in which animals defend and protect themselves—such as claws, fur, feathers, quills, shells, teeth, scent, tails, coloring, flying, running, climbing, burrowing, playing dead, etc.

How do animals find and store food?

Watch animals adapting to changes in temperature and moisture:

Stretching out to achieve maximum contact with damp earth or a
cool floor on a very hot day
Huddling up on a cold day
Puffing out feathers on a cold day
Standing in a sprinkler on a hot day or bathing in a puddle
A frog or toad buried in damp earth on a hot day

Can children use any of these same techniques?
Listen for the different sounds animals and birds make:

Guinea pigs chirping and crooning to each other
A rabbit thumping when frightened or angry
A jay scolding
A squirrel chattering for attention or when frightened
The songs of birds
The sounds of crickets and katydids
Dogs barking and growling
Cats purring, calling their babies, howling
A mother hen calling her chicks

Make a list of the different animals, birds, and insects seen on the
school grounds or in the neighborhood. Observe and discuss how each

finds food, water, shelter; how they care for their young; what they do
and where they go in winter.

Talk about the different body structures of animals and birds and how
they are used:

A cat's whiskers
A rabbit's large ears
A bird's foot
Different kinds of bird beaks
A squirrel's tail
A cat's claws and padded feet
A turtle's shell
A fish's fins

Look for footprints of animals and birds in damp earth and in the sandbox. Some tracks can tell a story. What part of the foot makes the imprint?

Notice the different hunting habits of dogs and cats—i.e., cats stalk quietly and pounce; dogs run down their prey by sheer speed and strength.

Watch a domestic cat stalking its prey and compare this to the behavior of a wild jungle cat.

**A WORD
ABOUT SCROUNGED
MATERIALS**

Many times in this book reference has been made to "found" or "scrounged" materials. Such materials introduce variety, relieve the budget, and encourage children to visualize new uses for some otherwise useless objects and materials. We cannot present here an exhaustive list of such resources. Each area of the country is different. Cities yield different possibilities from those of rural areas. What we offer here are some basic principles which may help a teacher explore her own environs for useful free "scrounged" materials.

Sit down with the yellow pages. Leaf through them to get ideas about kinds of industries that exist in your area. Speculate about the sorts of scrap the industries may actually have a problem disposing. For example, companies which make paper and boxes have many kinds of scrap: cardboard cores for rolls of paper; cardboard boxes which can't be sold because of an overrun, a poor ink, or a bad print job; large sheets of cardboard; and so forth. Electronics companies and appliance makers have all kinds of interesting packing materials, including Styrofoam and heavy cardboard in interesting shapes. Telephone repairers often discard the large wooden spools on which telephone cable is wound. Telephone installers have cable which, when the outer cover is removed, reveals numerous thin, brightly colored, plastic-covered wires. Printers dispose of their "ends"—the odd sizes of interestingly colored and textured papers and cardboards which are cut off when a particular printing order is trimmed to size. Small newspaper publishers often give away the ends of their huge rolls of newsprint if they are picked up by the teacher. One such roll end may supply classroom easels for many months. Factories which make floor tiles and carpet may have stray pieces and seconds. Stores that sell floor covering materials or wallpapers often give away their samples of out-of-date lines. If you live near a waterfront, all kinds of interesting crates and old lobster traps may be available.

In general, industries produce useful waste for which disposal costs money and time. Find out what they have in their "dumpster," or huge trash bin, and find out if there is a regular schedule for disposal. For instance, a city may always collect trash at one paper box company on Tuesday and Friday around noon. Those mornings are the best "trash-picking" times. A parent or community volunteer may enjoy making collections for you.

You will probably discover that among the parents of children in your class a number are employed in interesting lines of work which produce their own unique varieties of scrounge. Issue a list of your wants just to get them started thinking. But be prepared to cope with the influx of oddly shaped boxes and bags of materials. Perhaps you will ask a milk company to donate its discarded milk crates which can be stacked on their sides to make open storage bins for the various materials you will collect.

Get into the scrounge habit. It is one of the best ways to introduce a note of variety in your curriculum.

Scrounged materials make interesting raw materials and storage spaces, too.

HELPING CHILDREN LEARN FROM EVERYDAY ACTIVITIES

Throughout this book, we have been emphasizing the incidental learning that goes on in a good preschool program where children are allowed to explore their interests and teachers are wise, responsive resource people. Some children are curious and aware. They will ask questions or make their own deductions from daily activities and specially planned projects. For other children, however, the teacher needs to be more active in pointing out and stressing the skills and concepts to be learned.

Group meetings before and after an activity, such as a cooking or carpentry project, serve to insure that more children in a classroom will absorb the key points in a "lesson." Gathering the children altogether or in small work groups just before an activity begins gives the teacher a chance to find out what they already know. "If you were going to make some pudding for our snack time, what would you have to buy at the store?" "What do you call a person who builds things with wood and tools?" "How does a carpenter decide exactly where to saw a board to make it fit just right?" Leading questions like these help children participate in the planning process so that interesting new projects are not simply happenings in an already well-supplied classroom. As children mention what they think is required in the way of tools and materials, you can make a list for them to see. Write with a felt-tip marker in large letters and make a quick sketch of tools or ingredients or paste part of a can label or catalog picture beside the list. Don't expect children to be able to read the list; the goal is to impart the idea that a sequence of events are to take place or that the ingredients in a recipe cannot be left to chance. Gradually children gain a sense of logical planning, and some will benefit from the symbolic representation of three-dimensional objects or of a sequence of events that happen over time.

While engaged in the activity itself, continue to verbalize what you are doing and refer children to the chart you have made or your planning discussion. "Do you remember what we said we would need to buy at the store?" "Look at our chart and tell me what comes next after we have put the flour and the salt in the bowl together." "In our picture of a boat, which piece of wood goes first on the bottom?" Some complex activities need a lot of teacher assistance. One way to keep the children actively involved is to engage them in this type of discussion as you go along. Otherwise, some may lose interest as they remain mere spectators.

Similar techniques are valuable after an activity has been completed. "Before we eat our snack today, I am going to take a picture of our cookies so we can remember what you made." Sketching or photographing the various steps in a complicated process gives children a chance to savor the experience and also provides for the child who learns better by visually reviewing what is done. Some teachers like to keep a collection of posters or charts that were made during important activities all during the school year. Others keep a scrapbook that children can refer to, in which there are photos or sketches and a simple story line concerning important events in the classroom. A scrapbook of "things we have cooked together" or "what we made at the workbench" or "blockbuildings we wanted to save" will be a great source of pride to children. It provides a tangible record of progress and a way for some children to absorb and review concepts they could not fully grasp during a group experience.

SELECTED REFERENCE MATERIALS ON VARIETY IN THE CURRICULUM FOR TEACHERS OF YOUNG CHILDREN

Adkins, Jan. *Toolchest: A Primer of Woodcraft.* New York: Walker & Co., 1973.

Althouse, Rosemary. *Science Experiences for Young Children: Air; Colors; Magnets; Water; Wheels; Food; How We Grow; Pets; Seeds; Senses.* New York: Teachers College Press, 1975.

Austin Association for the Education of Young People. *Teaching with Nature.* Vol. 1. Washington, D.C.: National Association for the Education of Young People, 1973.

Belton, Sandra. *Sparks: Activities to Help Children Learn at Home.* New York: Human Sciences Press, 1976.

Blake, J., and Ernst, B. *The Great Perpetual Learning Machine.* Boston: Little, Brown & Co., 1976.

Blockbuilding (a filmstrip). Scarsdale, N.Y.: Steve Campus Productions, 1976.

Brown, Vinson. *How to Make A Miniature Zoo.* Rev. ed. Boston: Little, Brown & Co., 1957.

Bruno, Janet. *Cooking in the Classroom.* Belmont, Calif.: Lear Siegler/Fearon Publishers, 1974.

Buck, Margaret Waring. *Along the Seashore.* Nashville, Tenn.: Abingdon Press, 1964.

_____. *In Ponds and Streams.* Nashville, Tenn.: Abingdon Press, 1955.

_____.*In Yards and Gardens.* Nashville, Tenn.: Abingdon Press, 1952.

_____. *Small Pets from Fields and Streams.* Nashville, Tenn.: Abingdon Press, 1960.

Cadwallader, Sharon. *Cooking Adventures for Kids.* Boston: Houghton Mifflin Co., 1974.

Campbell, Robert. *How to Work with Tools and Wood.* New York: Pocket Books, 1972.

Caney, Steven. *Steven Caney's Play Book.* New York: Workman Publishing Co., 1975.

Chrystie, Frances N. *Pets: A Complete Handbook of the Care, Understanding and Appreciation of All Kinds of Animal Pets.* 3d rev. ed. Boston: Little, Brown & Co., 1974.

Collis, Margaret. *Using the Environment, 1. Early Explorations.* London: McDonald Educational, 1974.

Cooking and Eating with Children: A Way to Learn. Washington, D.C.: Association for Childhood Education, 1974.

Croft, Doreen. *An Activities Handbook for Teachers of Young Children.* 2d ed. Boston: Houghton Mifflin Co., 1975.

Early Experiences, A Unit for Teachers. London: MacDonald Educational, 1976.

Eckstein, Joan, and Gleit, Joyce. *Fun in the Kitchen.* New York: Avon Books, 1972.

Eliason, Claudia; and Jenkins, Loa. *A Practical Guide to Early Childhood Curriculum.* St. Louis: C. V. Mosby, 1977.

Ferreira, Nancy. *The Mother-Child Cookbook.* Menlo Park, Calif.: Pacific Coast Publishers, 1969.

Fiarotta, Phyllis, with Noel Fiarotta. *Snips and Snails and Walnut Whales: Nature Crafts for Children.* New York: Workman Publishing Co., 1975.

Frank, Marjorie. *Kids' Stuff Math.* Nashville, Tenn.: Incentive Publishers, 1974.

George Peabody College for Teachers. *Free and Inexpensive Learning Materials.* Nashville, Tenn.: George Peabody College for Teachers, 1976.

Greenberg, Sylvia, and Raskin, Edith L. *Home-Made Zoo,* New York: David McKay Co., 1952.

Hartley, Ruth; Lawrence, Frank; and Goldenson, Robert. *Understanding Children's Play.* New York: Columbia University Press, 1952.

Johnson, Georgia, and Povey, Gail. *Metric Milk Shakes and Witches' Cakes: Cooking Centers in Primary Classrooms.* New York: Citation Press, 1976.

Karnes, Merle B. *Learning Language at Home.* Reston, Va.: Council for Exceptional Children, 1977.

Kids Are Natural Cooks: Child Tested Recipes for Home and School Using Natural Foods. Cambridge, Mass. Parents' Nursery School, 1973.

Leavitt, Jerome E. *Carpentry for Young Children.* New York: Sterling Publishing Co., 1971.

Lincoln, Martha, and Torrey, Katherine. *A Workshop of Your Own.* London: Chatto & Windus, 1961.

Lorton, Mary B. *Workjobs; Activity-Centered Learning for Early Childhood Education.* Menlo Park, Calif., Addison-Wesley Publishing Co., 1972.

Martel, Jane. *Smashed Potatoes: A Kids-Eye View of the Kitchen.* Boston: Houghton Mifflin Co., 1974.

McClung, Robert M. *All about Animals and Their Young.* New York: Random House, 1968.

Nassau County Regional Office for Educational Planning. *While You're at It: 200 Ways to Help Children Learn.* Reston, Va.: Reston Publishing Co., 1976.

Noble, Judith. *Games Children Play and Learn from: Learning Activities for Young Children.* Dubuque, Iowa: Kendall Hunt, 1973.

Paull, Dorothy. *Yesterday I Found . . .* Boulder, Colo.: Mountain View Center for Environmental Education, University of Colorado, 1972.

Rudolph, Nancy. *Workyards.* New York: Teachers College Press, 1974.

Russell, Helen Ross. *Ten Minute Field Trips; Using the School Grounds for Environmental Studies.* Garden City, N.Y.: J. G. Ferguson, 1973.

Selsam, Milicent E. *Animals as Parents.* New York: William Morrow & Co., 1965.

Skelsey, Alice, and Huckaby, Gloria. *Growing Up Green: Parents and Children Gardening Together.* New York: Workman Publishing Co., 1973.

Stant, Margaret A. *The Young Child: His Activities and Materials.* Englewood Cliffs, N.J.: Prentice-Hall Inc., 1972.

Starks, Esther B. *Blockbuilding.* Washington, D.C.: National Education Association, 1960.

Stein, Sara B. *The Kids' Kitchen Takeover.* New York: Workman Publishing Co., 1975.

Sterling, Dorothy, and Lubell, Winifred. *Caterpillars.* Garden City. N.Y.: Doubleday, 1954.

Sterling, Dorothy, and Lubell, Winifred. *Caterpillars.* Garden City. N.Y.: Doubleday, 1961.

Taetzsch, Sandra Zeitlin. *Preschool Games and Activities.* Belmont, Calif.: Fearon Publishers, 1974.

Teale, Edwin Way. *The Strange Lives of Familiar Insects.* New York: Dodd, Mead & Co., 1964.

The Whole Learning Catalog. Palo Alto, Calif.: Education Today, 1976.

Wiseman, Ann. *Making Things, Books 1 and 2.* Boston: Little, Brown & Co., 1975.

Woodworking (a filmstrip). Scarsdale, N.Y.: Steve Campus Productions, 1976.

"Working with Wood." In *Creating with Materials for Work and Play,* Leaflet Number 5. Washington, D.C.: Association for Childhood Education International, 1969.

Young, Doris. *Kim's Cookbook.* Pawtucket, R. I.: Red Farm Studio, 1972.

Seven

Academic Preliminaries

The notion is widely held that abstract and symbolic learning is taboo in the preschool, that the primary focus should be the social and emotional growth of the child, that "real" learning begins only when the child enters first grade. We believe that the division between emotional and cognitive development is an artificial one, that they are interdependent, and that only an impoverished preschool does not hold intellectual development in high regard.

ACADEMIC SKILLS BELONG IN THE PRESCHOOL.

Some preschool programs attempt to foster intellectual growth by imitating the worst in traditional elementary education; these programs violate what we know about the nature and evolution of young children's development. Whether they be in elementary or preschool, rigid, mechanical procedures which group children regardless of interest and developmental level tend to have a high concentration of teacher verbalization and to promote skills that are devoid of genuine conceptualization. Furthermore, they run the risk of establishing negative attitudes toward the world of learning and ideas.

We believe that the child by his very nature is reaching out toward symbolic learning from the earliest days of his life and that the preschool years provide an important segment of this life-long learning process. The preschool experience is there to enhance every kind of learning for which the individual is ready and, more than that, to help him to become ready for more advanced ways of perceiving and conceptualizing. But its prime means of doing so is through the medium of the child's *own* play, his *own* interests. Young children are still finding out about the marvelous world into which they have so recently come. Their own curiosity, their delight in the use of their senses, their bodies, and their intellects must be the ground from which learning springs.

In the preschool, the young child must continue the development of the communicative skills begun in the family setting, for unless a child can learn to talk and to listen with understanding, it is futile to think that reading and writing will be meaningful to him later. He must encounter variety, gain all sorts of experience of the world about him out of which

Children's own play is their prime means of becoming ready for more advanced ways of perceiving and conceptualizing.

can grow his conceptual life. He must develop his powers of sensory discrimination gradually. Only if he can organize and apply the discoveries he makes and relate these to what the people around him tell and show him do they become fully his own.

Gradually, he learns that the world is a realm of regularities in which he can have confidence. (Every time he throws a ball up in the air it comes down; day follows night; fire is hot; ice is cold.) And he learns that he can do things (walk, run, balance, complete a puzzle, hammer in a nail, sing a tune); thus, he can have confidence in himself as a being with increasing control over the world, increasing ease in mastering problems.

Out of a wealth of encounters, he begins to shape abstract concepts— length, size, weight, space, time—and his powers of reason grow as he wrestles with the process of "if this, then that." In simplest terms, he tests his first hypotheses. ("If I put on this last, top block, I can make the roof of my building go up to a point like a real one.") He begins to be at ease with the attitude of questioning, of asking "why" and "how" as a means of learning and evaluating for himself, so that he no longer is dependent entirely upon stimulus from without to move him toward knowledge; instead, in a true sense, he becomes self-directive. His urge to learn springs from within. He has gained some notion of how to go about learning, and though he is still at the beginning of the long process of education, he is already approaching learning in a rational, humane way.

Children differ in their interests and capacities for learning academic skills.

The age at which young children show interest and capacity for learning academic skills varies widely as a result of native endowment and the kinds of situations within which the learning is being conducted. The reassuring thing about this variation is that, in time, most children become ready to learn. The important thing, within the wide normal range of child development, is not the exact moment when the child reaches this stage but that he should be encouraged and helped in meaningful ways when he does show readiness to begin. Few adults remember exactly when they began to read, but even many decades later, their use and enjoyment of reading is still affected by the early feelings they held about it.

The age at which young children reach the "ready to read and write" point seems to be determined both by their developmental level—with its emotional, physical, and intellectual components—and by their earlier experiences. For example, the child who has received little verbal stimulus will be delayed in language comprehension. The child with a physical handicap may be markedly slower in reaching the point where it is right for him to approach reading in any formal way.

Nor do children develop in an "all of a piece" fashion. A child may be able to perceive and recognize a form such as a circle or a triangle but still be quite unable to control his fine muscles sufficiently to draw the form for himself. A teacher must be aware of a child's background and predisposing circumstances and must be most keenly knowledgeable about developmental levels before she attempts to institute or to direct learning.

Preschools usually do not have formal periods for teaching academic skills. Reading is not scheduled for nine o'clock, for example, or arithmetic for eleven. Therefore, adults who are used to a formal scheduling of subject matter as the structure of the school day are apt to assume that the kinds of learnings which are basic to later school achievement are ignored in preschools. This may be true sometimes, but more often these learnings are very much present, though dealt with informally within the ongoing, fluid content of young children's concerns.

Skill learnings are integrated into the preschool curriculum.

Skill learnings at this stage should not necessarily be isolated. Instead, they must be interwoven throughout the school day, throughout the whole curriculum, just as their use is interwoven throughout our daily lives. Moreover, when taught at the receptive moment, they come through to the child with enhanced meaning. If the teacher shows a child how to write the letters of his name at just the moment when he is bursting with eagerness to write it himself on his own painting, this achievement is a far greater source of pride and satisfaction than the same task done routinely as part of a writing lesson. Having learned this magic symbol that means "self," the child uses it again and again—to sign an invitation to Mother to come to a holiday play, on the card he makes for his friend who is sick, on his own locker, on his paper kite. Learning skills are tools for all the rest of life. Taught when motivation to learn is high, they are grasped easily and used more freely and effectively. Learning becomes a process the child undertakes joyfully in the expectation of success.

MOTIVATION IS CRITICAL.

The opportunity to extend a child's skills frequently occurs because the teacher is alert to the potential within a natural situation.

Growth in language is a case in point. All later learning depends upon the child's ability to communicate. Knowing this, the skillful preschool teacher is continually enlarging her children's vocabularies; al-

TEACHERS MUST BE ALERT TO EVERYDAY OPPORTUNITIES TO FOSTER SKILL DEVELOPMENT.

lowing them to hear language used well in her choice of poetry, stories, and songs; helping them to express more clearly the ideas they are struggling to formulate; helping them to enjoy words. A group of small children kneeling at the foot of a ledge, thrusting their fingers deep into the cold, scratchy "crevices" the teacher has pointed out to them as they have climbed is having a language experience. So is a group chanting, "I'll huff and I'll puff till I blow your house down." Children learn language from one another, and the aware teacher provides opportunities for this sort of mutual growth. For example, when a child comments on the cricket found in the grass, "Oh, look at his *feelers* move!" the teacher gives the group the time needed—before moving on—for several children to talk about how crickets feel, what those things wiggling there on their heads are doing, and what keeps them safe.

The child who stands in front of the aquarium noting the fish can have his language and discriminatory skills enriched by the adult's verbalization:

"The neon tetra is the one with the stripe."
"Look at the platy's red tail."
"Notice where the catfish spends his time—at the bottom."

His language skills may also be enriched by his own spontaneous verbalizations:

"The little black fish with the blue stripe . . ."

Thus, whenever a child is exploring plants, leaves, animals, rocks, clothes, or faces, there is abundant opportunity to help him look critically, observe thoughtfully, and communicate propositionally.

Children can learn the usefulness and importance of written language before they are ready to write themselves. The atmosphere of the preschool classroom can easily encourage such realization. For example, in a group of five year olds, one little boy apparently felt the need for solitude. Working with concentration, he built himself a house of big blocks in a corner of the room and retired into it, turning his back on his busy friends. But his friends refused to leave him alone. They kept coming to call, appearing at his door and knocking or coming uninvited into his house. "Stay out!" said the would-be hermit, but they kept coming in. Finally, the child went to his teacher. "Print me a sign to put over my door," he requested. "Make it say, 'Keep out!' " The teacher did this. Armed with tape, the child affixed the sign to his lintel, surveyed it proudly, and announced to his nonreading friends with perfect faith (though he could not read it either), "It says 'Keep out!' " and retired to solitude. This time, his wish was respected. Restrained by the sovereign force of the written words (though no one could read them), all of the children conformed at last to the directive.

Why did they obey the sign? Why did the builder of the house turn for protection of his right to privacy to a printed piece of paper which neither he nor his friends could decipher? Why did it work when no one paid attention to his spoken word? Written language has power. Children know it. At four or five, they are already a bit blasé about talking. *Anyone* can talk. But writing—that's different. That's grown-up. There is a kind of magic in something that preserves thoughts and allows them to be retrieved unfaded.

In this same classroom, a child was sent down a flight of stairs to the school secretary with a written note. The child's wide eyes and sense of wonder when she came back—"She knew just exactly what to do because you wrote it down!"—showed that this insignificant errand performed successfully through the medium of writing had seemed to her a marvel of communications.

The teacher who helps a child who is still far too young himself to write to begin to get this sense of the value of written language will have enhanced the meaning for the child of the whole long—often dull— process of learning to read and write when he reaches the appropriate stage a couple of years later.

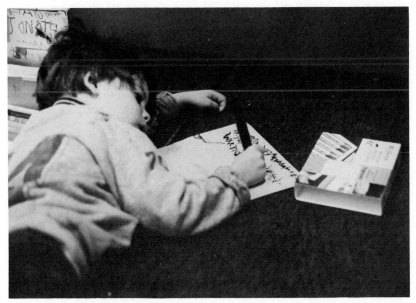

Children imitate adult writing before they learn how the letters really look.

Although the astute teacher will seize every opportunity to integrate learnings into on-going activities, there may be occasions when she will want to structure activities to provide focus on particular academic skills. In doing this, she should not plan an activity for the entire class or even a large group. We all learn skills individually at our own time; we do not line up groups of one-year-old children and teach them how to walk. Nor do we have a group of four year olds sit around waiting their turns to be shown how to use the scissors. We accept different rates for each child in these areas, but somehow we expect all children to want to hear the sound that *g* makes or to find the missing part at the same moment. This simply is not the case. The activities that a teacher plans should be planned for individuals or, at most, for small groups.

SOMETIMES YOU DO ISOLATE A SKILL.

There are a number of communicative, cognitive, and motor skills that the preschool teacher should be aware of and will want to foster. These are the "nuts and bolts," the foundation upon which reading, writing, and arithmetic skills are based.

SKILLS ON WHICH READING, WRITING, AND ARITHMETIC ARE BASED

Discrimination, Classification, and Seriation

Visual discrimination refers to the ability to differentiate the distinguishing features of objects, pictures, and other forms. Any time children work puzzles, match shoes, or play games like lotto and picture dominoes, they are practicing this skill. Eventually, they must be able to differentiate upper and lower case letters and word forms.

Auditory discrimination refers to the ability to differentiate sounds in the environment, as when a child hears the difference between the telephone and the doorbell or knows when his mother is speaking in a cheerful or angry tone. Eventually, children must be able to focus their hearing upon and to repeat the phonetic sounds in words and to associate these sounds with written symbols.

Classification refers to the ability to recognize likenesses and differences between objects and to group them accordingly. There are descriptive classifications based on physical criteria—all the red blocks, all the wood blocks, or all the circle blocks; functional classifications based on the interdependence of items—all the things we use in the kitchen, for instance; and there are categorical classifications, based on membership in a class (e.g., every member of the group is a tool, or an animal, or a toy).

Seriation refers to the ability to arrange objects in a series according to some specified order. Young children who play with nesting blocks that fit into one another or with the Montessori knobbed cylinders, which require them to fit the cylinders into their proper holes based on height and width, are practicing seriation.

Activities

The imaginative teacher will utilize a variety of amusing and provocative items to engage children's interests while cultivating these important skills.

Matching Objects and Pictures

The environment is full of opportunities for giving children practice in matching. Children can match mittens, rubbers, blocks, cars, pegs, buttons, beads, pictures—anything which is available in numbers of more than one. For instance, put one of a number of pairs of mittens in a pile. Let children draw one from a matching set of mittens placed in a bag or closed box and then find its mate in the pile.

Or ask a child to find a shell just like one that you hold in your hand or to put all the buttons like a given one into one section of the button box, all like that into another, and so forth.

Tracing Shapes and Objects

Children can match the shapes which they or you have traced and cut. They may trace objects in the room, cut out their tracings, and determine which tracing goes with which object. You can make various intricate free-form shapes for children to match. Children may wish to make their own lotto or picture domino games, drawing their own pictures or using duplicate pictures found in mail order catalogues or magazines.

Grouping Objects in the Environment

Again, the materials for sorting and classifying on the basis of specific qualities or attributes are abundant in the environment. Children can go outside, gather a number of objects, and return with them to the classroom. They then can talk about the materials. In what ways are they alike? How are they different? Which things could they put together in a group? What are some different ways they could group these objects?

They can sort a pile of clothing according to whether each item would be worn by men or women, adults or children.

Picture matching, as in lotto games, comes before symbol discrimination.

All the dollhouse toys could be placed in a heap. The children would then sort them according to which room they belong in.

Set aside a table on which you place a number of objects which are alike in some way (i.e., yellow, round, hard, soft, plastic, or metal) and have children add to it during the course of the day.

Almost any subject which is being developed in the classroom will lend itself to making paste-ups. Children can cut and paste onto a big piece of paper taped to the wall pictures of things that go in water, things that are hot, things that are cold, things that make us feel happy, things that grow in soil, and so forth.

Grouping Pictures

Or children can cut out and group all the shades of red or blue.

What's the same about a ball and a balloon? A plane and a ship? Which one of the following things is not the same as the others?

Talking about Likenesses and Differences

> One of these things is not like the other.
> One of these things doesn't belong.
> Can you tell which thing is not like the other
> Before I've finished this song?*

These activities can be extended to more difficult and complex topics: comparison of summer and winter, of a bird and an airplane, of mother's and father's work.

*Joe Raposo, "Which of These Things Is Not Like the Other?" Copyright© by Joe Raposo. Reprinted by permission of the author.

Attribute Blocks

Attribute blocks were developed at the Educational Development Corporation in Watertown, Massachusetts, to provide children with the opportunity to deal with problems involving classification and the relationships between classes. The blocks deal primarily with the attributes of size, shape, and color. An activities manual suggests activities for children as young as age four and complex enough for adults.

Matching Patterns

A number of materials provide children with the opportunity to match whole designs or patterns. You can start out by asking children to duplicate simple patterns made with beads or colored blocks. Then you can provide pattern cards with beads, parquetry blocks, pegboards, mosaic boards, or pattern blocks. Children are asked to duplicate the picture pattern with the blocks.

Tangram games published by McGraw-Hill take children a step further in developing spatial relations and are highly stimulating to some children and adults.

Seeing Sequence

From matching a series of beads, children can move on to seeing established patterns and sequences and guessing which bead would come next in a sequence.

They can look at photographs of a trip taken and put them in order according to the order in which they visited various places.

Or you can have a number of pictures which tell a story when put together. Children can be asked to put these in sequence.

Any time a child is asked to retell a story or to remember in what order various ingredients were added to make the bread or vegetable soup, he is practicing the skill of putting things in sequential order. You should be alert to this and focus on these opportunities rather than just assuming that they happen.

Ordering Pictures and Objects by a Rule

You can keep the materials for seriation activities stored in attractive containers like stocking or shoe boxes which will appeal to children and stimulate them to see what's inside when put into a pile. One might contain buttons to be ordered by size; another, pencils to be ordered by length. A third might contain scraps of Styrofoam cut up into graduated lengths.

Or you could provide packages of things which have been ordered by size, volume, length. Take one away and see if the child can replace it where it belongs.

Children might cut out strips of paper, ribbon, or string equal to their arm spans, their waists, or their heights and tape them to the wall— shortest to tallest or tallest to shortest.

Card Games

Fish

Concentration

Children love to play games of all sorts. Certain card games are particularly useful for practicing various skills. Children can play Fish with the colored Fish cards: "Do you have a red? A blue? A grey?" Or you could make their own Fish cards: "Do you have a ball? A chair? An airplane?" The game Concentration in which children turn all cards face down and take turns in turning over two cards to see if they match is a good one. Children can use a regular deck of cards, of course, but you may wish to start with pictures which you or the children have made or with sets like "Wildlife Concentration" available from the National Wildlife Federation in Washington, D.C.

Equipment: Small cardboard picture cards of objects that go together **Combination card games** (e.g., a cup and a saucer, a desk and a chair, a coat and a hat). *Action:* Children group the cards that have objects that go together.

Equipment: Groups of playing cards with pictures centering on a **Grouping card games** theme (e.g., kinds of stores with individual cards showing merchandise bought in different stores—such as tools for a hardware store, toys for a toy store—or kinds of rooms in a house with cards showing different furniture found in different rooms—such as refrigerator for the kitchen, bathtub for the bathroom). *Action:* Children group cards into areas (stores, rooms, etc.).

Games teach many skills.

Raggedy Ann, Candyland, Higgety-Piggety, and Winnie the Pooh are *Commerical Games* all commercial games which ask children to match colors or forms and require that they move in sequence and see parts of the whole. They make good classroom tools. Chutes and Ladders introduces numbers and gives children a sense of forward and backward movement.

Make a tape recording of common household sounds and let children *Listening to the Sounds in* identify them. Let them record their own voices and identify them when *the Environment* played back.

1. *Equipment:* All different kinds of usual school equipment that makes sounds, such as play telephones, cash registers, drums, bells, clocks; animals, such as birds, mice, etc. *Action:* After discussing sounds, children go on a "sound" hunt in which they attempt to find all the things in the room that make sounds.
2. *Equipment:* Different kinds of usual school equipment that make sounds (same as those already indicated—water faucet, typewriter, record player, etc.). *Action:* Children close their eyes while you or a child operates something in the room that makes a sound (turn on the faucet, click typewriter keys, etc.). Children guess the source of the sound.

3. *Equipment:* Rods of different materials, such as wood, metal, plastic (rhythm sticks, metal triangle beaters, etc.). *Action:* Children use the rods to produce different kinds of sounds by tapping different things in the room (a window, wooden table, a metal bookcase, etc.).

4. *Equipment:* None. *Action:* Children are in a group; one child is in the middle with his eyes closed. A child from the group calls him by name. The child in the middle attempts to identify the caller's voice.

Listening walk

Preparation: A motivating story such as one of Margaret Wise Brown's Noisy Books or discussion about sounds. *Action:* Children go on a walk to notice or discover all the different kinds of noises and sounds around them (such as an airplane flying overhead, a dog barking, men drilling in the street, automobile and truck engines or horns, etc.). A list of all the different sounds that were heard could be made either on the walk or upon return to the classroom.

Singing and musical games

Seek out songs, stories, poems, and finger plays which emphasize the identification of discrete sounds. Listen to jingles and nursery rhymes, especially those that emphasize a particular sound.

Rhyming

Equipment: Objects or pictures of objects whose names rhyme (e.g., *star* and *car*, *house* and *mouse*, *tail* and *whale*). *Action:* Children gather objects or pictures into rhyming groups.

Make up simple two-line jingles about familiar things or people. For example, you could ask, "Do you hear the words that sound alike in this jingle?"

> Today we're going to plant the seeds,
> I hope we don't find lots of weeds.

After rhyming words have been identified, ask the children to mention other words which rhyme. The rhyming words should only be heard; they should not be written.

Ask the children to choose the two words which rhyme in a group of three: *stop, gives, top*.

Listen for specific sounds.

Point out when words begin with the same sound: *book, Bobby, Billy*. Have children listen for words beginning with the same sound: *mild, mother, my*. Let children try to suggest other words beginning with that sound.

Give a number of words beginning with the same sound and one which begins differently. The children might clap as soon as the different word is pronounced.

Give some word pairs where one sound—beginning, middle, or end—is varied:

box—socks
pit—pin
pat—put

Preliminary Reading and Writing Activities

Language is a fundamental tool in learning and thinking. Without the abilities to listen and comprehend, to speak and make himself understood, the child cannot learn to read and write adequately. Motor skills are also important. Too often, we ask children to write letters before they have fine motor skills which are equal to the task. Other preliminary reading and writing activities should include much exposure to the printed letter.

Too much classroom conversation is of the management type: "Be sure *Conversation* to wear a smock if you're going to paint" or "Let's put these blocks away now." You, as a teacher, need to take time to listen to and talk to each child about those subjects which are meaningful to him—his family, his feelings, his projects. Encourage him to share his experiences and to discuss his ideas. Those children who do not respond to direct questions about what they think often respond to declarative sentences which say what they may or may not be thinking. For example, you might say, "You had such a good time visiting your grandparents" rather than "Did you enjoy yourself?" or "What did you do?" At the very least, you should spend a few moments each day *conversing* with individual children.

Children also learn from conversations with other children. Verbal interactions between children should, of course, be encouraged.

Give children opportunities to both hear and tell stories. Books are *Read books and tell* particularly effective language tools when used with one or two children *stories.* at a time. Start by looking at books and talking about them. Then move on to simple books with colorful pictures, short, clear texts concerned with familiar things, and a simple story line. (The "Golden Shape" books are excellent sources.) Later, read the more complex and wordy preschool staples.

When looking at books with small groups, you can use the books as take-off points for discussion:

What did that mean?
Did you like the way the story ended?
Have you ever had an experience like that?

A very good way of using books to develop expressive language skills *Story Dramatization* is to dramatize stories. Repetitive books like *Looking for Susie* by B. Cook or *Ask Mr. Bear* by M. Flack lend themselves to story dramatization particularly well. You read the book until it is familiar to the children; then you read and wait for the children to fill in words and phrases—in fact, most of the story. Children can then walk through roles as you read; they then act out the story and talk as much as they can following the visual clues in the book; finally, they tell and dramatize the story with no visual clues.

It is not always necessary to follow all these steps. The aim of the dramatization is to give the children a chance to place events in sequence correctly and to express the meaning of the words in a book.

Looking at and talking about pictures is a very effective way of prac- *Picture Interpretation* ticing language skills. You can talk about pictures with individuals and with small groups of children. The pictures should be large, attractive, meaningful. Some of the best show action or tell a story so that you can ask, "What's happening here?" to elicit the details or, "How do you think the little boy feels?" to elicit expressions of feelings. You can expand upon the children's responses to model the language form or introduce

Games that Involve Following Directions

new vocabulary. Some good pictures are available commercially from such sources as *Words in Action* by Holt, Rinehart & Winston and *Let's Begin* by Scholastic Books.

But there's value in keeping your own file of pictures collected from magazines and other sources so that you have greater variety and immediacy than a few sets of commercial photographs would allow.

Games can vary from those which require the understanding of very simple directions to those which are more complex. For example, games might range from "Stand up" to "Step over three blocks" to "Crawl under the table, knock three times, crawl back out to the window ledge, and stand up."

You can send children on a scavenger hunt. Hide some objects in advance in the classroom or outdoors. You can give clues orally; "At the back of the room, look under the broom." Or make up clue cards with simple words or pictures; for example, a card might have a picture of a broom and say, "Look under me."

Riddles

A very good receptive language device is the riddle, which may range from the very simple: "It's white and we drink it" to "I'm thinking of something that we use to buy things in the store, and it begins with *M*" to "It has eyes, but it cannot see."

Classification riddles: "I'm thinking of three things—leaves, bark, and branches." Have the child name a category into which all three will fit.

Children are usually stimulated to make up their own riddles after a time.

Jokes

The meanings of jokes are not always understood by young children. Share simple jokes, explaining the language if necessary. For example,

What did one hand of the clock say when he met the other?
I'll see you in an hour.

Labeling Objects with Printed Names

Preparation: Print the names of objects in the room—for example, a sign saying "Toad" on the terrarium where the toad lives and signs saying "Paper" where the paper is kept. *Objectives:* To encourage questioning of signs and realization that letters can stand for objects and can hold information.

Signs

Preparation: Place paper, pencils, and crayons near various areas of activity so that signs can be incorporated by children into play as needed. For example, signs can be made telling the names of block buildings; "Working" signs can be put in areas that need extra space or protection; "Quiet, Baby Sleeping" signs can be put in the housekeeping corner when children want minimal noise.

Action: Suggest signs as a help in extending or enforcing play. For example, seeing a child who is pretending to be a traffic-controller, ask him if he'd like a sign that says "Stop" and "Go." The child could make the sign and then, depending upon the child's developmental level, you could print the words for the child, ask if he knows the letters that say "stop" or "go," or provide a model of the words for the child to copy.

Alphabet letters

Preparation: Provide sets of alphabet letters in the room. Letters that are made of materials such as wood, wood covered with sandpaper, or plastic are usually more interesting for children to manipulate and more durable than those of paper or cardboard. *Action:* Children can feel, look at, and arrange the letters. For example, children who don't have the motor control necessary for writing letters can often perceive the letters and thus can "write" words such as their name with letters that are already formed.

Visual discrimination and matching letters come before real reading.

1. *Preparation:* Print children's names on their lockers or coat hooks. *Action:* Children can begin to identify their lockers and other children's lockers by their printed names as well as their position and contents. Children often begin to recognize one another's printed names in this way. **Children's names**
2. *Preparation:* Place pencils and crayons near children's art activities. *Action:* Print children's names clearly on their art projects. As a child begins to be ready, suggest that he might like to watch while you print the first letter of his name and then he might like to copy it. Through this process of observing and trying, many young children learn how to write their names. As children begin to make representational things in art, you can offer to print what they say about their product—e.g., "It's a merry-go-round of all different colors"—on the product.
3. *Preparation:* Take snapshots of children at the beginning of school and print out their names to go with their pictures on a display. *Action:* When children begin to recognize the names, they can enjoy a game in which the names and pictures are all mixed up and they straighten them out again. Later on, the pic-

tures can be grouped in different ways—e.g., under the letters of the alphabet which their individual names start with (Jeffrey's and John's pictures and names under the J, etc.) or under numbers indicating the number of letters in their names (Jeffrey under "7", John under "4," etc.).

Writing Stories

Preparation: Place paper, pencil, and crayons in various parts of the room.

Action: As children describe their experiences or make up stories, ask if they'd like to have them written down so they can take them home or tell them to the other children. Original stories can be encouraged by providing motivation, and you can be ready to accept dictation—for example, after Halloween place a table with drawing and writing supplies on it near Halloween pictures or decorations. Place a sign on the table saying, "What did you look like?" or "What did you do?" Children can then make pictures about their Halloween experiences, dictate stories, or both. Or the motivation could be an action-filled picture showing a situation with no ending but your questions: "What do you think happened? Why?" Frequently children want to tell stories about their pictures, and the adult can record these, too.

Primary Typewriter

This resource is a highly desirable piece of equipment in the preschool room. The teacher may use it to type stories dictated by the children or to type messages or directions for the children. Children often like to type themselves: exploring the keyboard at first, next learning to recognize upper and lower case letters, and then typing words and sentences that the teacher may provide for copying or that they may produce themselves.

Recipe Charts

Preparation: Make charts for cooking projects. The charts have pictures and words telling what to do; for example, there may be pictures of the ingredients (such as three eggs drawn and cut out with the words *three eggs* printed beside them) and processes (such as a sketch of the eggs being broken).

Action: Children "read" the recipe to find out what they do in the cooking process so that they can complete the project with minimal help.

Song Charts

Preparation: Make charts for repetitive songs that have several verses, such as "The Farmer in the Dell," "Looby Loo." Draw or cut out pictures that indicate what comes next (e.g., first a farmer, below him a picture of his wife, etc.) and print the words for the figures beside them (e.g., Farmer, Wife, etc.).

Treasure Hunt Walk

Preparation: Sketch pictures of objects that are found outside or paste the actual objects themselves on cards. For example, sketch or paste three red leaves or five short sticks and then print the names of the objects beside the pictures ("three red leaves").

Action: Children go on a treasure hunt walk in which they attempt to find the objects their card has pictured.

Signmakers give away remnants.

Companies that make signs will frequently give teachers their salvage material. Resourceful teachers will find samples of brightly colored and durable numbers and letters for children to trace, to spell with, and to manipulate.

Billboard companies will sometimes share massive sections of billboard posters full of letters which may be cut and used for various purposes, including homemade letter lotto games, board games in which a child spins and moves to the letter spun, etc.

Other salvage and remnant materials which can be obtained from commercial enterprises include leather, Styrofoam, foam rubber, scrap metals, printers' remnants, plastic scraps, cardboard boxes and tubes, and upholstery remnants.

Almost any large industrial manufacturer or supply company will have leftovers which the resourceful teacher can make use of.

Remnants are usually fine materials to use for improvising activities which give children practice in fine motor skills. Such practice is available daily in the cutting, tracing, and drawing activities of the classroom as well as in the using of specific materials like the primary typewriter, the alphabet board by Holt, Rinehart & Winston, and letter strip books with page sections children turn until they have three that match.

Practicing Fine Motor Skills

Still, it may be necessary to provide more specific finger and hand skill activities. Collect bowlfuls of salvage beads which can be strung with thin wire or fish line. Styrofoam pieces also may be sewn together with needle and thread to make necklaces.

You can make attractive and decorative signs with small beans, peas, and lentils. Write the child's name or any other sign he wants to make on a piece of cardboard. Then he brushes Elmer's glue on a letter and places beans on the glue. It takes concentration and skill, and the results are very pleasing.

Little by little, children become acquainted with numbers, quantities and other mathematical concepts which form the foundation of future learning in this area. Children vary greatly in the backgrounds with which they enter the preschool. A child may know that he is four years old, that he has one sister, that he wears two shoes. Another child may recognize the numerals on a clock, understand that a dozen is twelve of something, and know that he can buy a candy bar with fifteen pennies or a dime and a nickel. Whatever their experiences, children are usually fascinated by numbers and interested in activities which help them increase their understanding of mathematical concepts.

Preliminary Mathematical and Geometric Activities

In the preschool, you will want to give children opportunities to set up one-to-one correspondences—to determine when two groups have the same number of objects by pairing them. When, for instance, a child puts a napkin at each chair or gets a lollipop for every child at his table, he is setting up a one-to-one correspondence. When he puts a cover on each felt-tip marker or a cup in each saucer, he has set up a provoked correspondence.

One-to-One Correspondence

Children also come to understand conservation of volume or or grouped together but that the number of objects remains the same if none are added or removed. If a child is given a bunch of jelly beans, he has no more when he spreads them out in a line than when he puts them in a pile. This understanding is called conservation of number.

Conservation

Children also come to understand conservation of volume or amount—that the amount of milk in a tall thin glass is the same when poured into a shallow bowl if no more has been added or taken away—as well as conservation of length—that two sticks of identical length are still identical in length when placed side by side even if one is pushed a little to the right of the other. Teachers can and should provide experiences with measurement of lengths and quantities for children, although these experiences need not necessarily be made with the units that adults use; rather, such materials as yarn, string, ribbon tape, unifix cubes, and marbles can be used.

Number Operations

When a child says "1, 2, 3, 4, 5, 6 . . ." he is not necessarily indicating that he understands "sixness"—what *six* is. In the preschool, children need much experience with meaningful counting, with understanding that the name spoken when the last object is touched tells how many objects are in the group or set. Then they can add to and take away objects from sets and learn the meaning of *more* and *less.*

Using the Materials of the Environment

Once a teacher understands the skills that she wants to isolate and help children practice, the materials are near at hand. You do not need a closetful of expensive equipment, although some bought materials can be useful. The following is a partial list of materials which can be kept on hand for those moments when you want to help a child understand something mathematical: beads, buttons, straws, pipe cleaners, marbles, shells, clay, string, paper, cardboard boxes, jelly beans, poker chips, plastic miniature toys (cowboys, horses, and houses), and jars of all sizes and shapes.

Quantitative Three-Dimensional Relationships

Equipment: Wooden blocks in related shapes ranging in size from a few inches to several feet.

Unit blocks

Action: Children build with them on the floor and can discover various spatial relationships (e.g., two of the small rectangles equal the length of one large rectangle; two small triangles equal one small square).

Cuisenaire rods

Equipment: Groups of small wooden rods of relative lengths gathered in bags. There are ten different lengths of rods. The smallest is a cube; the largest is ten times the length of the cube. Each different length of rod has a particular color.

Action: Children originally use the rods for building on tables and gradually work into games involving size and number relationships (e.g., How many yellow rods are needed to make one green one?) and, eventually, as children get older, into games of multiplication and division, etc. Manuals come with the rods and describe the use of the rods and the progression of the game.

Unifix cubes

Equipment: A pool of 500 colored plastic cubes which fit together. Additional equipment includes inset patterns boards, a track which goes from one to one hundred, one to ten boats (holders), number indicators or caps, grids for assembling multibase structures, and others.

Action: Children put cubes together, build towers, measure, compare, place appropriate number of cubes in pattern boards or boats, cap with number indicators, etc.

Number activities games

Motivation to manipulate numbers is high when children are playing games, and much practice in meaningful counting—counting by twos, for example—in adding and subtracting, and in recognizing that written numerals can be obtained within the social framework that a game provides. Some games will be competitive; here, children will have motivation to learn additional skills by keeping score. Other games will not be competitive but played simply for the fun of it.

Children can bowl with blocks and a hard rubber ball or with cardboard milk cartons and a foam rubber ball. Each pin can be valued at one point or varied in value depending upon the level of children involved. A simple wire hoop attached to a cardboard backing can serve as a basketball net. Additional fine motor skill practice will accrue to the child who sews some netting to the hoop. With that and a foam ball, you play basketball, using any scoring method you wish. Bean bag toss and magnetic darts are popular games which lend themselves to tallying.

Some Games Involving Gross Motor Activity

Popular games like Chutes and Ladders and Casper the Ghost tell us a great deal about the kinds of activity that children enjoy. Effective board games can be created by teachers or children. Some simple, readily available materials that serve to stimulate this activity include signal dots, gummed stickers, felt-tip markers, large sheets of paper and cardboard, small rectangular boards, precut for the child, paper punches (for homemade dice, etc.), mosaic tiles, toy cars and trinkets (for markers), and plastic letters and numbers.

Board games

Teachers who may make board games will likely want to use more durable materials. Wood and enamel paint are recommended for greatest permanence and appeal. Items made from paper may be sprayed with clear plastic spray or covered with transparent contact paper. Usually it pays to use heavy cardboard, wallboard, triwall, tiles, Masonite samples, and other sturdy materials. Teachers will also want to give consideration to a game's aesthetic appeal, and this can be enhanced with large, clear letters, numbers, or illustrations that can be obtained from posters, discarded calendars, rubber stamps, transfer lettering, old catalogues, etc.

The spinner or die is usually the key to the game, telling the child where to go on the board, although one can use a pile of cards from which the child chooses the top one to serve the same purpose of telling how many spaces to move. Variations on simple spinners and standard dice are valuable. A spinner which reads something like the following

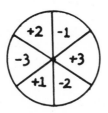

tells children to move ahead or back so many spaces. It can be used with an egg carton to be filled with marbles; the child spins to see how many he puts in or takes out. It can be used with a pole on which the child must place ten metal discs; the child again spins to see how many he adds or subtracts. Or you can make a pair of dice to serve the same purpose.

Use a soft foam block and cover it with a brightly colored fabric onto which you have sewn the configurations. One die could have the standard configurations; the other could simply have plus and minus signs.

Number-Sorter

Equipment: A flat board with clusters of wooden prongs. The first "cluster" is one prong; the second cluster has two prongs, and the clusters go up to five prongs. Fifteen rubber squares, each with holes from one to five, fit over the prongs.

Action: The child fits the three squares with three holes over the cluster of three prongs, and so on.

Number Puzzles

Equipment: A set of ten two-piece puzzles. One end of each puzzle pair has a number. Its matching end has the corresponding number of objects (for example, the puzzle piece with the number *five* fits onto the puzzle piece having a picture of five balloons).

Dominoes

Equipment: Domino sets come in various materials and sizes. The large wooden sets (about three inches by six inches) are most durable, most easily handled by younger children, but also most expensive. Children will enjoy making their own domino sets using paper punches or gummed circles.

Action: Younger children may enjoy matching them first; later, they will be able to "build" with them by matching ends; however, they will usually not be able to play the game of building with others, which involves taking turns, until they are four or five years old at least.

Number Board

Equipment: A board with ten small holes and the numerals one to ten written beside the holes in ascending order. There are ten pegs of different lengths (with the longest peg being ten times the length of the shortest) which fit into the corresponding holes. Fifty-five wooden washers accompany the board; each washer is of such a thickness that only one will fit on the shortest peg while ten will fit on the longest peg.

Action: Children arrange the pegs in ascending order and place the washers on the corresponding pegs.

Counting Cards

Equipment: Make large cardboard cards with visually or tactually interesting objects glued on them in different-numbered groupings and write the numeral opposite the group (for example, a card with five chestnuts or five pieces of brightly colored cloth grouped by three and two on one side of the card, the numeral five on the other side).

Counting Songs

Action: Sing counting songs, such as "Ten Little Indians," "This Old Man," "Roll Over."

Counting Books

Action: Read counting books, such as *One Snail and Me, Brown Cow Farm, My Red Umbrella, Brian Wildsmith's 1, 2, 3 Book.*

Measuring Activities

Kitchen Scales

Equipment: Kitchen scales.
Action: Children can weigh objects on kitchen scales as a means of learning the concept of absolute weight.

Balance Scales

Equipment: Balance scales (can be purchased or made).
Action: Children can compare weights of different objects on balance scales as a means of learning the concept of relative weight.

Clocks

Equipment: Actual clocks that tell time and faces of clocks with hands children can move.

Balance scales help children learn the concept of relative weight.

Action: Actual clocks to refer to in learning time ("At three o'clock—that is, when the little hand is at the three and the big hand is at the twelve—we'll go outside"); faces of clocks with movable hands so children can match the hands to the real time, can set the hands to tell the time they want in play, etc.

Equipment: Large indoor and/or outdoor thermometers.
Action: Children can learn the concept of measuring the temperature through reading the thermometer and experimenting with it (e.g., putting it near a radiator, then near an open window).

Thermometers

Action: Anything which grows is fun to measure. Activities can include marking and measuring children's heights on a paper reaching from the floor past the height of the tallest child. Compare heights at the beginning and end of the year; measure waists with a tape measure, size of feet by drawing around them on paper and then measuring with a ruler, or use a real shoe measure; measure with a tape measure how many feet children can jump, etc.

Tape Measures, Yardsticks, Rulers

Equipment: Plastic or metal cups and spoons.
Action: Cups and spoons for use in cooking, water play, sand and cornmeal play, etc. Through using these materials, children can begin to understand their related sizes (e.g., that two cups of the half-cup size will equal one cup of the one-cup size).

Measuring Cups and Spoons

Equipment: Make large calendars of the month with the blocks representing each day being several inches square. There is then space for pictures or writing so the calendar can be personalized to the particular group's experiences (for example, pictures or comments about events or activities of special interest—birthdays, holidays, field trips, or seasonal events such as the first snow or the first robin—can be added).

Calendars

Equipment: "Surprise" calendars, which are calendars made as those above except that each day is covered with a paper "door."

Action: Children open the "door" for the corresponding day and find a picture underneath telling something special about the day, the season, the activities of the group, etc.

Wooden Cylinders

Equipment: Large wooden blocks with holes filled with knobbed cylinders of varying depth or diameter.

Action: Children take out cylinders and attempt to replace them in their corresponding holes as a means of estimating depth and diameter.

Geometric Activities

Geometric Insets

Equipment: Brightly colored pieces of metal with a geometric shape cut out of each piece and knobbed.

Action: Children can use these insets as shape puzzles to be taken apart and replaced or as shapes to draw around.

Parquetry Blocks

Equipment: Wooden blocks, several inches in size, of varying colors and shapes (triangles, rectangles, etc.).

Action: Children fit the blocks together into different patterns or use the blocks for building.

Geometric Shape Puzzles

Equipment: Rubber colored puzzles of different shapes such as circles, squares. Each large circle is filled with smaller circles that fit tightly inside each other.

Action: Children take them apart, sort the pieces, and fit them together again.

Geoboards

A geoboard permits a child to invent and experiment with shapes even before he can name or draw them.

Equipment: A square board of almost any convenient size. Nails must be set into the surface of the board at regular intervals. Colored rubber bands are also necessary.

Action: Children pull rubber bands across the nails to form a great variety of geometric forms and colorful patterns. The geoboard can be used for various marble games too.

These materials, kinds of equipment, and activities provide the basis for a strong, rich preschool program. With their aid, the good teacher can awaken her children to many facets of the world and can help them to grow. But the aids themselves are inert; alone, they do nothing. Only when the teacher sets them to work does something begin to happen, for the heart of the preschool program is activity—planned, appropriate, stimulating—right for the children. The program is the medium for growth and for learning. When it is suitable, children swim in it as a fish swims in water, and supported by it, they flourish.

SELECTED REFERENCE MATERIALS ON INTEGRATING ACADEMIC PRELIMINARIES INTO THE CURRICULUM FOR TEACHERS OF YOUNG CHILDREN

Many of the books listed contain excellent suggestions for specific skill development activities for children.

Biggs, E. E. *Math for Younger Children.* New York: Citation Press. 1972.

Croft, Doreen. *An Activities Handbook for Teachers of Young Children.* Boston: Houghton Mifflin Co., 1975.

Elementary Science Study. *Attribute Games and Problems—Teacher's Guide.* Manchester, Mo.: McGraw-Hill Book Co., Webster Division, 1967.

_____. *Match and Measure.* Manchester, Mo.: McGraw-Hill Book Co., Webster Division, 1967.

_____. *Tangrams.* Manchester, Mo.: McGraw-Hill Book Co., Webster Division, 1968.

Eliason, C., and Jenkins, L. *A Practical Guide to Early Childhood Curriculum.* St. Louis: C. V. Mosby, 1977.

Engle, Rose. *Language Development Experiences for Young Children.* Culver City, Calif.: Lyon Publishing Co., 1972.

Frank, Marjorie. *Kids' Stuff Math.* Nashville, Tenn.: Incentive Publishing Co., 1974.

George Peabody College for Teachers. *Free and Inexpensive Learning Materials.* Nashville, Tenn.: George Peabody College for Teachers, 1976.

Goodacre, E. J. *Children and Learning to Read.* London: Routledge & Kegan Paul, 1971.

Karnes, Merle B. *Helping Young Children Develop Language Skills.* Arlington, Va.: Council for Exceptional Children, 1968.

_____. *Learning Language at Home.* Reston, Va.: Council for Exceptional Children, 1977.

King, Pat H. *Individualized Instruction: Games That Teach.* Encino, Calif.: International Center for Educational Development, 1971.

Lorton, Mary. *Workjobs: Activity Centered Learning for Early Childhood Education.* Boston: Addison-Wesley Publishing Co., 1972.

Noble, Judith. *Games Children Play and Learn From: Learning Activities for Young Children.* Dubuque, Iowa: Kendall Hunt, 1973.

Nuffield Mathematics Foundation. *Beginnings.* New York: John Wiley & Sons, 1967-1972.

_____. *Mathematics Begins.* New York: John Wiley & Sons, 1967-1972.

_____. *Checking Up.* New York: John Wiley & Sons, 1967-1972.

Russell, D., and Russell, E. F. *Listening Aids through the Grades.* New York: Columbia University Teachers College Press, 1968.

Sargent, Betsye. *The Integrated Day in an American School.* Boston: National Association of Independent Schools, 1970.

Sharp, Evelyn. *Thinking Is Child's Play.* New York: E. P. Dutton & Co., 1969.

Stant, Margaret A. *The Young Child: His Activities and Materials.* Englewood Cliffs, N. J.: Prentice-Hall, Inc., 1972.

Wedemeyer, Avarill, and Cejka, Joyce. *Creative Ideas for Teaching Exceptional Children.* Denver: Love Publishing Co., 1970.

The Whole Learning Catalogue. Palo Alto, Calif.: Education Today, 1976.

Eight

Understanding the Physical
and Social World

We know that children are living through experiences every day which **CHILDREN KNOW A** provide them with information about the physical and social world. **GREAT DEAL.** From the earliest ages, they toddle around their neighborhoods, walk up and down the aisles of a supermarket, experience changing weather—cold, wind, rain—and notice the changing seasons. They learn about their bodies. Sometimes they have a pet. Certainly, they observe plants and animals and other people in a multitude of situations. They eat a variety of foods, notice the variety of housing, ride in or on many vehicles and wear garments appropriate to the situation. The more perceptive the child, the more details he notices: people have black, brown, blond, red, curly, straight, wavy hair; animals have hair too, but it differs from human hair; hair is distributed in different places on the body, etc. *But* this mass of information and detail can be meaningless to the young child unless he has help in sorting it all out and unless it can be related meaningfully to his own experiences.

WHAT IS THE
RESPONSIBILITY OF
THE TEACHER?

When a child asks how the water gets into the sink, the teacher must be **Finding Out What's** able to help him sort out the information he already has about water and **Known** pipes and sinks:

How do you think it gets there?
What do you see that helps it get there?

She must then help him gain new information through a wide range of **Providing New** activities and experiences: **Information**

Walking to the basement to look at the pipes
Examining valves
Talking to the plumber or janitor
Looking at books

157

Relating the New and the Old

Then she can provide consolidating experiences, helping him relate what he already knows with his new information so that his understanding is increased.

CHILDREN NEED TO KNOW ABOUT THEIR OWN ENVIRONMENTS.

Many adults either seldom look closely at physical and natural phenomena around them or look without really seeing. As in other areas of curriculum, we are interested in fostering children's abilities to see things accurately, to be able to describe what they see, and to begin to understand the relationships among things which happen around them. The alert teacher sees the possibilities for increasing what children will see. She encourages comment and discussion because these let her know what the children are seeing and, more important, what they are understanding. She asks a lot of questions, open-ended, wondering questions, which don't imply that there is only one "right answer" but which inspire children to look for possible answers. Some children come to school with a rich background of experiences which make them ready to wonder and ask questions. Others will have a paucity of experiences, and the teacher will have to work slowly and carefully to awaken and sustain a similar degree of curiosity in them. Traditionally the teacher of young children has relied upon spontaneous opportunities to accomplish the goals of fostering curiosity about experiences and increasing knowledge and understanding of the world. When a child brings in a piece of moldy bread or a doll from England, when he asks why the sun goes away, the usual approach is to exclaim what an interesting thing or question this is and put the object—if an object is involved—on a table for all to look at. Occasionally, there is a suggestion that the class find out more about the object or question, and some nearby reference book is sought out. More often than not, however, the whole incident is soon forgotten.

The Case for Planning

For most children and teachers, this approach is not adquate. Even when a teacher recognizes a good learning opportunity (and this occurs less often than we'd like to believe), she frequently lacks the time, knowledge, or self-confidence to proceed. She responds at the moment and moves on. In so doing, she not only stifles budding curiosity but also inhibits future questions and speculations.

How can a teacher respond to things a child introduces?

She can welcome a child's contribution and look at it with genuine interest. She can find a suitable place to display it where other children will be able to see it. She can extend this visual experience by suggesting activities for the children to do: for example, develop an adjective word list about the object, find pictures of it in reference books, find other objects as big as, as round as, or the same color as the one being viewed. The teacher can also help the child find answers to his questions by setting up new experiences that will challenge him to examine relevant material.

Suppose a child brings a bird's nest to school.

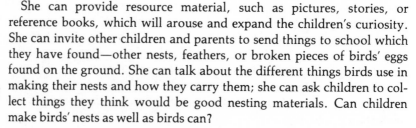

She can provide resource material, such as pictures, stories, or reference books, which will arouse and expand the children's curiosity. She can invite other children and parents to send things to school which they have found—other nests, feathers, or broken pieces of birds' eggs found on the ground. She can talk about the different things birds use in making their nests and how they carry them; she can ask children to collect things they think would be good nesting materials. Can children make birds' nests as well as birds can?

By genuinely expanding a single incident in this way, the teacher can let all the children know that their contributions are valued as something important rather than as mere diversions from what the teacher had meant to talk about that day.

Have children examine the bread. What do their senses tell them? How does it look? How does it feel? How does it smell? Then go home; find out about mold. What is it? What does it need to grow? What kinds are there? Where does one find it? How does it reproduce? Is it harmful? With some solid information, the teacher then should be able to plan activities which will allow children to explore the dimensions of mold.

If a child brings in a piece of moldy bread and you don't know anything about mold

When a teacher recognizes that a particular topic is of interest to some children or when she decides for other reasons that some area of information should be explored with some children, she can proceed in the following way:

HOW DOES THE TEACHER PLAN?

1. Gather all the information she can about the topic, whether it be the circus, houses, hair, shoes, bones, roads, or dinosaurs, and think through the key concepts related to that topic.
2. Capitalize on an existing interest or motivate the children to be interested.
3. Gather appropriate materials and a variety of activities for children through which they can gain information and/or consolidate what information they already have.
4. Try the activities and explore the materials before introducing them to children.

Hair is a subject with which we are all familiar but about which we are seldom extensively informed. It is so much a part of us that we tend to take it for granted. Yet there is much about hair which, when investigated, could lead children to a wider understanding of themselves and their differences from and similarities to other people and animals.

What *is* hair? How does it originate? What are its properties? What are the differences between men's and women's hair? Between the hair of people of different races? Between animal hair and human hair? How is hair taken care of? How does it relate to our other body functions? How does weather affect hair? Who are the professionals who deal with hair? How do hair styles symbolize our feelings and values?

The teacher gathers a great deal of information, not all of which is necessarily appropriate for young children. She may find good resource people among the parents in her own class or in the surrounding community. She may find good reference material in a local public or school library or in literature distributed as a public service by various scientific and educational organizations. Books which are written for elementary school children, if they are based on accurate scientific knowledge, can provide good, understandable information for the preschool teacher. The power of this knowledge is that it enables the teacher to serve as a resource person, to stimulate and encourage the interests of children as they take different turns and directions. The teacher needn't fear the unexpected because she's thought about it—or at least is willing to think about it.

The teacher becomes the resource.

How is this knowledge transferred to children?

While it's the task of the teacher to think through the information and to plan appropriate activities for children, it is through their experiences that children gain information. And here is where the creative abilities of the teacher are taxed. For she must provide opportunities for the children to interact with the world, to explore it, to talk about and learn from their interactions and explorations.

What are the activities through which children gain information and understanding?

In planning activities for children, the teacher should strive to use the following avenues imaginatively: actual experience with and observation of a phenomenon, experience somewhat removed through various audio-visual aids, wise and judicious use of books, and the spoken word—hers, an expert's, the children's.

Direct Experience

There is no substitute for direct experience. Children should be given many opportunities to see, touch, feel, manipulate, taste, and in other ways absorb firsthand information about a given subject. This experience is particularly possible in the areas of natural phenomena.

of mold

Children can observe mold on bread, meats, oranges. They can observe what happens when mold is cultivated in conditions of cold and in warmth, in darkness and in light, on bread and on wood.

of trees

Children can be led by sensitive teachers to be aware of the different branch patterns of trees in winter—to observe how trees look from below, looking straight up the trunk; to identify different kinds of bark through feeling. Does the wind sound different through different kinds of trees? Is there any tree you can recognize by smell? What kinds of wood from trees can you recognize? How? How does rough wood feel compared to planed, sanded, and polished wood? Do you know how trees are cut and processed for lumber? Have you seen this done?

with shoes

Look carefully at shoes. How are they made? What are their parts? How are they put together? Why are they different sizes? What are they made of? Where do the materials come from? How do the different parts feel? Smell? How many different kinds are there? Why do we wear them? The sensitive and perceptive teacher is alert to the manifold opportunities for children to observe and be aware of what they experience, whether it be shooting off a water rocket, examining a lock of hair, giving attention to the sound of the rain, or simply watching the fish in the aquarium.

To the greatest possible extent, the teacher avoids being verbal and concentrates on what children can see, feel, and hear.

The Field Trip

One of the most effective ways of providing firsthand experience for children is the field trip. Trips are an excellent way of giving young children ideas to talk about, to build with, to paint, and to act out. They can give children immediate experience with the facts of the social sciences; they can provide the foundation for teaching language and reading. They are one of the best avenues of learning for every age. The circus is brought to life by the children's being there in a way which is unmatched by any other activity. One can talk about how houses are built for days yet achieve less than could be achieved with one visit to a nearby construction site where the process can be observed.

The limitations of the field trip

There is nothing magical about just getting out of the classroom. In order to be worthwhile, the field trip has to be chosen wisely and planned well. We all know of disastrous field trips; certainly there are those that are simply a waste of time. Like any other activity, the field trip pays the most dividends when it is done well.

How, then, does one choose a site for a field trip? One has to think both about the *type* of place one will visit and the mechanical aspects of size, distance, and complexity of the site. What are the children interested in at that moment? What kinds of things are they investigating? The field trip ought to pertain to other things going on in the classroom and be relevant to the interests of the moment. The site of the field trip may be a place where children are able to see something happening, where a product is manufactured, or where a substance is changed from one state to another. Ideally, it is a place where children are able to manipulate some things—where they can touch, try out, use things.

How does one choose a field trip site?

Thus, if children are exploring the topic of food, they might go to someone's yard and harvest the vegetables. They might visit a nearby farm where they could feed some of the animals. They might visit the kitchen of a restaurant when food was not being served or visit a specialty market, such as a seafood store, noting all the kinds of fish and perhaps purchasing some for cooking in the classroom. They might also visit a bread-making, candy-making, or tunafish-canning facility. All these places could be relevant to the interests of the children and could provide very rich learning experiences if well handled.

From a mechanical point of view, trips should not be to far-away places, nor should they be long and fatiguing. Sometimes, the site is within the school building itself. Other fine trips are within walking distance of most schools: a road being repaired, a tree being cut down, cardboard cartons being manufactured. . . .One shouldn't plan to travel far, and one shouldn't plan to stay too long. One should also choose to visit simple, uncrowded places. Too much noise and confusion will defeat an otherwise productive field trip.

A good field trip involves preparation of both teacher and children. As part of the teacher's preparation, she should take the trip first herself. She should become familiar with the place. What is of particular interest? What can she point out? What questions can be raised that will help children observe well? The teacher should talk in advance with key people. She should explain the ages of her children, what she hopes for them to gain from the experience, why it is important to help them locate the good places for learning.

Planning a field trip

During the trip itself, the teacher is alert. She stays close to the children, listens to them, talks with individuals about their experiences, and answers questions they may have. Mostly, she watches. She may take slides profitably either then or on her earlier visit to use in follow-up activities in the classroom. But picture taking should not be done at the expense of alert attention to the children. Each child is having an individual experience and, to the greatest extent possible, the teacher should allow the children to move slowly, to drink in what they want, to go at their own paces.

Taking the trip

Field trips should not be taken in isolation, for they are an integral part of the curriculum. They are chosen because they grow out of an interest, are prepared for as part of a larger activity, and should be built upon after they have been taken. Class books with photographs, displays of

Back in the classroom

objects, and conversations are all ways of extending and consolidating the experiences of a field trip. Children should not always be asked to paint a picture of what they remember or liked best. They should be encouraged to play out in the way most suited to them. While some children, on returning from a trip to a bird sanctuary, might wish to move like birds, others might wish to build the sanctuary in blocks. Still others might pore over picture books, make a bird feeder, or investigate the properties of wings. The teacher needs to bring into the classroom the props and supplies that relate to the trip so that it can be reenacted in any way that will be helpful to the children.

But what if children can't have firsthand experiences? Aren't there other ways for them to get information?

Obviously, one can't learn everything through firsthand experience; even though it's essential for teachers to provide as many opportunities as possible for such learning, there must be other kinds of activities happening at the same time. There *is* a place for words in the preschool as a means of extending information. The teacher may look at an aquarium with children and label the fish. She may have a discussion with a small group of children about how babies grow, about a child's trip to Mexico, or about the bones in our bodies. And the teacher may use the vehicle of a total-group discussion to impart and share information, feelings and attitudes.

*The Group
Discussion*

Is there a place for total-group discussion in the preschool?

There is some dispute as to whether young children ought to be required to take part in total-group discussions and as to whether such discussions are helpful. If they are, what is the role of the teacher? To a large extent, teachers have to make individual decisions about some of those questions and do what is comfortable for themselves and their particular group of children. However, some guidelines may be set.

Skills are not appropriate for group "discussions."

For the most part, skills are not an appropriate lesson topic for a total group. Some teachers, under the guise of "discussion," call the group together in order to instruct them in how the letter "s" sounds or in how to play a number game. On these occasions, each child must wait his turn and watch while every other child has his. While some teachers in some classes get away with this, it's done at a great price to children who must curb, for what is usually a long period of time, their natural inclinations to talk and move. Furthermore, children vary greatly in their capacities in the skills areas, and it would be impossible to devise a lesson or "game" which is appropriate for the levels of fifteen different children playing in the same way at the same time. A third disadvantage of this kind of total-group "activity" is that it is planned, initiated, and directed by the teacher. She takes the lead and carefully controls whatever is to take place. Children have no opportunity to alter events; indeed, they are usually chastised for changing the subject or for giving a creative answer.

But honest discussion is different.

But if teachers and children want to enter into honest dialogue to share ideas, information, and questions, then the group can provide a stimulating and provocative base. Suppose the teacher wants to introduce the topic of people's homes or the idea that certain people—architects—design buildings which are not all alike. She might read a book about homes (for example, *A Home for Everyone* by Betty Miles) and then discuss with the children their own homes. There is probably much that each child could contribute about his home, and the process of listening to others would stimulate him to think about aspects of his home about which he had never previously thought. Some questions that children may begin to think about during the discussion are:

Who lives in my house?
What does it look like?
What color is the outside?
Is it old or new? Big or little?
How many floors does it have? Rooms?
How many windows are in my room?
What color is my room?
What material is my house made of?

Or the teacher may want to deal with issues with affective implications:

Has anyone ever been afraid of a house?
What makes people afraid?
How does it feel to be afraid?
Are grown-ups ever afraid?
What do you do when you're afraid?

Both the teacher and the children can learn from a small-group discussion.

Such discussions, although initiated by the teacher, are really carried on by the children. Each child is likely to have something to contribute, and the process of hearing what the others have to say is enlightening. Even children who do not speak up will be benefitting from the opportunity to extend their understanding.

Furthermore, the teacher learns. She learns where her children are in relation to a particular topic. She may learn about some of their concerns and misconceptions. She certainly learns a little about each of them. She is not a choreographer—she has not figured out in advance exactly what will be said. She's a skillful leader of and participant in honest sharing of ideas and information.

Under these circumstances, small-group or total-group discussions can be valuable.

How do you motivate a discussion?

Sometimes a teacher would like to find out what children know or think about a particular topic. Perhaps she wants to know how much information her children have about the circus. In this case, she simply asks, "Who can tell us about the circus?" However, a question of this sort is usually answered enthusiastically by children with a lot to say, while the others feel quite left out. Often, a good discussion involving all the children can be stimulated by the introduction of a device—a lion tamer's whip, a clown's costume, or a trapeze, for example. Such a device not only triggers the memories and experiences of the children but also serves as a focus for those children who may not have had previous experiences.

An object often helps.

Books, too, stimulate discussion and are sources of information.

Additional potent sources of information for children are books. Books may be used by individuals and by groups. The range of experiences provided by them is enormous,* but among their purposes for young children is the information that can be gained from the written word. When children cannot learn something from firsthand observation and experience, when they cannot learn something from the word of their teacher or classmates, they can nearly always find a book which will give the information desired. Thus, reading is an activity which is priceless for both teachers and children.

Can audio-visual aids be helpful?

A fourth major source of information to children—and one intimately related to books—is, the audio-visual aid. Included among such aids are:

Charts or study prints
Films
Film loops
Filmstrips
Records
Slides
Tape recorders

While audio-visual aids are the next best thing to direct experience, they are frequently under-utilized by teachers in the preschool. This may be because teachers in general are not very concerned about planning for the extension of curriculum with young children. Or it may be that there are not very many good aids readily available to teachers of young children. But the children themselves love to look at pictures and slides, and pictures can add immeasurably to their knowledge and understanding of a topic. The teacher can frequently get commercial slides of subjects (e.g., birds, their feeding habits, their nests, their young) which she would be unable to take herself. The Audio-Visual Services of the Smithsonian Institution in Washington, D.C. has a range of slides, as does the Encyclopedia Britannica Corporation, the Hubbard Scientific Co., of Northbrook, Illinois, and The Society for Visual Education, Inc. in Chicago.

The best thing about slides is that any teacher is capable of taking them herself. The alert teacher will have her camera on a field trip or personal vacation to catch the road being cemented, the ship being built, or the banana trees growing in the South. And these slides will serve as an in-

---

*For a fuller explication of this idea, the reader is referred to chapter four.

valuable teaching resource, for pictures often convey far more than words, especially when trying to help young children understand new concepts. A further advantage of slides is that they may be looked at through a viewer individually or in groups. Children can be shown how to handle slides carefully and then be left free to examine a set of slides independently and at their own paces.

Filmstrips are a somewhat less successful aid, partly because of the general quality of filmstrips available and partly because of the medium itself. They cannot be used as flexibly as slides; it's difficult to zero in on one frame and one is unlikely to want to show a whole strip. Individual filmstrip viewers, however, can be set up on any table near an electric outlet, and children frequently enjoy using them independently.

Film loops are a relatively new medium. Small film cartridges are inserted into the film loop machine, and film is projected onto a corner of a wall where an individual or a small group can watch without inconveniencing others in the class. The loop plays continuously until the machine is stopped, thus allowing children to see the same two- or three-minute piece of film as frequently as they wish.

Films, of course, have to be used judiciously with young children, but in recent years, some companies have put out some nice ones: "Animal Homes" and "The Water Says" by Churchill Films (662 North Robertson Boulevard, Los Angeles, California 90069); "Sheep and How They Live" by AIMS Instructional Media; "The Family Farm" by Sterling Educational Films. For information about films, the teacher may contact Federal Marketing Services, Alexandria, Virginia 22307, or write directly to film producers for catalogues (ABC Media Concepts, New York, New York 10019; Oxford Films, Inc., Los Angeles, California 90038; NBC Educational Enterprises, New York, New York 10020; AIMS Instructional Media Services, Inc., Hollywood, California 90069).

Teachers should check local libraries for sources of films and *preview* films that might be shown. Most are inappropriate, but if a good one is found, it can be a fine source of information for the children.

SOME SPECIFIC EXAMPLES OF HOW TO PROCEED

With the preceding information as background, we now will develop here two topics in the physical and social sciences which are related to one another—plants and soil; we will also suggest possible activities for a third and more unusual topic—hair. We hope that these will give the teacher an idea of how to proceed, will be a model for developing her own ideas in other areas. Almost any topic is appropriate for development: frogs, wood, space exploration, farms, cans, shoes, rocks, bones, food, weather, blood. The teacher need be guided only by her own interests and those of the children.

Integrating the Curriculum

Some of the activities require a teacher to plan for and purposefully stimulate the goings-on. Others develop through children's spontaneously expressed interests or in incidental happenings in the environment.

Some of the activities are, frankly, for the purpose of giving children specific information. Others help children develop cognitive skills—observing likenesses and differences; sorting, grouping, and classifying; measuring, charting, recording. Still others focus on language skills: extending vocabulary, offering opportunities to express facts and ideas, to ask questions, and to relate sequential events; and listening to others.

Finally, there are activities that allow children the opportunity to express themselves through art, dramatic play, dance, music, storytelling.

Some Pitfalls

To execute a plan of this sort, the teacher needs interest in and appreciation of the topic herself, a good degree of actual knowledge, and the willingness to use all avenues of activity creatively and flexibly to help children gain new knowledge and understanding.

PLANTS

Plants in any classroom help to make it look lived in and cared for; even in a city classroom, the teacher can find some sorts of plants that will grow in this environment. If she has a window which gets several hours of sun per day, she can choose from quite a variety. If the windows get no sun, the choice is more limited, but there is still much that can be done. During the winter, the teacher will need to know how cold the classroom gets at night or on weekends and choose the plants accordingly. If they must be moved frequently, she can place them on a tray or a board for greater convenience.

Investigating plants can help children notice and appreciate variety, provide them with the opportunity to experience the labor, devotion, and satisfaction involved in gardening, and help them absorb some basic concepts about life processes. But it is a broad topic, and much the same information could be arrived at through a study with a narrower focus, such as a study of a vegetable farm, or with an even narrower focus, a study of the carrot. The teacher must be guided by her own and the children's dispositions in this matter.

Some Key Concepts Related to Plants

Plants are living things and, as such, undergo a cycle of growth, maturation, reproduction, and death.

Plants require the support of water, air, light, and certain nutrients to grow and live.

Plants vary widely in appearance—from trees and bushes to grasses and grain to ferns and mosses to fungi and algae.

Plants and their products are needed by people and animals who would perish without them. Most of our food is of plant origin.

Some Information about Plants for the Teacher

A plant is any member of the vegetable kingdom. Although everything which grows in the ground is a plant, most plants are green.

The roots grow beneath the soil and take in the water and food which the plant needs; they also anchor the plant.

Stems transmit water and food upward and outward through the extremities.

Leaves give excess moisture; when exposed to sunlight, they convey water, carbon dioxide from the air, and nutrients from the soil into the food and plant material essential for growth.

The flower is the part of the plant which is often colored and sometimes scented. In the center of the flower are the most important parts: the stamens, which bear pollen, and the pistil, which is connected to the ovary. These are necessary for the production of seeds and fruit.

When a bee or other insect brings pollen from one flower to another, seeds begin to form in the flower's ovary. Gradually, the ovary grows, the petals fall off the flower, and the ovary is left to grow and ripen.

Every plant has its own kind of fruit. The fruit contains the seeds which can grow into a new plant—if they fall on or are planted in suitable ground. Seeds are inside some fruits and on the outside of others.

A seed contains a tiny plant, food for the plant, and a seed coat for protection.

Some plants are grown primarily for flowers, some for shade and ground cover, and some for food.

Man is dependent upon plants for such foods as fruits and vegetables and wheat to make bread. Meat, milk, and eggs come from animals which in turn feed on plants.

We use plants and their products in a variety of ways—as an energy source (wood, coal), as materials for our homes and clothes (cotton, wood, straw), as decoration, as paper, and as a source of pigments and chemicals.

The lives of many people—and even whole regions—revolve around plants. From the growing of cotton, corn, or coffee to the harvesting of timber or hemp, plants are important to economies.

Buy some plants for the classroom. Identify and examine the leaves and stems. Stimulate children to note how quickly philodendrons spread and grow or to examine different colored coleus leaves. Have ivy in a low hanging pot and set up a responsibility chart for its care. **Some Activities for Children**

Have cacti planted in a soil of sand and earth in a container with good drainage, covered with one-half inch of gravel. Let children touch them, observe the different shapes, notice how little water they need in comparison to other plants; thus, the children will begin to understand how different plants have different needs. *Observation*

Look at *stems* on flowers, green plants, bushes, and trees. Find that some are woody, while others are soft; some are thick, others, thin; some are rough, others, smooth; some are short, others, long.

Display different types of stems in the classroom. Group them. Encourage descriptive words. *Discussion*

Bring in celery. Identify the parts, place in water with food coloring, cut the stem, and look at it with a hand lens to follow the course of the colored water. *Doing*

Collect and examine samples of *leaves* with the children. Note the shapes, vein patterns, and edges. Feel the leaves, front and back. Use a hand lens.

Group leaves according to shape, size, color, and tree leaves as compared to flower leaves. Identify species.

Tape leaves to a table. Cover with paper and make crayon rubbings.

Watch one tree as it develops through the fall, winter, and spring. Make picture charts of the changes.

If there is a fruit tree in the neighborhood, encourage the children to notice it periodically.

Discuss why leaves fall. Do all trees lose their leaves? Find trees which do not.

Bring in many kinds of *flowers* and let the children examine them extensively to see and smell differences.

Group flower samples or pictures of flowers according to color, size, smell, etc.

Show slides of different flowers. Close-up shots can sometimes show parts more clearly than the naked eye.

Dissect flowers and examine with a hand lens. Point out the stamen and the pistil. Discuss the functions of these parts.

Watch bees lighting on flowers. Discuss what they are doing. (They come to get nectar at the bottom of the petals. In reaching for the nectar, they rub pollen off the anthers.)

Talk about what the children like about flowers. Discuss how flowers make you feel. Encourage them to note the colors and smells. Bees are attracted by the same stimuli.

Visit a nursery but go there yourself first. Arrange to go into the greenhouses. Buy seeds, soil, peat moss, and pots.

Bring in many kinds of *seeds*, including nuts, grains, and fruits. Observe. Taste. Feel.

Mix different kinds together. Group into separate piles.

Find different kinds of seeds forming on plants. Note their size, shape, and color.

Soak a lima bean seed in water for about an hour. Open and examine an embryo inside.

Plant large seeds—lima beans, corn, beans, in a glass container filled with cotton balls soaked in water. Watch the formation of the root structure.

Place cuttings of coleus, impatiens, begonia, or torenia in clear glasses of water and watch root formation. Plant the cuttings at different stages and see how much root is required for the plant to survive.

Plant some fast-growing seeds—grass, clover, rye, peas, and beans in several inches of sphagnum moss in a bowl. Moisten. Keep in a dim, warm spot until seeds come up. Then move to the light. Measure and record daily growth.

Watch plants bend toward the light. Turn some but don't turn others. Observe growth and keep a record of it.

Vary conditions of moisture. Watch for different rates of growth.

Plant varieties which take a longer time to sprout, including familiar vegetables and flowers.

Grow a plant which produces *fruit,* such as an ornamental pepper plant, a gourd, or a tomato plant in a large pot. Watch the fruits develop from bud to blossom to fruit.

Open one of the fruits and look at the seeds. Discuss the cycle of seed, plant, flower, fruit, and seed again. These can be seen all at once.

Open several different kinds of fruit—grapefruit, pomegranate, apple, peach, avocado, watermelon. Taste. Smell. Examine the seeds. Can children remember what fruits the seeds are from?

Plant a garden outside.

Some planting hints

Use potting soil from a nursery or make your own from sand, sphagnum moss, and soil.

Choose appropriate containers. Clay pots are excellent, but they lose moisture quickly. Plastic pots retain moisture longer. Peat moss pots may be placed in a garden at a later date. Flats accommodate many seeds.

Plant indoors and transplant at a later date, unless it has already been warm for some days and chances of frost at night are minimal.

Either place the containers in a refrigerator box with a clear cover or, as an alternative, cover the plants with a glass plate or clear plastic sheeting.

Lima beans, corn, carrots, radishes, and sunflowers are a few of the hardier seeds and can survive without meticulous care.

In spring, if you have outdoor space, you may with to start a garden. Dig up the sod (find the worms), dig the ground well to aerate it, and get rid of large rocks. Rake the ground smooth; mark off rows with a stick or handle; water the furrows and sow seeds evenly; moisten the newly planted seeds with a hose or watering can.

Plant seeds which will produce quickly.

Take photographs of the children planting seeds, watching the seeds come up, and transplanting them. Write down stories the children dictate about the seeds and make books.

Activities relating plants to other areas of the curriculum

As children talk about the plant activities, record some of their words and read them to the children later.

These are only suggestions.

Visit a fruit and vegetable stand. Buy vegetables to make soup.

Use vegetables to do printing. Use toothpicks and scraps to make sculptures.

Visit a pumpkin or squash farm; select one vegetable for the class. Roast the seeds; salt and eat.

Visit an apple orchard. Slice, peel, eat, and cook apples. Make applesauce, apple juice, apple pancakes.

Encourage the children to move to music as leaves do in the wind.

Use citrus fruits to make orange juice, lemonade, and fruit salad.

Discuss how important such fruits are for healthy bodies.

Introduce other foods that come from plants.

Have a seed contest with watermelon slices; see who has the most seeds per slice. Let each child estimate how many seeds he has before counting. Let children group seeds in different ways and see that they always have the same number.

In wintertime, put sunflower seeds in an outdoor birdfeeder and then watch for birds.

Make beanbags. Fill material with beans and seeds and sew up the bags. Use beanbags as balance material; a book weighs _____ beanbags.

Glue seeds on top of letters, numbers, and words to make a sign; make seed designs (free form).

Make a collage of flowers and corresponding seeds.

Make a garden mural by spreading a large sheet of paper on the floor and letting children paint together. Or make a mural by letting children cut and paste pictures of flowers, fruits, plants, or any other topic heading on a large sheet of brown paper taped to a wall.

Make a flower arrangement on waxed paper, put another piece on top of it, and iron the two pieces together.

Do potato sculpture with potatoes, toothpicks, and assorted scraps.

Use blades of grass to dip through paint and make designs.

Use long, dry grass for weaving.

View the film "Tomatoes—From Seed to Table" by AIMS Instructional Media, 1970.

Post and discuss at appropriate times the study prints of "Common Fruits" and "Common Vegetables" published by the Society for Visual Education.

A Bibliography of Children's Books on Plants

Books for children about plants should be read throughout the course of the unit, and the children should be encouraged to write or draw their own stories. The following books are recommended:

Adelson, L. *Please Pass the Grass*. New York: David McKay Co., 1960.

Black, I. *Busy Seeds*. New York: Holiday House, 1970.

Buella, C. R. *A Tree Is a Plant*. New York: Thomas Y. Crowell Co., 1960.

Carle, E. *Tiny Seeds*. New York: Thomas Y. Crowell Co., 1970.

Hudlow, Jean. *Eric Plants a Garden*. Chicago: Albert Whitman & Co., 1971.

Krauss, R. *The Carrot Seed*. New York: Harper & Row, 1945.

Lubbell, W. *Green Is for Growing*. Chicago: Rand-McNally, 1964.

Parker, B. *Garden Indoors*. New York: Row, Peterson, & Co., 1944.

Peterson, M., and Peterson, M. *The Story Book of Foods from the Fields*. V. H. Winston & Sons, 1936.

Selsam, M. *Play with Plants*. New York: William Morrow & Co., 1949.

_____. *Seeds and More Seeds*. New York: Harper & Row, 1959.

_____. *The Tomato and Other Fruit Vegetables*. New York: William Morrow & Co., 1970.

_____. *Vegetables from Stems and Leaves*. New York: William Morrow & Co., 1972.

Soucie, Anita Holmes. *Plant Fun: Ten Easy Plants to Grow Indoors*. New York: Four Winds Press, 1974.

Sullivan, G. *Plants to Grow Indoors*. Chicago: Follett Publishing Co., 1969.

Trimby, Elsa. *Mr. Plum's Paradise*. New York: Lothrop, Lee & Shephard, 1977.

Webber, I. *Up Above and Down Below*. Glenview, Illinois: Scott, Foresman and Co., 1943.

Wood, D. *Plants with Seeds*. Chicago: Follett Publishing Co., 1963.

Zion, G. *Plant Sitter*. New York: Harper & Row, 1959.

Where do I go from here?

Green plants are only a beginning. Working with plants can stimulate interest in the earth, soil, worms, animal homes, and rocks. It can lead to a consideration of the role of the farmer, the trucker, the grocer, the cook, and the shopper. It can lead to an appreciation of the principles of supply and demand or of differences in geography and its effect on plant growth. This can lead to the study of children from other lands. What foods do they eat? Certainly, the study of plants can be related to issues of health, ecology, and environmental pollution. Consideration of the ways people use plants will lead to discussions about food, rubber, lumber. And it can go on and on. The alert teacher reflects upon the interests and questions of the children and is guided by these in her planning of classroom activities.

SOIL*

All children respond to digging in the mud.

All children respond immediately to the calming pleasure of digging in the mud, an absorbing activity that frees the mind to ponder questions or

---

*Many of the following ideas related to soil were contributed by Judith B. Hanselman while she was a student at Tufts University.

to take flights of fancy. The progression from simple digging, watering, squeezing, and dripping to the following activities is natural and easy. The teacher should be prepared to follow the children's interests and direct them only when necessary. This involves much thought and preparation on the teacher's part, but the added child involvement and learning are well worth the effort.

Soil is generated through decomposition of rock and organic matter. There are different kinds of soil. Soil is lost through erosion. In some cases, man can control erosion. Man uses the soil directly as do the plants that grow on it. Other animals, birds, and insects use the soil, too.

Some Key Concepts Related to Soil

The earth's outer layer is the crust which is made up of soil and rock. We use the topsoil for growing things in many areas—it is only about twelve inches deep.

Weathering (the break-up of rocks) is caused by the action of air (wind and chemicals in the air), water (rain, freezing water in the cracks in rocks, chemicals in the water, and glaciers), and plants (roots grow in the cracks in rocks and split them further; chemicals are produced by the plant roots).

Soil is produced by the decomposition of rocks, plants, and animal matter.

Already created soil is carried from one place to another by air and water and gravity in the process of erosion. Soil moves from hill to valley and from valley to ocean floor.

The main types of soil, which are classified by particle size, are clay, silt, sand, and gravel.

Loam, with which one gardens, is a combination of silt, sand, and organic matter called humus.

Plants grow in soil when provided with water and light.

Soil is a habitat for many kinds of animal life—ranging in size from single-celled amoebae, which are not visible to the unaided eye, and small insects, which are scarcely visible, to the better known ants, centipedes, and worms. Larger animals, such as chipmunks and woodchucks, may live in larger burrows in the ground.

Adobe bricks can be made out of sandy clay mixed with water and some grass or straw and baked in the sun for two weeks.

Red construction bricks are made of clay that is dried and then baked in kilns at 1600-2000 degrees Farenheit.

Some Background Information for the Teacher*

Take a walk outside the classroom and *collect soil* from different places. Place the soil in box lids or jars and label them. Notice where the soil is replaced by something else, such as concrete or asphalt. What grows in the soil around the school? What would grow in the classroom?

Let children squeeze the soil. Does it stay in a ball? Note that it's made of different sized pieces. Use a hand magnifying lens to examine soil carefully. Separate some of the little and big pieces.

Ask each child to bring a shoebox full of soil from around his house. Display samples on a shelf or table and *compare the soils*. Notice the differences in color (brown, tan, yellow, white, gray) and texture (sticky, clay, sandy, pebbly, crumbly loam). Group samples according to color

Some Activities for Children

---

* This information will help the teacher be better prepared to move in the directions that seem appropriate to the children she is teaching. It is not included to be shared with children as it is.

or texture and label. Add samples of very different soils (sand from the beach, pebbles from a stream bed) if there is not a great deal of variety.

Put various soil samples in suitable containers and *plant* a variety of seeds in different samples. Use clay and sand as two of the types. Make sure there are drain holes in all of the containers. Dandelion seeds or milkweed, acorns (saved, chilled, and soaked), white pine seeds, found in pinecones and only retrievable when the cone is dried and opened up, make good examples. If the pinecones are fresh and haven't been through a winter, then put them in the freezer for a week so they will sprout. Label and, if appropriate for your group, keep a chart of how soon they sprout and measure them as they grow. Their growth should be followed and noted verbally if no chart is made. Notice which ones sprout first as well as those which don't seem to be growing as well.

You might want to *make soil* by breaking up poorly consolidated rocks with a sledgehammer in a box. Some good rocks to use might be the soft red siltstone found in the Connecticut River Valley and the slate, shale, and rotting granite from Massachusetts and Maine. A rock supply store may be able to furnish some sandstone. The rock dust and small chips will look like sand. Add ground-up leaves in order to make soil. The rotten leaves can be ground up in a hand food grinder or between two rocks: one flat and one round. Discuss how this process happens in nature as well as how long it takes. Observe parts of leaves in the samples that were brought from home.

Look for a *humus pile* or piled leaves under bushes or shrubs and investigate them. The leaves will be wet, partially rotten, and dark in color. Observe the worms and insects among them. Natural topics of interest will be the origin of leaves, what is becoming of them, and what things are using the leaves for a home.

When collecting soil from around the school, take along some containers with lids so that the children can bring back part of an ant colony. Keep ants from different hills separate or they will fight and not make colonies. *Make an ant farm*; put two pieces of glass held about one inch apart in a frame. Add soil and pack firmly. Put ants on top of the soil and observe them daily. Are they all working on the tunnels? Are they trying to get to the bottom?

If the children discover worms when looking in the decaying leaves, bring some leaves and worms back in a container. *Make a worm garden*; take a large jar or terrarium and layer soil, sand, and humus. Put the worms and leaves on the top and keep moist. Cover the whole terrarium to keep it dark so that the worms will stay on the upper levels to feed and will be easy to see. Observe and discuss what the worms eat, how they get through the soil, what they do to the soil.

Try to find a place where you can *dig clay*. Ask the local Department of Public Works, a builder, or the building inspector of the town for possible sites. The clay does not have to be fine; the sticky yellow kind will work well. If the clay is too sandy or too sticky, add some commercial clay to it. Work the clay through a screen to remove pebbles and leaves. This reinforces the concept that while the clay is soil, it is mostly of the clay type. Discuss the different types of clay and what would happen if sand and humus were added to it.

Let the children *work with the clay* in any way their imaginations dictate. Discuss with them the uses of clay for dishes, bricks, pipes.

Children will enjoy investigating their worm terrarium day after day.

If the idea of concrete comes up, explain the difference between clay and concrete. If feasible, *make something of concrete*—a miniature road, an edging for a flower bed, a base for some outdoor toy. The mixture (which comes premixed under the trade name "Sakrete") can be stirred in a plastic tub. Try it out yourself first. Be sure to protect your hands with gloves, preferably plastic or rubber coated; otherwise, the skin will become dried out and cracked.

Visit a cement plant. Observe how they make big batches of cement and how they load a cement truck. Or watch a cement truck pour out its load at a building site.

In addition, you will want to look at and read books at the appropriate times. The following list contains some suggestions for children:

A Bibliography of Children's Books on Soil

Bendick, Jeanne. *All around You: A First Look at the World.* New York: McGraw-Hill, 1951.

Darling, L., and Darling, L. *Worms.* New York: William Morris and Co., 1972.

Keen, M. L. *The World Beneath Our Feet; The Story of Soil.* New York: Julian Messner, 1974.

Krauss, R. *The Carrot Seed.* New York: Harper & Row, 1945.

Lauber, Patricia. *Earthworms, Underground Farmers.* Champaign, Ill.: Garrard Publishing Co., 1976.

Parker, B. M. *Soil.* New York: Row-Peterson Co., 1943.

Simon, S. *Discovering What Earthworms Do.* New York: McGraw-McGraw-Hill, 1969.

Stevens, C. *Catch a Cricket.* New York: Young Scott, 1961.

Udry, J. M. *A Tree Is Nice.* New York: Harper & Row, 1956.

Wensberg, K. *Experiences with Living Things.* Boston: Beacon Press, 1966.

Wong, H. H., and Vessel, M. *Our Terrariums.* Reading, Mass.: Addison-Wesley, 1969.

Parker, A. *Terrariums.* New York: Franklin Watts, 1977.

HAIR*

Occasionally, teachers will want to develop more unusual topics, like "hair." One would first think about the relevant information and key concepts. In the interest of brevity, we present only a few suggestions of activities for children to indicate how such a topic might be developed.

Motivating Interest

The initial activity to arouse interest in children may come from the children themselves. A child may comment, "I just got a haircut" or "I have the same color hair as Jonny" or "Why is Becca's hair so curly?" At these times teachers can pick up on the interests of the child and extend his learning experiences as far as time and his interests permit.

In some cases, the teacher will want to initiate the motivating activities. She might place some big, colored pictures of hair on the wall with mirrors placed below. Or she might have on display a group of inexpensive wigs which the children would look at, try on, and talk about. Questions would undoubtedly ensue.

Once introduced, there is no definite pace at which these activities should proceed; nor is there a sequence or schedule. The teacher is aware of children's interests and questions and capitalizes on these as they occur.

Some Activities for Children

Look at each child's hair. Compare lengths, texture, color, straightness. Tape samples of hair on cards and group on a large chart according to these attributes or others.

Cut locks of interested children's hair (with permission from both children and parents). Put the samples into separate little plastic boxes. Children can match the samples in the boxes to their classmates' hair. The teacher may want to put written names or photographs, depending upon the ages of her children, on the bottom of the boxes for self-corrective feedback.

Look at and discuss pictures of hair of people of different races. Discuss what functions hair serves. If both parents and child agree, bleach one hair on a child's head and measure its growth every week. Or find a child with very straight bangs and note where on the child's face the ends fall each week.

Expose a bare arm to cold air. Watch goose pimples arise accompanied by hair sticking up. Discuss the implications of this phenomenon. This experiment may also be done by tickling one another lightly.

Look at and discuss pictures of animals and their hair. What function does hair serve for them? Bring in sheep's wool or horse hair.

With the naked eye and under a microscope, look at a human hair and an animal hair obtained from furs or rugs.† Compare. Place animal skin hair samples from furs or rugs in a cardboard box. Guess by feeling what hair belongs to what animal.

Let children try on wigs and compare the way they look. Take pictures and let children tell how they feel with one hair style or another.

Bring in appropriate equipment and set up a barber shop or beauty salon in the dramatic play area. Use wigs, empty spray containers, and

---

*Some of the following suggestions for activities related to the topic "hair" were contributed by William Salter while a student at Tufts University.

†If a microscope is used, be sure that children understand its use and purpose. Learning Things, Inc., Littleton, Massachusetts 01460 puts out a 25x to 100x "superscope" which may be used by young children.

other equipment in dramatic play. Set hair samples with pins, clips, and rollers. Watch the differences that arise.

Bring in pictures of parents, grandparents, and great-grandparents. How has hair styling changed over time? Discuss balding, differences in old hair and young hair. .

Possible field trip sites include: a men's barber shop, a women's beauty salon, an animal beauty parlor, a zoo (to observe animal hair), a wig factory, a wig shop, or a salon.

Read books: for example, *Straight Hair, Curly Hair* by Augusta Goldin.

When the children no longer seem interested, no longer ask questions **How do I know when to** or participate eagerly in activities, then it's time to stop. The teacher may **stop?** have weeks more of investigation that she wants to pursue, but she must be tuned in to the clues that a topic has run its course with a group of children.

It should be clear that a teacher must observe what the children are do- **EPILOGUE** ing and listen to what they are asking carefully, thoughtfully, constantly. She must be able to recognize—and to accept—the level at which each child is working and allow each to function there for so long as the process is satisfying and productive to him. But when the symptoms of dissatisfaction or boredom appear, she must be there, ready to ask the right questions, to provide the experiences which will let him move on. Teachers must know when to sit back and let the children do their own struggling with a situation. By the same token, they must also know how to intervene when the time for encouragement or stimulation has come. At that point, it is essential to plan: to extend and clarify the children's ideas, to introduce new ideas and information, and to be critic or questioner or resource person in the fullest sense. To fill these roles effectively, the teacher must study the subject and personally investigate and explore the activities and materials to be used with children.

SELECTED REFERENCE MATERIALS ON INTEGRATING ACADEMIC ENVIRONMENT FOR TEACHERS OF YOUNG CHILDREN

The following list contains a few suggestions for reference materials which will provide good background reading for teachers. Some also have illustrations which would be appropriate for children.

Althouse, Rosemary. *Science Experiences for Young Children: Air; Colors; Magnets; Water; Wheels; Food; How We Grow; Pets; Seeds; Senses.* New York: Teachers College Press, 1975.

Baker, S. *The Indoor and Outdoor Grow-It Book.* New York: Random House, 1966.

Blough, G., and Schwartz, J. *Elementary School Science and How to Teach It,* 4th ed. New York: Holt, Rinehart & Winston, 1969.

Brandwein, P. F., and Cooper, E. K. *Concepts in Science—Beginning Level.* New York: Harcourt Brace Jovanovich, 1972.

Carmichael, V. *Curriculum Ideas for Young Children.* Los Angeles: Southern California Association for the Education of Young Children, 1971.

_____. *Science Experiences for Young Children.* Los Angeles: Southern California Association for the Education of Young Children, 1969.

Cobb, V. *Science Experiments You Can Eat.* Philadelphia: J. B. Lippincott, 1972.

Craig, G. *Science for the Elementary School Teacher,* 5th ed. Waltham, Mass.: Blaisdell Publishing Co., 1966.

Hildebrand V. *Introduction to Early Childhood Education.* New York: The Macmillan Co., 1971.

Hone, E., et al. *A Sourcebook for Elementary Science,* 2d ed. New York: Harcourt Brace Jovanovich, 1971.

Ladybird Natural History Book. *Plants and How They Grow.* Loughborough, England: Wills & Hepworth, Ltd. (Available from Merry Thoughts, Inc., Pelham, New York 10803).

Leeper, S.; Dales, R.; Skipper, D.; and Witherspoon, R. *Good Schools for Young Children,* 3d ed. New York; The Macmillan Co., 1974.

Paul, A. *Kids Gardening.* Garden City, N. Y.: Doubleday, 1972.

Paull, Dorothy. *Yesterday I Found . . .* Boulder, Colo.: Mountain View Center for Environmental Education, 1972.

Sargent, B. *The Integrated Day in an American School.* Boston: National Association of Independent Schools, 1970.

Science 5/13 Series. London: McDonald Educational Corp., Schools Council Publications, 1972.

Shuttlesworth, D. *Exploring Nature with Your Child.* New York: Greystone Corp., 1952.

_____. *The Story of Ants.* Garden City, N.Y.: Doubleday, 1959.

Taylor, B. *A Child Goes Forth.* Provo, Utah: Brigham Young University Press, 1972.

Wastridge, E. R., editor. *Nuffield Junior Science: Teacher's Guide 1, Teacher's Guide 2, Plants and Animals.* London: William Collins Sons & Co., 1967.

Wurman, Richard, S., editor. *Yellow Pages of Learning Resources.* Cambridge: The MIT Press, 1972.

Textbooks intended to be used by children of elementary-school age also sometimes provide good illustrations for preschool children as well as ideas for a very simplified presentation which can help the teacher in making her plans. The publishers named below and others have such material available at the kindergarten and first-grade level. (Be sure to get teacher's annotated editions, and remember that they are not to be used by children as textbooks but, rather, by teachers and older children as reference material!)

Allyn & Bacon, Inc., 150 Tremont St., Boston, Mass. 02111. *Exploring Science.*

Ginn and Co., Statler Building, Back Bay P.O. 191, Boston, Mass. 02117. *Science Today and Tomorrow.*

Harper & Row, Publishers, 49 E. Thirty-third St., New York, N.Y. 10016. *The Today's Basic Science Series.*

D. C. Heath & Co., 285 Columbus Ave., Boston, Mass. 02116. *Science for Work and Play.*

Holt, Rinehart & Winston, Inc., 383 Madison Ave., New York, N. Y. 10017. *Understanding Science Series.*

The Macmillan Co., 60 Fifth Ave., New York, N. Y. 10011. *The Science Life Series.*

There are many excellent series, most of them fairly new, which are written for primary-school children to read themselves. These make excellent teachers' references and can be consulted by children with a teacher's help. The illustrations in most of them are very good.

Basic Science Education Series. New York: Harper & Row. Primary level.

Encyclopaedia Britannica True-to-Life Books. Chicago: Encyclopaedia Britannica, Inc.

Golden Library of Knowledge Series. New York: Golden Press.

Golden Nature Guide Series. New York: Simon & Schuster.

How and Why Wonder Books. New York: Grosset & Dunlap.

"Learn About" Series. Racine, Wis.: Whitman Publishing Co.

Let's-Read-and-Find-Out Science Books. New York: Thomas Y. Crowell Co.

My Easy-to-Read True Book Series. New York: Grosset & Dunlap.

Question and Answer Series. New York: Golden Press.

"True Book" Series. Chicago: Children's Press.

Webster Beginner Science Series. New York: McGraw-Hill Book Co.

Nine

Adapting to Learning Problems in the Classroom

Teachers in the natural setting of the classroom have an opportunity and a responsibility to know more about the individual ways in which children learn.

TEACHER ASSESSMENT OF CHILDREN IN THE CLASSROOM

Thus far in this book, most of the material has centered around child development. It has guided the teacher in setting the stage for a program in which the children actively collaborate in deciding what kinds of learning will take place. The children's own discoveries, questions, problem-solving efforts, and striving for mastery have supplied most of the energy and initiative needed to develop a curriculum. Accordingly, teacher and children share responsibility. There is a tacit assumption that if the teacher is a good provider, her well-organized and motivated students will be able to select their own "work." Their aggregate experiences will provide a foundation for more formal "academic" work.

For some children, learning at school is not so easy. In some cases, the child's basic constitutional endowment—the ways in which his body and mind are put together and organized—makes active collaboration with the teacher in a regular class much more difficult. In other cases, experiences prior to school have not been able to fully support development and learning. In either case, the teacher must take a much larger share of the responsibility for deciding what the child needs to learn and how to arrange a special environment in which he can do so effectively. Assessing learning problems in preschoolers is not an easy task, for their behavior is not yet very differentiated; they are vulnerable to temporary changes and emotional upsets. In addition, goals and expectations are not usually clearly stated (e.g., in contrast to reading or writing achievement). More customarily, the most overriding global objective is based on the premise that children will "learn how to learn."

Preschoolers may seem to have "problems" that are really just transitory phases of their normal development. Such developmental peaks and valleys are best taken at face value. Too much alarm over such phases creates anxiety which may add to the problem. This section of the book presents a way of understanding children's "abilities and

When is a problem a problem?

179

All children reverse letters when they are first learning.

disabilities" that helps to broaden the development framework used in other sections of the book. Remember that young children develop unevenly—in spurts—and that they may reflect temporary changes in their environment and family situation quickly. A problem is a problem only if it continues over a significant length of time, resists casual efforts to help, or impedes the child in his daily functioning. For instance, most children reverse letters while they are first learning to write; this is not cause for alarm. But a child who continues to reverse letters after he has had coaching and practice and who is also awkward and poorly coordinated may indeed be in for difficulty in "academic" learning. A preschool teacher may be the first person to notice these characteristics. Her job is to observe accurately, ask questions, plan strategy, and test out various hypotheses. If the problem still exists, it is often helpful to discuss it with a consultant or supervisor. Such a person may have further suggestions to try out or may help the teacher know when it is time to make a referral for a professional evaluation.

A Framework for Observations

Most teachers have impressionistic ideas of what their children can and cannot do. John is "good at puzzles"; Cindy "knows her numbers." It is more helpful (and more interesting) to be able to say, "John can do an eight-piece interlocking puzzle. He uses a visual searching method rather than trial-and-error." "Cindy counts by rote to twenty but is just beginning to have a real sense of what numbers mean. She can 'show me two blocks' but beyond four, she just jumbles a bunch together and looks questioningly." One must be a shrewd and disciplined observer to gather such details about each child in a group of fifteen or twenty children. If you spend several hours a day for several months or a year with a given group of children, you have all that's needed to be a good, accurate observer; you may simply need a framework for organizing what to look for and what you have found out (i.e., a way of thinking about children more than a specific list of things to do or tests to give).

You may set aside ten minutes a day to try out some tasks with individual children or small groups. Or, keep a good outline form or checklist in your pocket so you can easily make note of your observations. Every few weeks you can check to see what big gaps there are in your information and make a special effort to gather observations in those areas.

Children's behavior can be categorized under several major headings, which are artificially separate since they are really intertwined. But by observing discrete functions, you can assess "target" behavior and plan an individual program rather than using a "shotgun" approach.

Here is an outline of major headings:

1. *Motor Development*—How the child manages his body and what he can do with it—fine and gross motor coordination and related factors.

2. *Language Development*—How the child communicates with others; his understanding and use of words and ability to express himself.

3. *Cognitive Development*—How the child understands and organizes his world—what he "knows."

4. *Social-Emotional Development*—How the child is able to interact with other people; how he handles and expresses his feelings and emotions, his play, and his personal habits.

In the next section of this chapter these major headings will be broken down into component parts with suggestions for curriculum and tasks to help a teacher chart how far a child has progressed. The final section is a discussion of individualized teaching or "tutorial" work as a way to stimulate children's strength and remedy deficits.

MOTOR DEVELOPMENT

One of the first things you may find out about a child is how he moves and handles his body. This is basic to what he can *do*. Children with significant motor coordination problems have a harder time with many things. They are likely to develop an image of themselves as incompetent and to have trouble in social situations. Problems in coordination are often related to problems in perception, which in turn, influence school learning.

To assess motor development, you can observe the child in numerous real-life situations as well as some that you can easily "stage."

Gross Motor Skills

Try to get an overall impression of the skill and comfort with which a child accomplishes common activities, whether or not he seems to know his own limits, and whether he dares to try things within a realistic range. One has to separate *preferences* for certain types of activities from *active avoidance* patterns (e.g., Is this a child who can climb well on the jungle gym but who would rather work with crayons and paper at the table? Or is this a child who feels frightened and insecure about trying things with his body and therefore makes up excuses for spending all his time in sedentary pursuits or as an onlooker?).

Useful activities for observation: How does the child get into and out of a chair at the table? Watch how he adjusts its position if it's not close enough to a table. Does he get down, walk around, and give it a push as a toddler might; or can he skillfully hitch himself forward in the chair to just the right position?) How does he negotiate stairs? Is he always holding the railing or needing a hand to hold? Can he go up and down with *parallel steppage* —with both feet resting on every step—or *alternating steppage*—one foot to each step with continuing motion forward? Can he jump easily from the last step? The next to the last step? Is this an enjoyable accomplishment? A painful concentrated effort?

Is his gait wide-based and cautious like a toddler's, with upper body weight poorly balanced, or can he move with assurance, swinging arms and body weight to match the rhythm of his feet? Can he stand on one foot? Skip? Jump over a puddle or beyond a chalk line? How well does he throw and catch a ball? Can he kick a ball that is rolled to him?

Laterality and Directionality

The sense of sidedness within one's own body and the ability to project this sense or image onto objects perceived outside one's self is essential for learning to read. Does the child have a definite hand preference? Does he know which are his right and left hands and use the labels correctly? Can he indicate which hand he likes to use for drawing? Eating? If handedness does not become clearly established, a child is more likely to have problems with skilled motor movements and learning to read.

Does the child use the two hands interchangeably depending upon where an object is for which he is reaching; or does he rearrange the environment in order to use his preferred hand for skilled tasks? When first acquiring a new skill, the child may only be able to do it with the preferred hand. For simple tasks, once the skill is established, he may again do it more casually with whichever hand happens to be more convenient at the moment. Pouring juice is an example of a skill which might go through these stages; drawing, writing, or throwing would normally be done only with the dominant hand. Therefore, one may have to observe a range of activities in order to draw conclusions.

The presentation of activities is important for efficient observation of handedness. For instance, if you repeatedly pass a juice pitcher to the child so that the handle is pointed at his midline, with which hand does he reach for it? Is it always the same one? If you hand him a crayon, pair of scissors, or a spoon, which hand is used? Which hand is used for building with one-inch cubes or other small objects? Can he transfer buttons or raisins from one container to another with either hand? Does it require more concentration and more time with the hand that is not preferred? Is a pincer grasp well developed in both hands or only with the preferred hand?

Can the child follow directions such as "Touch your left knee" or "Touch your right ear with your right hand"? Does he kick a ball with the foot on the same side as his hand preference? If you demonstrate use of a paper telescope and then hand it to him, does he use the eye on the same side as his hand and foot preference? (Some children who do not have a consistent hand/eye and footedness have learning and perceptual difficulties. *Others do not.* This is just one of a number of clues worth noting).

Can the child play simple follow-the-leader or mirroring games which involve touching various body parts, raising arms or legs in symmetrical patterns, moving just one arm or leg, working on the diagonal (i.e., raising one arm while lowering the other)? Observe how easily the child performs these skills. Can he isolate one part for a movement while the other remains still, or does the other creep up and reflect the movement in the other side of the body? Can he imitate your movement in one smooth motion while watching you, or must he keep checking visually and comparing his position with yours?

The child needs not only specific skills that involve use of his body but *Body in Space* also an integrated way of coordinating all his parts in relation to each other and within his environment. Some children seem awkward and clumsy; they are always bumping into things and people, knocking down or spilling things. Others seem quick and agile, as though they enjoy using their bodies and know where all their parts are, how much room they need in which to move, how to anticipate the moves of others. One gets a general impression of his sense of his body in space merely from observing a child in common classroom activities. More specific activities for observation follow.

Arrange loose floor tiles or squares of construction paper in a pattern on the floor and ask the children to walk across the room stepping only on the designated squares. What happens when obstacles are in the path? Does it take concentration to get past a doorsill, a wrinkle in the rug, several chairs or play objects on the floor? Walk on a sidewalk without stepping on the cracks. Build an obstacle course out of classroom equipment and watch how children negotiate it. Include such things as a table to crawl under, two chairs placed close enough so that children have to turn sideways to squeeze through, a broom handle or yardstick across two chairs to crawl under, a small obstacle to step or jump over. Can the child follow directions, such as "Stand in front of, behind, on top of, or beside the chair?"

Skill in using the hands and ability to coordinate hands and eyes are **Fine Motor Skills** important in daily living and essential in most school activities. Schoolwork demands the ability to manipulate tools—pencils, scissors, paste, math and science materials. Has the child developed a precise pincer grasp and fine finger control? The following are the usual steps a child goes through in developing this skill:

1. A full-arm sweeping motion involving one whole side of the body
2. A fisted grasp from the elbow
3. A full-palm grasp
4. A precise opposition of thumb and index finger, the so-called pincer grasp that distinguished man from other animals

Opportunities to observe: How does the child manipulate zippers or buttons, pick up a small juice cup, pick up an M & M or a raisin, pick up one-inch cubes or small building blocks, select beans from peas in a dish of collage materials, separate blue buttons from red buttons, hold a crayon or pencil, manipulate scissors, place pieces in a puzzle, hold a spoon or a fork?

Many of the tasks and accomplishments discussed in this whole section **Perceptual-Motor** on motor development assume that the child's senses are intact and that **Development** he can coordinate not just his hands or his body but also his *perception* of the world. To select blue buttons from red, one's eyes must help one's brain receive accurate information about size, color, relative position, and distance. This information must be coded and signals sent to the muscles of the fingers and arms. Some children *see* well but cannot relate what they see to what their bodies must do. Much of school learning, indeed much of *living*, involves reliable coordination of visual information with motor actions. "Pour your juice up to the blue line." "Cut out a circle and paste it on your paper." "Draw a circle around three red balloons." "Draw a line between the pictures of things that belong together."

Whenever a child has trouble accomplishing a motor task, it is good to ask whether something goes wrong with the kind of information his muscles are receiving. To test this out, set up situations in which the child's *perception* can be evaluated separately from his ability to carry out a direction demanding a motor response. Instead of doing a puzzle that involves placing various geometric figures in their places, ask the child to tell you whether two shapes you point to are "just the same." Or say, "Put your hand on the square." "Tell me to stop pouring when the juice is up to the blue line." These tasks also involve a certain degree of conceptual development: *knowing* about squares, lines, colors. Most areas of skill are overlapping—which is exactly why such careful observation is necessary.

SPEECH AND LANGUAGE DEVELOPMENT

A child's ability to communicate in words strongly influences his social development and his success in school. Most of the facts and concepts to be learned have to be conveyed in words. Most of the interactions through which learning occurs take place in language exchanges. *Speech* usually refers to the technical aspects of sound production, voice tone, quality and rhythm, and vocabulary development. *Language* is the more complex process of putting ideas and words together in grammatically correct fashion to understand and communicate to others. Speech and language development depend upon several factors: the child's intelligence; the amount of appropriate language stimulation in his environment; his ability to hear; his ability to *discriminate* accurately language sounds from the background of all the other sounds in his environment; his ability to *perceive* these language sounds in the brain (i.e., to attach meaning, to *structure* them into units or words), to *associate* these words with prior experiences, and to *store* them for future use; and his ability to recall these units or symbolic representations of experience, group them in new combinations, and send messages to the small muscles of mouth and throat in order to *communicate*.

The process by which children learn language and the difficulties they have with it are complex and mysterious. We can observe only a child's mouth, lips, and tongue, listen to his sounds, and observe his behavior to check his understanding. When he has problems with language, we cannot easily tell just where he gets off the track. By contrast, when a child has difficulty doing a puzzle, we can watch and analyze exactly how far he gets and what his difficulties are. We can demonstrate and coach and even guide his hand. We can try it ourselves to gain a better sense of what skills are involved. In language, there are many fewer guideposts. There is no good simple way to check what happens inside a child who hears something and cannot reproduce it, one who gets the order of words mixed up in a sentence or cannot remember tomorrow what he seemed to know today, or one who can use words and sentences spontaneously but cannot respond to the demand to answer a question.

In addition, emotional factors may complicate the whole process of acquiring and using language. For instance, a child may be so shy that he worries his teachers by never talking in school, yet he chatters to his mother on the way home.

The language environment we create in most preschool classrooms—similar to that of a noisy cocktail party—is helpful to the normally functioning child and the child who is simply a little slow or who has lacked stimulation. To the child with specific difficulties in any aspect of the complex task of making sense out of sound, the enriched preschool environment is frequently detrimental. It may increase his burden by overloading his capacity to discriminate, structure, and associate sounds without offering any concrete assistance. It also may increase the teacher's difficulty in accurately observing the language skills of individual children. The presence of a great deal of background noise and the normal interruptions of an active classroom make it hard to hear the fine details of what children say and equally hard to remember the particular deficits long enough to record them. (These are *exactly* the difficulties many children experience). Keeping a checklist and pencil nearby helps. The following is a beginning list of things to listen for and try out:

Vocabulary

How extensive is the basic working vocabulary of the child? Does it include all of the main parts of speech—verbs, nouns, pronouns? Does the child seem to enjoy trying out new words and phrases? Lotto cards and picture dictionaries are good tools for testing vocabulary. Be sure at first that the child understands the idea of pointing to or covering up a certain picture. Then it is possible to test his receptive vocabulary by asking him to "Show me the . . ." or "Point to the . . ." Later one can ask him "What is this called?" or "What is the name for this?" so that he has to be able to use the word correctly in order to answer. By mixing these types of activities, you also quickly discover how fast the child is able to acquire new words.

Articulation

The clarity with which the child can pronounce individual sounds also is noticed easily in everyday speech. Normally, children do not pronounce all the sounds in the English language correctly until age six or even later. Vowel sounds come first, followed by most of the simple consonants formed in the front of the mouth with lips, tongue, teeth: *m, d, b, p, t*. Sounds such as *f, s,* and *v* are more difficult, and combinations such as *th, br, bl,* and *sl* normally are perfected later still. It takes a sharp ear to note exact difficulties: is it an omission ("bock" for block) or a substitution ("bwock" for block)? Since people of any age tend to make articulation errors with greater frequency when they are tired, excited, rushed or tense, note whether there is a pattern to the occurrence of the error. That is, does the error occur when the child is under pressure to make a contribution at circle time but not during relaxed sandbox play? An articulation problem is often a fine motor problem. For whatever reason, the child simply cannot handle his tongue.

Language Processing

Because teachers have most of their contact with children who do speak normally, their attention to children's language often has been confined to vocabulary and articulation. But recent studies have added to our awareness and understanding of language processing problems which are often at the root of serious behavior and learning difficulties. Since a language problem may precede a reading problem, there often are significant clues in the preschool years as well as numerous opportunities to assist a child before a problem becomes serious.

Language difficulties can be divided into *receptive* and *expressive* areas. Receptive language comes first. If you have been around a toddler just learning to talk, you know he understands things that he can't yet use in his own speech. He needs a store of words to draw from before he can talk.

Receptive Language

Having a serious *receptive language* problem is similar to being deposited suddenly in a foreign country where you do not know any of the language. Nothing is understandable. In fact, you may not even be able to sort out the rapidly produced sounds to know when a word or sentence ends or a new one begins. Gradually, you realize that a group of sounds often go together and happen at the same time that someone reaches for your hand in a greeting. You have discovered the word "hello." For some children, everything they hear is equally difficult to fathom. They may even appear to be deaf, retarded, or psychotic because they are so unable to rely on language.

Assessing a receptive language problem is not easy. You may see a child who does best in situations where he knows a reliable routine and everything is orderly, who gets upset and confused when things are noisy or disorganized. He may seem to understand you very well and to be quite intelligent—sometimes—yet act as though he doesn't hear or isn't very smart at other times. Try simplifying your own words and illustrating what you say with a gesture or a dramatic mannerism. Test out whether he can follow a direction equally well without gestures or other visual clues. Notice whether he seems to watch you very carefully as you talk; children with receptive problems often become skilled at picking up meaning from contextual and visual clues.

Is it deafness?

Distinguishing between a severe receptive language problem and deafness is exceedingly difficult. The final decision must be made by an experienced audiologist or language specialist. The casual observer often may think a child with a receptive language problem is deaf, while parents and teachers who know him best will have observations to prove that he hears even soft sounds in many situations. The task is to distinguish whether sound gets in but cannot be "coded" into something meaningful. In such cases, a child often will start to ignore most language sounds while he responds well to concrete environmental sounds of similar loudness. When mother says, "Go open the door and see if the newspaper is here," he looks at her in confusion. He has heard a glob of undifferentiated noise yet he knows she wants something because of her expression. But if the paperboy comes and makes even a soft noise on the porch, the child knows what that means through his own repeated experience. He goes to get the paper on his own initiative. A child like this may actually reject a hearing aid; it raises the level of his confusion but does not help him organize the incoming noise.

Auditory memory

Auditory memory is part of receptive language since one has to hold onto sounds long enough to do something with them. To check auditory memory, try a "listening game." For example, say some numbers and see if the child can say them just the same way. Try three numbers that are not in sequence, such as three-six-four. If the child is successful, try a series of four numbers, then five until failure occurs. The same game can be played with nonsense words and then sentences. The child may be able to repeat, "The cat ran up the tree" (six words) but not, "The big, black cat ran up the tall, green tree" (ten words). Be systematic about the numbers or sentences used because it will help *you*, the observer, to remember what the child is able to do.

Following commands is another simple check on auditory memory. "Close the door" is easier for the child to remember than "Close the door and then bring me the book." "Put your juice cup on the tray, throw your napkin away, and then get your mat for rest" is still more difficult at first attempt but is an example of a routine that a child may know so well that the verbal command no longer tests auditory memory.

Having an *expressive language* problem is similar to having a word **Expressive Language** "on the tip of your tongue." Chances are that the harder you try to remember it, the less likely you are to do so. Later, when the pressure is removed, the word will "pop into your mind" (or onto your tongue). It was there all the time, but you couldn't withdraw it from storage.

When the difficulty is at the expressive level, a child will be able to respond to things you say and directions you give. He may give very concrete one-word responses. But when the situation calls for something more abstract or more complicated or when there is pressure to talk fast or answer questions, he either will withdraw and remove himself from the situation or show signs of intense frustration.

An important clue is that his language lags noticeably behind his other development. From many other factors, you will be certain that he is intelligent.

There are all degrees of language processing problems, ranging from something so minor that it shows up only when a child is tired or under pressure to something that is quite incapacitating. A receptive problem is generally more serious than an expressive one. When language doesn't get in, the child is totally dependent upon his own observational capacities to make sense of his experiences and relationships. When viewed in this context, difficulties with articulation and vocabulary are relatively minor.

Language is intertwined intimately with most aspects of cognitive **COGNITIVE** development, thus making it difficult to separate the two even for pur- **DEVELOPMENT** poses of discussion. Cognitive or conceptual development refers to what the child *knows.* Some schools expect a child to "know his colors," a few letters of the alphabet, and his name and address before entering kindergarten. However, remembering by rote and truly *knowing* are really very different. A child who rattles off the days of the week may not know that Saturday and Sunday are weekend days or be able to tell you what comes after Wednesday. Least of all does he know that days of the week are a way of ordering time.

For later success in school, the child's total cognitive framework is what matters. Whether he knows squares from circles is eventually not important; rather, his ability to select and apply these specific concepts in order to solve problems he has never met before is.

Kamii,* who has studied the application of Piaget's principles to a **A Cognitive Framework** preschool curriculum, mentions several broad areas of cognitive

*Constance Kamii, "A Sketch of a Piaget-Derived Preschool Curriculum Developed by the Ypsilanti Early Education Program," in *History and Theory of Early Childhood Education,* ed. Samuel J. Braun and Esther P. Edwards (Worthington, Ohio: Charles A. Jones Publishers, 1972) pp. 295-313.

development in which the child must acquire competence. She outlines the following:

Physical knowledge: The observable properties of objects and physical phenomena. The child must develop "a repertoire of actions he can perform on objects." He must become curious about what might happen and learn to make predictions.

Logico-mathematical knowledge: The relationships among objects, including ideas of classification, seriation, and numbers.

The structuring of space and time: Concepts of size, shape, and time sequences; the ability to deal flexibly with these concepts.

Social knowledge: Social conventions and sensitivity to situations that require certain behavior.

Representation: The representation of things and ideas (symbols), as through imitation, and the use of arbitrary signs—most especially language.

Assessment Activities

In a quick assessment of cognitive development, one pays attention to the child's general fund of knowledge as well as to his execution of specific school tasks. This assessment assumes that if you tap an isolated skill, you get some sense of the child's overall cognitive functioning. Does he have general information about the world around him: names of objects, the materials things are made out of, where common things come from? Does he know names of shapes, colors, relative sizes, body parts, denominations of money, periods of time? Can he sort and categorize what he sees? For instance, if you present him with a collection of common household objects, can he pick out the *round things*, the *blue things*, the *things to eat*, the *things we wear*, the *smallest thing*, the *heaviest thing*? Each of these concepts involves knowing a whole class of things that go together and knowing what attributes include or exclude something. Some quick measures of conceptual development are to ask the child to place an object, such as a block or a ball, *on, under, on top of, beside,* or *behind* a chair. Arrange a collection of varying cardboard shapes (or the familiar parquetry or attribute blocks) that also vary in size and color. Ask him to show you the "large blue square" or the "small red triangle." If this proves too difficult, remove one attribute (such as size) entirely and give him only two to deal with. Place a pile of small blocks on the table and ask him to give you two blocks or six blocks. Divide the blocks into two piles with an uneven number and ask him, "Are these piles the same?" and then, "Which pile has more blocks?" Ask a few standard questions: How old are you? When is your birthday? What day is today? What state do you live in? Which is larger, a horse or a dog? How many wheels does a car have? In winter, is it cold or hot? Is a baby old or young? What is two plus four? What kind of vegetables do you like?

Notice how dependent nearly every one of these tasks is on knowing (i.e., remembering and applying) a concept based on language. It is difficult, though not impossible, to assess some aspects of cognitive development without relying on language. Children's spontaneous block building reveals concepts of size, weight, and space. Completion of some kinds of puzzle tasks may help. Placing colored blocks in a certain sequence begun by the teacher may be useful (such as alternating red and blue or one yellow and two green). Perhaps this is the place to underline the fact that children who have not had stimulating experiences with language or those for whom English is not the primary language may have difficulty with many of the tasks outlined in this entire section. They may not have an inherent disability, but they still do have a "problem" in our schools!

Thus far in this chapter, we have considered areas of development in which there are some specific tasks and accomplishments which can be observed. Yet the child's emotional-social behavior, his play, and his personal habits bind these skills and knowledge together and represent his attempt to integrate them into a functioning whole. His behavior in relationship to other human beings, his capacity to ask for and appropriately use help, and his ability to initiate play represent his capacity to occupy his time; they represent how he has glued together the interrelated capacities so that they stick properly. Teacher observations about social and emotional development present some difficulty. The teacher must be aware of self (e.g., whether she likes or dislikes a particular child, whether she and the child rub each other the wrong way or communicate unusually well with one another may actually say as much about the teacher and the classroom as they do about the child). Nevertheless, there are some useful observational guideposts.

Erikson, in *Identity and the Life Cycle*, has provided us with a useful framework for understanding children's emotional and social development. From his stages of psychosocial development in the human life cycle, the earliest three—*trust, autonomy,* and *initiative*—are helpful landmarks to an understanding and assessment of the development of preschoolers.

SOCIAL AND EMOTIONAL DEVELOPMENT

Being able to ask for and accept help is important.

The stages lead from one to another and influence the success with which each succeeding social and emotional task can be coped. However, all children—and indeed all of us—have similar dilemmas as reflected in Erikson's formulations of the stages of our emotional life and personal relationships. Remnants of those aspects which were not fully resolved arise again at times of stress. For this reason, teachers need to be sensitive to themselves and their personal reactions as they attempt to evaluate children.

Trust

Basic trust is established in infancy. It encompasses an expectancy that needs will be fulfilled, that closeness and intimacy will be safe and rewarding, that physical comfort will be available when needed, that one belongs to someone else, that frustrations can be mutually regulated, and that new experiences are interesting to explore and the unknown is not unduly fearsome.

Observational Guideposts in Basic Trust

Relationships

Notice the child's way of dealing with new situations—people, materials, places—and his way of asking for and accepting help when it is needed. Does he act as though people and the environment are predictable and reliable? How much help does he need to determine this predictability? In other words, must the teacher take extra precautions to prepare him for her comings and goings, for changes in routine and room arrangements? Is he interested in trying out new materials and activities? A new classroom area or arrangement? Is a walk or trip an interesting adventure or a stimulus for whining and clinging to the teacher? What happens when he gets stuck on a difficult activity? Can he ask for an appropriate amount of help and accept it if offered? When routines change or unexpected things happen, can he tolerantly give them a try? When he gets hurt or is tired or sad, can he accept some comfort and recuperate adequately? When unfamiliar adults are present in the classroom, can he get acquainted comfortably or does he cling to his familiar teacher and withdraw? Most "experienced" preschoolers can do most of these things with comfort. They like school and take a lot on faith, having decided their teacher is reliable and the environment basically predictable. But all children will have periods of illness, fatigue, or momentary preoccupation when it is more difficult to answer these questions affirmatively. What should concern the teacher is the child with trouble in a number of these areas that lasts over a period of time in spite of appropriate help and whose pervading characteristics are clinging, whining, and reluctance to enter situations.

Play

The infant explores the properties of simple objects in his environment. He mouths and feels things. His own fingers and toes provide playthings. He picks things up and drops them. Eventually, he discovers that something dropped out of sight is not gone forever.

Personal habits

The infant is totally dependent on others for his care. During this period, his rhythms of eating, sleeping, and eliminating become established. Gradually, he learns to recognize the inner feelings that signal his needs and to read the environmental cues that those needs are to be met—footsteps, kitchen sounds, and so forth.

Autonomy

The toddler and the two year old are busy establishing their autonomy. This stage encompasses the discovery that one's behavior is one's own to control. The child experiments with his strength, his capacity to say "yes" or "no" and to make decisions; he learns how much he can control significant others. He holds things and then lets go, hoards and collects, piles things up, carries them around, puts them in their proper places. He wants to do things for himself and has giant struggles with his

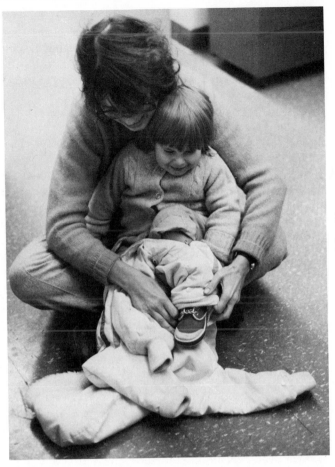

The toddler needs help with clothing.

caretakers when he must give in and accept help, guidance, or control from others. He learns to make choices, to "boss things around," and to gain gradual independence.

Children who are still working on establishing their own autonomy *Observational* use a great deal of "no," "mine," "do-it-myself" in both words and ac- *Guideposts in* tions. With autonomy successfully resolved, they can make appropriate *Autonomy* distinctions. Does the child have a sense of what is his and a willingness **Relationships** to defend it, coupled with an openness to let others have their due? Does he collect materials for the sake of having them and then not use them? Is he more concerned about who has how much of what materials than about how the material can be used? Can he decide what he wants to do and work on it, or is he wandering about unable to make choices? Has he a sense of mastery and accomplishment that need not always be measured by hearing someone else say "good boy"? Can he show pride when he has done something well? Can he move through a routine and respond to the "rules of the house" without engaging in a control struggle over changing activities or taking directions from others? When he can't get his own way, does he throw a tantrum and continue to resist, sulk, or withdraw? Most of these characteristics are expected to a certain degree in two year olds, but when they still pervade a four year old's behavior and relationships, they occupy too much of his and his teacher's time. They also impede learning because they interfere with the give-and-take relationship necessary for teacher and child to work together on tasks.

Play

The child's play represents an integration of his cognitive and his social/emotional development. The toddler pushes a toy car on the floor. He is doing something active. He may name the object and relate it to the family car, but he probably won't go much farther. He does not have elaborate ideas about other cars nor fantasy stories of adventures in which the car is involved. He is content to push it back and forth repetitively and alone. If other children are present, each needs his own car. They cannot wait or share.

The three year old has elaborated his play. The car is going somewhere. It meets other cars. People ride in it. It needs a road and a garage. What happens to the car is still very much tied to the child's own immediate experience, but when other children join in the play, there is some interest in each other's cars and fleeting cooperation. But each child may have his own ideas about what the car is doing, where it's going, and who's riding in it. Other children can move in and out of the play without causing great notice or disruption, but each child is still bound up in his own ideas and experience.

Personal habits

The child's independence in taking care of his own personal needs is of great importance to both teacher and family. The manner in which a child takes care of his toilet needs, dresses himself, and handles himself in meal-time, snack-time, and rest-time situations tells a lot about him. With the advent of more and more day care, a greater number of teachers and caregivers are involved in these events with children for a significant part of the day. Even in half-day programs, children have snacks, put on outdoor clothing, and take care of their bathroom needs. In addition, when teachers and parents communicate freely about the child's home and school behavior, it is often not "academics" so much as these "habits" or "training" areas that parents of younger preschoolers want to talk about.

The toddler has just achieved enough physical coordination to begin to be toilet trained. He needs help with clothing, reminders, a schedule, and someone to take most of the responsibility off his shoulders.

He feeds himself except for cutting meat and eating difficult things such as soup. He begins to eat most of what the family eats. At school, he chews cookies, manages to hold a sturdy cup but he does have spills and may not know the limits of his own capacity. He takes his shoes and socks and jacket off but can't do much of his own dressing. He adapts as a grown-up helps him into clothing. He may pull up a zipper if it is started for him.

The three year old has achieved more skill and independence. He is toilet trained but has an occasional accident. He handles himself without much direct help at meal and snack time. He is learning to pour his own juice. He dresses himself except for articles of clothing that have difficult fasteners. He can put on shoes and socks but can't tie the shoes.

Initiative

Children who trust adults and have established their own separateness and independence are ready to imagine new social roles and intellectual tasks. They fantasize about the active persons they wish to be and the varied roles they wish they could take on. They like to imagine what is possible. They develop friendships among both children and adults—people outside the immediate family become significant to them. They begin to have a life of their own which parents and teacher do not fully

Three year olds can handle themselves without much direct help at snack time.

share. They develop skills and work toward their potential capacities. They reach out with language, beginning to learn about more abstract things removed from their immediate concrete experience and products of their own imagination. They become independent and responsible for their own behavior a large part of the time. They develop an identification with persons of the same sex and an awareness of differences in what males and females can be and do. As an aftermath, they conclude they will need more growth and learning before they can realize some of their fantasies.

Four and five year olds can usually work and play independently for *Observational* considerable periods of time. They enjoy acquiring skills and using *Guideposts in* language as a tool. Can the child handle his body with comfort and ease *Initiative* to move about his school environment and work on activities? Does he **Relationships** enjoy being active and trying out complicated physical tasks? Does he explore and look for new things to do? Will he offer to help out with a hard task and with a sense of his own competence to take care of things? Is he developing concepts—expressed in language—which help him compare himself and his world to things not directly experienced? Does he demonstrate an imagination and an enjoyment of his fantasy life? Does he gain satisfaction working and playing with other children, collaborate with them to accomplish things, and differentiate roles in play? In dramatic play, does he try out roles of people he admires and wants to be like? Is he aware of and able to respond to the feelings of others? Can he comfort another child and share another child's pleasure in an accomplishment?

Four and five year olds need other children and have new ideas to **Play** keep the play going. For example, in his car play, elaborate accessories begin to appear—a street with signals and signs, tunnels, and toll

As they develop, children begin to have a life of their own that adults do not fully share.

bridges. The car has a destination, a place which the child may never really have visited, and persons with different roles who help it get there—policemen, gas station men, etc. The type of car is one the child *wishes* he might have. Other children are essential. They may have different roles in the play, each of which is important and probably has to be replaced if one child leaves. There is some agreement as to what the play is about. If the car has to go all the way to New York, a conspiracy may develop: "Let's make it have a flat tire along the way." Such adventures can become elaborate, and in the process, various children try out different roles.

Observe children's play carefully over a period of time. When assessing a particular child, note what interests and themes recur and especially whether there is a shift or elaboration of interests as time passes. Note what roles the child habitually takes on in play and whether he always insistently casts others in particular repetitive roles. Normally, children will express interests and preferences in their play but will also be flexible enough to try other ideas or shift roles occasionally.

Personal habits

Four and five year olds are fairly independent about taking care of their personal needs. Eating, dressing, sleeping, and eliminating fit into a routine that goes along reasonably smoothly. They need help and support, but the struggles of toddlerhood have been left behind. They manage most of their own clothing and even learn to tie shoes. They take responsibility for coming in from play to take care of their own bathroom needs. They become interested in "helping" parents and teacher with chores—preparing food, cleaning up, putting things away, choosing clothes. They imagine being like the grown-up who does these things and may take on more than they really can manage.

Children's difficulties in habit training areas usually have more to do with their sense of competence and independence and their wish to become more separate beings from their parents. There are normal fluctuations due to fatigue and temporary illness or the birth of siblings, but beyond these, continued failure to develop independence and regression in habits already developed suggest a need to remain little and be cared for as a much younger child.

The teacher's assessment task is a difficult one. Children with problems in learning and behavior do not always make it easy to decide what factors are primary. Difficulties in social and emotional development can slow down or grossly distort a child's progress in acquiring skills required for school performance. On the other hand, specific difficulties in handling stimuli, coordinating eyes and hands, or acquiring language can stand in the way of the development of independence and a sense of autonomy and mastery. Therefore, it is essential for teachers to gain an impression of the whole child into which to fit the more detailed observations of his specific learning capacities.

INTERRELATEDNESS OF PROBLEMS

PROVIDING FOR SPECIAL NEEDS

The Teacher's Role

If one goes to the trouble to observe and record the strengths and deficits of individual children, it follows that a curriculum and instructional arrangements should be tailor-made to provide for individualized needs that have been discovered. Within a given classroom of fifteen or twenty children, there frequently will be several who need work on auditory/language activities, a few with a weakness in the perceptual-motor area, and so forth. The teacher may feel helpless in meeting all these needs individually yet find she can group two or three children together. At first, she may wonder how she could possibly devote time to this. Yet closer analysis may show that the child who is distractible and has perceptual-motor difficulties really *takes* her time (often not very constructively) by resisting the standard fare, demanding attention, pulling her away from other children, disrupting others, or destroying their work. Were the teacher to plan and organize a program around his particular area of difficulty, she might give him not only skills but also the sense of belonging and confidence which he needs in order to become more cooperative and pleasant to have around. Chances are that two or three other children also could use the same kind of assistance but simply are less obtrusive in their expression of need.

There is a more subtle deterrent to individualized teaching than the concern for lack of time: many teachers feel very unsure about whether it is "good" for such young children to be assigned structured work or to be expected to produce a finished product. They feel that a child will not like anything he has not self-selected and that he will not like the *teacher* who makes him do something he didn't choose. A teacher often expresses this fear of being intrusive and disrespectful of children's feelings. What is forgotten is that children *feel good* about the sense of mastery which they may gain from struggling with something difficult and learning how to deal with it. For the child who easily can gain this feeling within the routine of regular classroom events, such arguments are unnecessary. The child with a deficit, however, may only experience repeated failures and frustrations.

Another dilemma often is expressed by the teacher in her lack of recognition that it may be necessary and essential to be "bossy" (i.e., to convey to the child a sense of knowing what is good for him). Such a stance takes a certain missionary zeal that rubs against the grain for some teachers who believe the child's individual rights to self-discovery are of primary importance. However, good individualized teaching remains faithful to the core understandings of a good developmental approach; children develop at different rates and in different ways but, generally, they follow an expectable unfolding sequence. Children on one end of a continuum move along smoothly, step by step. They seem to teach themselves and use the teacher as a resource and interested collaborator. Children on the other end of the continuum have a struggle with everything; they miss out on certain basic building blocks for later skills. Their difficulties are compounded the longer they go unattended, and serious emotional problems soon may be added to their learning problems. Most of all, such children generally do *not* take the initiative to even approach the very activities they most need in order to acquire skills. Teachers can confuse the concept of "readiness" with waiting too long.

Arranging the Environment

Certain basic provisions within the physical environment of the classroom will remove from the teacher's shoulders much of the burden for individualizing the curriculum. For example, children who have trouble selecting an appropriate level and amount of stimulation from an enriched preschool classroom are helped when the noise level and the visual distractions are reduced. Some children are helped by facing toward a blank wall rather than out into the classroom. Others need a colored paper placemat to define their work area. A work table that is partitioned off to make a little cubicle or an "office" helps the child to focus his attention and keep his materials from getting mixed up; it also makes it easier for the teacher to provide him quickly with some special work—a simpler puzzle, an envelope of shapes to sort, a special record to listen to. A cardboard table-top divider (two pieces of slotted heavy cardboard assembled in criss-cross fashion) quickly makes four small individual work spaces which one teacher can supervise while still keeping an eye on the rest of the class.

Being sure one activity is put away before another one is laid out reduces visual distraction and gives children a sense of the beginnings and endings to activities. Removing noisy pounding toys and musical instruments from some areas of the room or declaring them "off limits" during part of the day helps lower the general noise level for children with an auditory distraction problem or for those who simply need help concentrating on language development. A rug or sponge mat in the building block and wheel toy area markedly reduces the sharp sounds of wood banging on hard floor. Using classroom furniture to make many small, partially enclosed areas and cut down on large, open running spaces tends to enhance an atmosphere of concentration and privacy.

Choosing Individualized Remedial Activities

The problem areas and assessment tasks outlined in the first part of this chapter are the very same areas and activities that will be useful in individualized tutorial work in the classroom. They draw upon the teacher's knowledge of development, ability to observe, and upon the materials available in nearly every preschool room. Though some teachers may custom design a game or puzzle to help a particular child's problem, the basic concept usually will not deviate very far from what is already standard fare in classrooms. The teacher may decide she needs a set of puzzles made from cardboard that enable her to present a sequence of puzzle tasks in graded order of difficulty: one-piece, two-piece, and four-piece noninterlocking ones to build up toward a two-piece interlocking one, and so forth. But puzzles as such are not new; all classrooms have them, and most children enjoy them. The teacher's observational ability and her willingness to *expect* the child to do a given piece of carefully chosen work makes the difference. If she finds herself saying, "He can't do puzzles," she must examine how and when he gets stuck and program a series of progressively more difficult puzzle experiences that back up several steps before his stumbling point. They must lead him gradually, with a series of small successes up to or around his point of difficulty and help him go on. That is what good tutorial work is all about.

Elaborate materials are not necessary. A sense of how to arrange things in order of difficulty is the basis for good tutoring, combined with a fund of ideas for alternate ways to get at a difficulty. For instance, if a child has trouble with eye-hand coordination, as manifested by an inability to copy shapes, the teacher may first try giving him plenty of individual practice in copying the shapes she wants him to learn. But she may find that the shapes need to be larger; that stencils of cardboard allow the child to trace the raised edge with his finger and get the *feeling* of the shape in his muscles; that he needs to draw the shape with his index finger in wet sand or clay where his muscles will feel the resistence of the plastic medium; that he can "fill in the dots" if she makes a page of free-form or geometric shapes drawn in dotted lines*; or that he needs to play lotto with shapes and have lots of experience with matching and sorting shapes where the primary skill is visual recognition and little fine coordination is demanded. Knowing how to back up several steps along the developmental sequence of learning to draw shapes as well as knowing how to move sideways into parallel skills is an example of the essence of a tutorial approach.

When a learning problem has been identified in a young child, a teacher who has not had specialized training may feel overwhelmed by the difficulty of the task that lies ahead. She may feel that only someone with background in working with special-needs children could know what to do or where to start. Or, she may feel terribly frustrated when a child seems to be making only very slow progress. In these situations, it is possible to lose one's bearings, to push a child too hard or not hard enough.

A thorough knowledge of the developmental sequence and an ability to outline *behavioral objectives* will ease these problems. We have

Setting Concrete Objectives

---

*Children with special problems sometimes need work with teacher-made patterns. These have their place, but this should not be taken as license to introduce predrawn bunny rabbits or Halloween pumpkins in an art program! That is an entirely different matter. For further thoughts on this subject, refer to chapter two.

already referred to the importance of knowing what steps or subskills are involved in the development of a specific skill or way of behaving. What distinguishes a special educator from a "regular" teacher is the ability to outline for each child a series of concrete minigoals that are manageable and reachable, and that allow the educator to objectively observe achievement. To return to an earlier example, when a child is having problems in learning it is not sufficient to say, "I want John to be good at puzzles by the end of the year," or, "Cindy needs to know her numbers before she goes to first grade." "Knowing numbers" and "doing puzzles well" are far too global. Using these amorphous goals, a teacher may never have analyzed the task a child is performing or carefully observed where the child gets stuck. The child then experiences a vague feeling of not living up to the teacher's expectations, yet never clearly knows what the expectations are. The teacher feels frustrated because the vague, globally stated goal may be two years in the future for John or Cindy.

Restated in terms of behavioral objectives, becoming "good at puzzles" might sound like this:

> **General goal:** By December, every time he tries John will be able to complete an eight-piece, noninterlocking puzzle while working alone at a table without teacher assistance.
> **Specific behavioral objectives:**
> 1. John will first learn to select a puzzle, remove all the pieces, and place them face up on the table.
> 2. By Thanksgiving, John will be able to try each piece individually by trial and error and respond to a teacher's verbal coaching.
> 3. Next, John will be able to work independently on a puzzle, asking for help when he needs it.
> 4. By Christmas vacation, John will complete the puzzle while working alone without teacher help.

Clearly, even after reaching these four specific behavioral objectives, John would still have a long way to go to be "good at puzzles." New general objectives could be outlined, however, and might include completing a simple four-piece, interlocking puzzle in which each piece represents a distinct part of the whole picture—a whole arm or the wheel of a truck, for example. Subsequent general objectives would include working with interlocking puzzles in which the shapes of the pieces do not relate to the subject of the picture and in which the pieces are more numerous, smaller, and increasingly similar in shape.

By outlining a general goal and several achievable minigoals, or behavioral objectives, both teacher and child acquire checkpoints for achievement. The teacher has many opportunities to say, "Good boy, John, you did it," and John begins to feel like a competent person where puzzles are concerned.

A behavioral objective normally includes three parts: (1) a statement about a specific observable behavior (completing an eight-piece, noninterlocking puzzle), (2) a statement about the conditions under which the behavior will take place (while working alone at a table without teacher assistance), and (3) a statement about the criterion for success (every time he tries). While daily working objectives do not need to be so elaborately spelled out, one must keep the three elements in mind in order to establish realistic goals for a given child and to evaluate progress.

Most teachers find that when they have been able to analyze a task and outline developmentally appropriate, concrete minigoals, children are almost always able to achieve these goals in a reasonable period of time. Their sense of mastery and the teacher's feeling of competence are both enhanced. Many "behavior problems" wither away when these achievable goals are outlined.

Behavioral objectives are also effective for dealing with children's social and emotional difficulties. Global goals such as "getting along with other children," "making friends," "behaving well at circle time," or "developing a good self-image" are too vague and long-term. An understanding of component steps and appropriate developmental expectations is necessary. For instance, to "get along with other children," a child needs play skills, interests, a capacity to sit still and wait for a turn, the ability to be in physical proximity to others without feeling vulnerable or defensive, the ability to state likes, dislikes, and needs verbally or through some other mutually understood means, and so forth. When a child cannot "get along with other children," a teacher must be able to observe the current baseline behavior: what the child is able to do and exactly what happens when things go wrong. Perhaps Melissa grabs toys from others. She needs a concept of possession, awareness of the concrete meaning of "taking turns," words that will work for her ("I had it first," "May I have it next?" "When you're done, can I have it?") an ability to wait for an answer after having used these words, and an ability to select another toy or amusement while waiting her turn. She also may need a way to summon a teacher's assistance in negotiating with other children. These subskills can be outlined so that both Melissa and the other children know what she is working on and so that her teacher can chart her progress.

Setting Goals for Social and Emotional Growth

Behavioral objectives and ideas about positive reinforcement or "behavior modification" often go hand in hand. Both concepts can arouse irrational reactions in adults who do not fully understand them. As a management strategy for children with behavior and learning difficulties, positive reinforcement is quite useful.

Reinforcing achievement

Basic assumptions in reinforcement theory are that (1) merely by being together, people influence each other's behavior all the time, and (2) behavior that is followed by attention, reaction, or a reward is likely to be repeated, whereas behavior that elicits no response from the environment is likely to diminish. For most children, the attention of the teacher is a powerful motivating force. By looking or not looking, by moving closer, or farther away, by saying "good boy" or "stop that," a teacher reinforces (influences) behavior all day long. Those who defend the use of reinforcement simply say that when a teacher understands how her behavior affects particular children and when she carefully analyzes what children need to learn, she can use her behavior to skillfully influence what children's behavior will be likely to increase or decrease.

Let's go back to "being good at puzzles." We will assume that John wants to gain his teacher's attention. To help get him interested in puzzles, she may decide that she will go toward him and speak to him whenever he is in the puzzle table area. If he sits down with a puzzle, she will sit beside him. When he correctly places a piece in the puzzle, she will comment, "nice work," "good boy," or "you did it;" or she may pat his shoulder or arm or even give him a hug if she knows that physical contact means more to him than words. Having carefully observed what he can already do with puzzles (his baseline behavior), she already knows how much independent work he can tolerate and how much frustration he can bear before reinforcement is provided. Perhaps she needs to place a puzzle piece halfway into it's space so that a small movement will finish the job and give her an immediate opportunity to say "good boy." perhaps John has reached the point where, if she helps him with placing the first four pieces so the field is narrowed down, John himself can finish the last four while she merely watches. She can then give him a hug for a completed piece of work. This is the kind of reward system that sensitive caregivers use continually with little children. By saying that we are using "positive reinforcement," we are simply agreeing to bring contingencies more into our consciousness and control. Provided the tasks for children to accomplish are developmentally appropriate and broken into manageable steps, there need be nothing artificial, intrusive, or overly controlling about the use of reinforcement. *Setting appropriate behavioral objectives is the first step.*

CASE EXAMPLE

Bobby, who was almost five, had been in a four-year-old class all year in school. He was interested in letters and numbers, had good language skills, and, in fact, seemed quite bright. But all year he had struggled to learn to write his name even though he had been recognizing it and could say the letters out loud for over a year. He had trouble remembering which hand to use to hold the crayon, and sometimes he started at the right side of the paper instead of the left. Sometimes his *b*s looked more like *p*s or *d*s.

When he was still having the same trouble in March and getting angry with himself about it, his teacher decided it was time to take a closer look. She watched Bobby carefully for a few days and began to notice that he often bumped into things around the classroom. Outdoors when the class was climbing and sliding, Bobby often held up the line because it took him longer to execute the activity. When some of the children started a follow-the-leader game walking along a log and climbing over a box, Bobby was the first one to fall off. Indoors, he avoided most of the table activities, such as cutting and pasting, or always asked the teacher for a lot of help. She had never realized this before; he made such interesting conversation about what he was doing that she had enjoyed helping him. He kept talking all the time and got others to do a lot of his work for him. When that wasn't successful he whined and complained that he was tired.

When Bobby's teacher began to put these observations together, she decided to try out a few special tasks with him. One day she asked him, "Which hand do you like best to color with?" Before Bobby could answer, he looked puzzled, glanced first at one hand and then the other, and, finally, hesitantly, held up his right hand. The teacher asked, "Do you think that's the same hand you use for a fork when you're eating?" Bobby wasn't sure. By now the teacher had watched long enough to be pretty certain that Bobby was more proficient when he did use his right hand. "Bobby, do you want to try an experiment? Let me watch you write your name with this hand (right) and then with that one (left). Let's see which one works best." Bobby was interested, and, indeed, he did a better job with his right hand. He could see the difference when he looked at the two attempts on his paper.

The teacher suggested, "Let's try something for a few days to help you remember which hand works best. I'm going to tie this green ribbon on your right wrist every morning when you come in. When you do things with crayons and scissors, see if you can remember to use the hand with the ribbon on it."

This attempt worked pretty well, but still Bobby started his name anywhere on the paper and often ran out of room; the letters were still sometimes upside down and sometimes backwards. "Here's another thing for us to try, Bobby. I'm going to put this green X over here on the left side of your paper. That says, 'Go.' Start there when you write your name." In the meantime, outside on the playground, the teacher helped Bobby throw, catch, and kick a ball, reminding him to "use the green ribbon side." At music time, she had the class do "Looby Lou" ("You put your right hand in, you put your right hand out").

For six weeks, they worked together on many little activities to help Bobby become more aware of the sides of his body and the fact that his right hand was more skilled. He liked working on these things with her and sometimes came to remind her if she forgot to give him his green ribbon in the morning. Still, he was getting letters mixed up, and still, he was the slowest person at active games on the playground.

Since the end of the year was approaching, the teacher decided it was time to talk to Bobby's parents about her observations. She described her six weeks' effort to help Bobby with his problems and what kind of difficulties he might have later in school if his difficulties should continue. She told them she felt they needed to see someone who was more experienced with these problems than she. The parents were very concerned about the problem and about wanting Bobby to do well in school. They agreed to call the local public school guidance department and ask where to go for an evaluation of Bobby's problem. Meanwhile, the teacher agreed to continue working with Bobby for the remaining six weeks and made some suggestions to the parents about things to try at home. They decided to talk together again before school closed.

SUMMARY

Because children are individuals, they grow in different ways and at different rates, some with great ease and others with rough spots along the way. Teachers of preschoolers see behavior in the raw. Most developing problems have early clues which a shrewd observer can distinguish. Assessing a possible problem is like solving a mystery—looking for clues, discarding the false ones, figuring out what relates to what, trying out various hypotheses. Proposing a possible solution to the question of what's wrong or who the culprit is helps to suggest a plan of action. In contrast to much of early childhood education, which invites the child to self-discovery in a cafeteria array of goodies, good individualized teaching provides the particular nutrients in just the amounts needed to help make up for specific deficiencies.

SELECTED REFERENCE MATERIALS ON LEARNING PROBLEMS FOR TEACHERS OF YOUNG CHILDREN

Baldwin, Victor L.; Fredericks, H. D.; and Brodsky, Gerry. *Isn't It Time He Outgrew This.* Springfield,Ill. Charles C Thomas; 1973.

Barnard, Kathryn E., and Powell, Marcene L. *Teaching the Mentally Retarded: A Family Care Approach.* St. Louis: C. V. Mosby, 1972.

Barry, Hortense. *The Young Aphasic Child: Evaluation and Training.* Washington, D.C.: Alexander Graham Bell Association for the Deaf, 1961.

Bentley, William G. *Learning to Move and Moving to Learn.* New York: Citation Press, 1970.

Bereiter, Carl, and Engelmann, Siegfried. *Teaching Disadvantaged Children in the Preschool.* Englewood Cliffs, N. J.: Prentice-Hall, Inc., 1966.

Blank, Marion. *Teaching Learning in the Preschool.* Columbus, Ohio: Charles E. Merrill Publishing Co., 1973.

Bleck, Eugene E., and Nagel, Donald. *Physically Handicapped Children: A Medical Atlas for Teachers.* New York: Grune & Stratton, 1975.

Braley, William, et al. *Daily Sensorimotor Training Activities: A Handbook for Teachers and Parents of Preschool Children.* Freeport, N. Y.: Educational Activities, Inc., 1968.

Braun, Samuel J., and Lasher, Miriam G. *Are You Ready to Mainstream? Helping Preschoolers with Behavior and Learning Problems.* Columbus, Ohio: Charles E. Merrill Publishing Co., 1978.

Brutten, Milton; Richardson, Silvia O.; and Nangel, Charles. *Something's Wrong with My Child: A Parent's Book about Children with Learning Disabilities.* New York: Harcourt Brace Jovanovich, 1973.

Cameron, Constance. *A Different Drum.* Englewood Cliffs, N. J.: Prentice-Hall, Inc., 1973.

Cratty, Bryant. *Movement, Perception, and Thought: The Use of Total Body Movement as a Learning Modality.* Palo Alto, Calif.: Peek Publications, 1969.

Croft, Doreen J., and Hess, Robert D. *An Activities Handbook for Teachers of Young Children.* Boston: Houghton Mifflin Co., 1972.

Eisenson, Jon. *Is Your Child's Speech Normal?* Reading, Mass.: Addison-Wesley Publishing Co., 1976.

Engel, Mary. *Psychopathology in Childhood.* New York: Harcourt Brace Jovanovich, 1972.

Erikson, Erik H. *Identity and the Life Cycle.* Psychological Issues Monograph #1. New York: International Universities Press, 1959.

Fallen, Nancy H. *Young Children with Special Needs.* Columbus, Ohio: Charles E. Merrill Publishing Co., 1978.

Finnie, Nancie. *Handling the Young Cerebral Palsied Child at Home.* New York: E. P. Dutton & Co., 1968.

Getting Your Baby Ready to Talk; A Home Study Plan for Infant Language Development. Los Angeles: The John Tracy Clinic, 1968.

Glasscote, Raymond, and Fishman, Michael, et al. *Mental Health Programs for Preschool Children.* Washington, D.C.: Joint Information Service, 1974.

Golik, Margaret. "Strictly for Parents: A Parent's Guide to Learning Problems." Quebec: Quebec Association for Children with Learning Disability, 1969.

Gordon, Ira J. *Baby Learning through Baby Play: A Parent's Guide to the First Two Years.* New York: St. Martin's Press, 1970.

Gordon, Ira J.; Guinagh, Barry; and Jester, R. Emile. *Child Learning through Child Play: Learning Activities for Two- and Three-Year-Olds.* New York: St. Martin's Press, 1972.

Granato, Sam, and Krone, Elizabeth. *Day Care: Serving Children with Special Needs.* Washington, D.C.: United States Department of Health, Education and Welfare, 1972.

Groht, Mildred A. *Natural Language for Deaf Children.* Washington, D.C.: Alexander Graham Bell Association for the Deaf. The Volta Bureau, 1958.

Hainstock, Elizabeth. *Teaching Montessori in the Home.* New York: Random House, 1968.

Hamblin, Robert, and Buckholdt, David, et al. *The Humanization Processes: A Social Behavioral Analysis of Children's Problems.* New York: Wiley-Interscience, 1971.

Heisler, Verda. *A Handicapped Child in the Family.* New York: Grune & Stratton, 1972.

Humphrey, James H., and Sullivan, Dorothy D. *Teaching Slow Learners through Active Games.* Springfield, Ill.: Charles C Thomas, 1970.

Itard, Jean-Marc-Gaspard. *The Wild Boy of Aveyron.* New York: Appleton-Century-Crofts, 1962.

Jedrysek, Elanora, et al. *Psychoeducational Evaluation of the Preschool Child.* New York: Grune & Stratton, 1972.

Jones, Beverly, and Hart, Jane. *Where's Hannah: A Handbook for Parents and Teachers of Children with Learning Disorders.* New York: Hart Publishing, 1968.

Karnes, Merle B. *Helping Young Children Develop Language Skills: A Book of Activities.* Arlington, Va.: The Council for Exceptional Children, 1968.

Kastein, Shulamith, and Trace, Barbara. *The Birth of Language: The Case History of a Nonverbal Child.* Springfield, Ill.: Charles C Thomas, 1966.

Lagos, Jorge C. *Seizures, Epilepsy and Your Child: A Handbook for Parents, Teachers and Epileptics of All Ages.* New York: Harper & Row. 1974.

Lee, Laura L.; Koenigsknecht, Roy A.; and Mulhern, Susan T. *Interactive Language Development Teaching.* Evanston, Ill.: Northwestern University Press, 1975.

Lehane, Stephen. *Help Your Baby Learn: 100 Piaget-Based Activities for the First Two Years of Life.* Englewood Cliffs, N. J.: Prentice-Hall, Inc. 1976.

Levy, Hanine. *The Baby Exercise Book.* New York: Pantheon Books, Random House, 1973.

Meyers, Elizabeth S.; Ball, Helen H.; and Crutchfield, Marjorie. *The Kindergarten Teacher's Handbook.* Los Angeles: Gramercy Press, 1973.

Mindel, Eugene D., and McCay, Vernon. *They Grow in Silence: The Deaf Child and His Family.* Silver Spring, Md.: National Association of the Deaf, 1971.

Orem, R. C. *Montessori and the Special Child.* New York: Capricorn Books, 1970.

Painter, Genevieve. *Teach Your Baby.* New York: Simon & Schuster, 1971.

Park, Clara Claiborne. *The Siege: The First Eight Years of an Autistic Child.* Boston: Little, Brown & Co., 1967.

Ross, Dorothea M., and Ross, Sheila A. *Hyperactivity.* New York: John Wiley & Sons, 1976.

Ross, Alan O. *Learning Disability: The Unrealized Potential.* New York: McGraw-Hill, 1977.

Rutter, Michael. *Helping Troubled Children.* New York: Plenum Press, 1975.

Safer, Daniel J., and Allen, Richard P. *Hyperactive Children*. Baltimore: University Park Press, 1976.

Safford, Philip L. *Teaching Young Children with Special Needs*. St. Louis: C. V. Mosby, 1978.

Sharp, Evelyn. *Thinking Is Child's Play*. New York: E. P. Dutton & Co., 1969.

Shaw, Charles R. *When Your Child Needs Help*. New York: William Morrow & Co., 1972.

Spivack, George, and Shure, Myna. *Social Adjustment of Young Children: A Cognitive Approach to Solving Real Life Problems*. New York: Jossey-Bass, 1973.

Stewart, Mark A., and Olds, Sally Wendkos. *Raising A Hyperactive Child*. New York: Harper & Row, Publishers, 1973.

Taetzsch, Sandra Zeitlin, and Taetzsch, Lynn. *Preschool Games and Activities*. Belmont, Calif.: Fearon Publishers, 1974.

United States Department of Health, Education, and Welfare. *Responding to Individual Needs in Head Start*. DHEW publication no. (OHD) 75-1075. Washington, DC.: United States Department of Health, Education, and Welfare, 1975.

Weikart, David P.; Rogers, Linda; and Adcock, Carolyn. *The Cognitively Oriented Curriculum*. Washington, D.C.: National Association for the Education of Young Children, 1971.

Weiss, Helen Ginandes, and Weiss, Martin S. *Home Is A Learning Place*. Boston: Little, Brown & Co., 1976.

Wing, Lorna. *Autistic Children*. New York: Brunner/Mazel, Publishers, 1972.

Wood, Mary M. *Developmental Therapy*. Baltimore: University Park Press, 1975.

Index

Activities, learning from everyday, 131–32
Alderson, B., 62
Alexander boxes, 35
Alphabet letters, 146–47
Anderson, H.C., 64
Animals in the classroom, 126–30
    introducing, 127
    planned or spontaneous experiences
        with, 127–30
    provision of experiences with pets, 126
    suitable, 127
Art
    appropriate materials, 22–29
    collages, 34–35
    conceptual freedom and, 18–19, 20
    "dictated," 20
    early representational stage, 21–22
    importance of, 18–19
    individual differences and, 39–42
        children's preferences and, 41–42
        frustration, 40–41
    and "junk," 33
    motivation and, 36–38
    praise, 38–39
    printing, 29–31
    scribbling, 20–21
    sculpture, 31–33
    significance of, 17
    straws, 33–34
    undesirable methods of teaching, 19
Ashton-Warner, S., 67
Attribute blocks, 142

Audio-visual aids, 164–65
Auditory memory, 186–87
Autoharp, 49–50

Balet, J., 70
Ballatine, W., 63
Bartók, Béla, 53
Behavioral objectives, 198–200
Bernstein, L., 52
Bishop, C., 64
Block play, 116–20
    props for, 118–19
    rules for, 118
    storage and display of blocks, 117–18
    teacher's role in, 120
    types of, 117
    visual skills and, 119–20
    vocabulary building and, 119
Body in space, 183
Book making, 66
Branley, F., 67
Brown, M.W., 57, 62, 73, 144
Bruner, J., 1
Buckley, H., 57, 62, 63
Burton, V., 64

Calendars, 154
Card games, 142
Carle, E., 59
Carpentry, 120–26
    arrangement of the working area
        for, 123–24

Carpentry *(continued)*
  choosing nails, 122–23
  insuring success in, 124–26
  selection of materials for, 120–22
  skills to be learned, 120
  storage of materials, 122
  tools, 122
  values of, 120
Carson, A., 62
Carson, D., 62
Cedarbaum, S., 67
Chalk, kindergarten, 23
Childhood, importance of understanding, 3–9
Chomsky, C., 66
Clocks, 153
Cognitive development, 187–89
  areas of, 187–88
  assessment of, 188–89
Cohen, M., 69
Collages, 34–35
Comparison activities, 141
Conceptual freedom in art, 18–19, 20
Conklin, G., 67
Conservation of number and volume, 149
Conversation, 145
Cook, B., 145
Cooking, 111–16
  anticipating problems, 114–15
  hidden learnings, 113
  materials for, 115
  presenting the activities, 113–14
  things to try, 115–16
  using natural foods, 112–13
Cooney, B., 73
Counting activities, 152
Crayons, 23
Cuisenaire rods, 150
Curriculum
  spiral, 114
  teacher's role in, 106–8
  variety in, 105–8. *See also* Animals in the
    classroom; Block play; Carpentry;
    Cooking; Water play
Cymbals, 49

Dalgliesh, A., 67
Dancing. *See* Rhythmic movement
d'Aulaire, E., 67
d'Aulaire, I., 67
Deafness, 186
Death, books relating to, 72–74
Dietz, B.W., 53

Direct experience, 160
Directionality, 182
Dominoes, 152
Drums, 48–49
Dunn, P., 65

Early representational stage in art, 21–22
Engvilk, W., 62
Environment, what children need to know
    about, 58. *See also* Field trips; Hair;
    Plants; Soil
Erikson, E., 67, 189
Ets, M.H., 63

Fassler, J., 72, 73
Felt-tip pens, 23
Field trips, 160–62
Finger painting, 28–29
Fisher, A., 65
Flack, M., 58, 145
Fontane, T., 73
"Free" or "scrounged" materials, 130–31
Frustration, 5, 40–41
  in art experiences, 40–41

Gag, W., 61
Games
  board, 151–52
  commercial, 143
Geoboards, 154
Glues. *See* Pastes
Goldin, A., 175
Goldreich, G., 71
Gongs, 49
Grimm's fairy tales, 63
Grollman, E.H., 73
Group discussions, 162–64
Grouping activities, 140–41

Hair, 174–75
  activities related to, 174–75
  motivating interest in, 174
Hefler, R., 65
Herzka, H., 62
Hoban, R., 63
Hoban, T., 65
Hoffman, P., 69

Justus, M., 65

Kamii, C., 187
Keats, E.J., 69
Kellogg, R., 21

Kesselman, W., 70
Kessler, E., 62
Kessler, L., 62
Klein, N., 71
Krasilovsky, P., 62
Krauss, R., 62
Kunhardt, D., 59

Lanes, S., 57, 64
Langstaff, J., 70
Language development, 137–38, 184–87
    articulation, 185
    expressive language problems, 187
    language processing, 185–87
    in the preschool program, 137–38
    receptive language problems, 186–87
    vocabulary, 185
Larrick, N., 61
Lasker, J., 71
Laterality, 182
Lear, E., 64
Learning, cognitive-developmental point of
        view of, 4–5
Learning problems. *See also* Cognitive develop-
        ment; Language development; Motor
        development; Social-emotional
        development
    case example, 200–201
    interrelatedness of, 195
    observation and, 180–81
    providing for special needs, 195–210. *See
        also* Teacher's role
Leavitt, E., 51
Lenski, L., 62
Leonni, L., 64
Lewis, C., 51
Lewis, R., 65
Lewis, S., 59
Lexau, J., 69
Lindgren, A., 67
Listening, as activity for developing skills,
        143–44. *See also* Music
Literature
    bibliography of, 75–104
        animals and creatures, 76–78
        bibliographies of multiethnic books, 78
        books about children's literature, 78–80
        children in school, 80–81
        children's concerns, fears, and special
            needs, 81–83
        close relationships: family and
            friends, 83–85

    concepts and academic preliminaries,
        85–88
    good stories with real plots, 88–89
    humor and nonsense, 89–90
    international friends, 90–93
    minority groups, 93–96
    nature and science, 96–97
    poetry, songs, and verse, 98–99
    religion and holidays, 99–100
    sex role diversity, 100–101
    the urban community, 101–3
children's ages and, 61–68
    five year olds, 64–68
    four year olds, 63–64
    three year olds, 62–63
    two year olds, 61–62
fantasy in, 59–60
finding good, 57–58
key to publishers, 104
language and illustrations in, 59
presentation of, 58–59
social issues and, 60–61
sources for media books, 103
sources for reviews, lists, and
    evaluations, 103

McCord, D., 65
McLeod, E., 64
Matching activities, 140, 142
Measuring activities, 152–54
Measuring cups and spoons, 153
Mendoza, G., 64
Merriam, E., 71
Minarik, E., 65
Minority groups in books, 68–70
Motivation, 5, 36–38, 42, 137
    presentation of topics and, 37–38
    self-, 36
Motor development, 181–84
    fine motor skills, 183
    gross motor skills, 181–83
    perceptual-motor development, 183–84
Munavi, B., 59
Music
    instruments, 48–50
    learning to listen, 45–46
    singing, 46–48. *See also* Songs
    sources for, 55

Names, children's, 147–48
Ness, E., 69
Niles, J.J., 53
Numbering activities, 150–52

Oil-base pastels, 23
Olatunji, M.B., 53
O'Neil, M., 67
One parent homes, books about, 72
Ordering/sequencing activities, 142

Paints (poster or tempera), 26–28
    brushes, 27
    containers, 26
    tips for using, 27
Paper, 24–26
    activities for use of, 26
    construction, 25
    finger paint, 25
    manila, 25
    newsprint, 25
    salvage or remnant, 25–26
    shape, 26
    size, 24–25, 26
Parenting, 10–11
Parents and the school, 9–12
Parish, P., 67
Part, T., 53
Parquetry blocks, 154
Pastes, 23–24
    commercial, 24
    homemade, 23
    white all-purpose glue, 24
Paston, E., 62
Payne, E., 63
Perception and motor skills, 183–84
Perrine, M., 67, 70
Peterson, H., 67
Piper, W., 61
Planning, 158–66. *See also* Field trips; Group
        discussions.
    methods of, 159
    need for, 158
    resource people and, 159
Plants, 166–70
    activities related to, 165
    activities related to other curriculum
        areas, 169
    books about, 170
    hints for, 168–169
    information about, 166–67
Play, 2–3, 192, 193–94
    problem solving and, 2
    as research, 3
    role of, 1–3
    teachers and, 2–3
Pocket Songs, 49
Potter, B., 57, 63, 64

Praise, 38–39
Printing, 29–31
    thing, 30–31
    vegetable, 29–30
Psaltery, 49

Reading activities, 144–49
Reinforcement, 199–200
Resonator bars, 49
Rey, H., 58, 63
Rhythmic movement, 50–53
    direction and control of, 52
    dramatic play and music and, 51–52
    environments for, 50–51
    selecting music for, 52–53
Riddles and jokes, 146
Rorkham, A., 62

Sage, J., 63
Scales, 152–53
Scarry, R., 62
Scissors, 24
Scott, H., 69
Scribbling, 20–21
    materials for, 21
    as nonverbal self-expression, 21
    stages in, 21
Sculpture, 31–33
    box, 32
    manipulative modeling materials, 31–32
    other bases, 32
    wire, 32–33
Segal, G., 71
Self-confidence and art, 19
Self-expression and art, 18–19
Sendak, M., 57, 64
Serfazo, M., 65
Dr. Seuss, 63, 64
Sex-role typing in books, 70–72
Shay, A., 67
Shulevitz, U., 62
Skills, academic
    activities for developing, 39–44
    auditory discrimination, 140
    classification, 140
    isolating, 139
    language development, 137–38
    mathematical/geometric activities, 149–52
    in the preschool program, 135–36, 137
    reading/writing activities, 144–49
    seriation, 140
    stages in learning, 136–37
    visual discrimination, 140

Skills, motor, 149, 181–83
    fine, 183
    gross, 181–83
Slobodkina, E., 63
Social-emotional development, 189–95
    autonomy, 190–92
    initiative, 192–95
    personal habits, 192, 194–95
    play, 192, 193–94
    trust, 190
Soil, 170–73
    activities related to, 171–73
    books about, 173
    important information about, 171
Songs, 46–48
    encouraging children's participation, 47
    introducing, 46–47
    games, 47
    types, of, 46–48
    use of folk, 53
Speech development. *See* Language
    development
Steptoe, J., 69
Stevenson, R.L., 65, 70
Stick and gum materials, 29
Storage of art materials, 35–36
Stories
    dramatization of, 145
    reading and telling, 145
    writing, 148
Straws, 33–34
Sylva, K., 2

Tape measures, yardsticks, rulers, 153
Tapes, 28
Teacher's role, 3–9, 157–58, 195–200
    arranging the environment, 196
    assessing learning problems, 195–96
    choosing remedial activities, 197
    cognitive-developmental point of
        view, 4–5
    levels of expectation, 6–7
    recognition and understanding of children
        as "children," 3–4
    relationships with parents, 10–11
    setting goals for social-emotional growth,
        199–200
    setting objectives for children with
        learning problems, 197–99
Thermometers, 153
Three-dimensional materials, 29
Tom-toms, 48–49
Tracing activities, 140
Tresselt, A., 73
Triangle, 49
Typewriter, primary, 148

Udry, J., 69
Unifix cubes, 150
Unit blocks, 150

Viorst, J., 72–73

Waber, B., 64
Water play, 108–11
    making arrangements for, 108–10
    related learning in, 110–11
Wildsmith, Brian, 62
Wilkenson, B., 64
Witte, E., 59
Witte, P., 59
Writing activities, 144–49

Zaffo, G., 62
Zolotow, C., 71, 72